Sweet Songs for Gentle Americans

The Parlor Song in America, 1790-1860

Nicholas E. Tawa

Bowling Green University Popular Press
Bowling Green, Ohio 43403

Library of Congress Catalog Card No.: 78-71394

ISBN: 0-87972-130-8 Clothbound
0-87972-157-X Paperback

Cover design by Michael Gurtzweiler

CONTENTS

Preface

Interest in the nineteenth-century parlor song has increased in recent times. This music has become the subject of a few informative papers, the main element of several well-received concerts and the featured matter of a handful of recordings.

Nevertheless, though trustworthy information on vital aspects of this music is lacking, the parlor song remains a concern of few scholars. We are grateful for the one or two careful studies embracing the subject that have been published, particularly Oscar Sonneck's and Richard Wolfe's exhaustive bibliographies of secular music published in America before 1825. However, the little that has been written in book-form which focuses directly on the parlor song as often as not fails to stand up under careful scrutiny. The author has tried to study all recent secondary sources of information. In many instances they remain uncited in the text. Convinced of the compelling need to rethink the entire subject, he has preferred to go back to the original documents and re-examine the genre from the viewpoint of its American musical public.

Until recently, most writers on the subject have been enthusiastic amateurs. They have given us several histories of popular song usually consisting of catalogues of song titles, anecdotes on the lives of composers and singers, chit-chat on the conception and reception of famous compositions, and perhaps some selections of music, which in many cases are disfigured and distorted by editorial amendations to lyrics, melodies and accompaniments. In too many such publications, misinformation lurks in every sentence and in every measure of music.

A book is needed that aims less to popularize the subject and satisfy a mass-taste for amusement and nostalgia, more one that with scrupulous regards for scholarly procedures examines those important topics which are keys to the understanding of the genre: what it is; why, by whom, and for whom it was written; its textual and musical commonplaces; and the characteristics of its lyrics and music.

With some trepidation this kind of study is attempted here. The author tries to establish a reliable foundation upon which others can build. At the same time he expects that future investigators will correct the errors that inevitably invest groundbreaking work of this sort.

As the argument progresses, each step is documented and illustrated. To aid comprehension, most musical references are to the carefully selected group of complete compositions reproduced in facsimile in the Musical Supplement at the volume's end. These pieces can serve also as representative examples of the types of song most popular among Americans living in the years before 1860. In large part the selection is based on the frequent occurrence of these compositions in hundreds of still extant private collections of music from the years under study. All songs mentioned in the text and found in the Supplement are prefaced with an asterisk.

Since works such as these were the main form of secular musical entertainment for millions of early Americans and played a significant role in our cultural history, it would seem that the time has arrived to review them without the value judgments, prejudices, errors and half-truths which mar much of the existing literature on the subject. Instead, the author hopes to offer some insights for comprehending the genre as a whole, its function in American life and its perception by the society that called it forth. Principally, the countless songs contained in over 500 privately-bound volumes of sheet music, now deposited in Houghton Library of Harvard University and in the Brown Collection of the Boston Public Library, have been analyzed in order to form a basis for many of the conclusions reached.

For reasons the author advances in Chapter 1, the time-span 1780-1860 is divided into three historical periods: Period I, 1780-1810; Period II, 1811-1840; Period III, 1841-1860.

Chapter 1

Clarifications

From 1790 to 1860 the members of the urban middle class found pleasure and meaning in hundreds of modest vocal compositions, sacred and secular. These works comprised the greater part of the available musical literature of the time. For many people what eventually was known as the parlor song had a special attraction. Its examples embodied a wide spectrum of commonly-held ideas in a form readily understood and deeply satisfying. Its beauty arose from a lyric that expressed a human experience shared by most members of the American society and from a melody that augmented the lyric. Thousands of parlor songs were issued in sheet-music format and printed in songbooks, as well as in musical and other periodicals edited for the genteel reader. Parlor works were heard in the homes of educators, lawyers, large landowners, merchants, financiers and industrialists; in short, in the homes of those who had achieved some measure of economic and social success.

Less well educated and sophisticated Americans, however, began to take up the parlor song from the 1830s on. Realizing that a larger public now existed, American song composers and music publishers issued compositions that were uncomplicated enough to be accepted as "music for the millions." Many such songs, by composers like Marion Dix Sullivan, Isaac B. Woodbury, Stephen Foster and George Root achieved a popularity that reached into every household. The many articles on these works in the musical periodicals of the fifties, the increasing number of letters from rural areas to these same periodicals, and the immense quantity of copies of the songs sold throughout the United States attest to the importance of this musical manifestation.

It is noteworthy that the parlor song evolved during an era when the time and energy of the people of the United States were primarily directed toward finding solutions to the political and economic problems stemming from the growth and development of a new and burgeoning nation. Although little time and resources were left for the nurturing of a sophisticated musical culture such as symphony, chamber music, and grand opera, parlor song that was easily performed and comprehended met a definite need.

As parlor songs became a more and more accepted vehicle for entertainment, the purchasing of such works in sheet-music format and the collecting of them in privately-bound volumes became popular with many members of the middle class. Most of the sheet-music published from 1790 to 1860 that is available today consists of simple songs written by British or American composers and published in the Britsh Isles or the United States. About a third is piano music, usually dances, marches, quick steps and variations on favorite melodies. Once in a while the easier keyboard sonatas of minor composers are found. A small number of vocal works, most of them issued after 1850, are by German, French and Italian composers.

Countless examples of these musical pieces are still extant in American libraries. Many of their original purchasers are known, making possible not only a study of individual preferences in music, but also the role of music in the lives of the men and women who valued this aspect of American culture.

The Three Periods of Parlor-Song History

The urban centers of America grew swiftly in the last two decades of the eighteenth century. Many residents of cities like Philadelphia, New York, Boston and Baltimore hungered for musical entertainment. They began to seek out the diversions offered in concert hall and musical theater. A number of the educated and well-to-do from outlying areas commenced paying visits to the nearest towns, where they conducted necessary business, made household purchases and explored the delights of music, dance and drama.

Scarcely any Americans had the training or disposition to play in orchestras or sing on the stage. Musicians had to be imported. During the years immediately after American independence, emigrant British singers, instrumentalists and composers made up the greater part of the professional musicians in America. They performed in American concert halls, theaters and pleasure gardens, and introduced Americans to the graceful and melodious songs that were favorites in England. Entranced by the compositions, Americans purchased them to enjoy in their homes.

The affluent amateur musician from about 1790 through 1810 sometimes ordered his music directly from London. But normally he purchased it from one of the music stores opening in the largest urban centers along the Atlantic seaboard. Some music-store proprietors, like William Blake of Boston, George Gilfert of New

York, and Benjamin Carr of Philadelphia commenced issuing their own musical publications, mostly reprints of London compositions, a few the creations of British composers resident in America.

It is clear from the private music collections from these two decades that amateurs enjoyed the excitement of programmatic piano works depicting battles and storms at sea. Their patriotism was at white heat, thus their love for national songs. Their tenderer emotions were exercised mainly by ditties on love. A typical collection by an amateur musician might include piano pieces like Kotzwara's ubiquitous *Battle of Prague,* the popular *Washington's March,* variations on *Yankee Doodle,* and one or more of the many sets of cotillions and country dances arranged by favorite dance masters, especially those of William Francis and Pierre Landrin Duport. It would include also patriotic songs such as *Rise, Columbia,* words by Thomas Paine and adapted to the melody of *Rule Brittania,* or *Hail Columbia,* words by Joseph Hopkinson to the tune of the *President's March.* One or two compositions might be by British composers resident in America, like Benjamin Carr's *The Little Sailor Boy* and Alexander Reinagle's *Cousin John.* But the bulk of the collection would consist of currently popular songs composed by musicians in London, like James Hook's *Within a Mile of Edinburgh,* William Shield's *Old Towler* and Reginald Spofforth's *The Wood Robin.*[1]

Speaking generally, the three decades from about 1811 through 1840 were a transitional period in the history of American parlor song. American vocalists like Mrs. Burke and Mrs. French began appearing alongside the British professional singers. Few as they still were, American song writers like Oliver Shaw, Thomas Weisenthal and John Hewitt began to win a following. More and more of the most successful compositions were composed by British musicians resident in American—three of them, William Dempster, Charles Horn and Henry Russell. The bulk of the music issued in America, however, still continued to come from composers working in London.

Scores of new publishers made their appearance during these thirty years, some in cities distant from the Northeastern seaboard: Benjamin Casey in New Orleans, Charles Gilfert in Charleston and William C. Peters in Louisville. Because of the wide choice of titles and competitive pricing, almost all parlor songs purchased by amateurs during this period are from American, not British, firms. Moreover, the parlor-song public began to embrace Americans from the affluent almost to the ranks of the laboring classes, and from areas as far westward as the Mississippi River.

Regrettably, the author has seen no group of music pieces that can be identified as once belonging to someone of strictly limited means. The extant collections are those of upper- and middle-class amateurs. These were members of families which preserved and passed on their belongings from one generation to another or, in the instance of the song collections, donated them to libraries. The contents of the bound volumes indicate their former owners no longer sought out the descriptive piano works that had once stimulated their parents' generation. Nor do the music lovers seem as aggressive about their patriotism, at least not from 1820 on. The incidence of songs on love of country and defiance of enemies decreases. What they do treasure is songs depicting the gentle affections. The song titles alone indicate the changes that have taken place. A typical collection from the years 1811 through 1840 might well include such favorite American compositions as Oliver Shaw's *Mary's Tears,* Thomas Wiesenthal's *Take This Rose* or John Hewitt's *The Minstrel's Return from the War.* Popular songs written by British composers in America, like Joseph Philip Knight's *She Wore a Wreath of Roses* or Henry Russell's *Woodman! Spare that Tree* would be far more evident than American ones, as would be American reprints of London publications like Thomas Moore's *My Heart and Lute,* Thomas Haynes Bayly's *Long, Long Ago* and Henry Bishop's *Home, Sweet Home.*[2]

The next period, from 1841 through 1860, saw an immense increase in the parlor-song public, now numbering many thousands of Americans from the Atlantic to the Pacific Oceans. These years show a dramatic rise in the number of American singers and composers. Well-attended concerts given by native troupes (the Hutchinson Family, Ordway's Aeolians and the Alleghanians, to name three) featured parlor works written by American-born composers, among them Marion Dix Sullivan, Stephen Foster and George Root. Not only the well-to-do but miners, city laborers, farmers and slaves were described as singing parlor works like Sullivan's *Blue Juniata,* Foster's *Old Folks at Home* and Root's *Rosalie, the Prairie Flower.* British compositions continued in favor mainly among the higher social classes. Three examples of the most popular of the British songs are Crouch's *Kathleen Mavourneen,* Blockley's *Love Not!* and Balfe's *I Dreamt that I Dwelt in Marble Halls.*[3]

The three periods just described represent different musical eras in the history of parlor song in the United States. The years of British domination, between 1790 and 1811, are henceforth designated as Period I. The years that saw the rise of American singers and composers, 1811 to 1841, Period II. And the years of American ascendancy in the writing and public performance of parlor songs, 1841 to 1861, Period III. The demarcations are useful ones for the purposes of this study. One should understand, however, that no distinct stylistic divisions are intended.

A final observation is made here. No matter what the period of the music's origin, individual songs popular in one section of the country were found to be popular in all settled parts of America. To give two instances from the forties, *Woodman! Spare that Tree!* by Henry Russell and *'Tis Midnight Hour* by an "Amateur" were heard in concerts as far north as Chicago and south as New Orleans, and were purchased by amateurs in widely-scattered areas of the country.[4]

Explaining the Parlor Song

What are the parlor songs enjoyed by so many early Americans? Their texts are almost always the creations of contemporary British or American lyricists, scarcely any of them major poets. Their tunes come mostly from contemporary British or American composers practised in the writing of popular music of this sort. Some melodies are adapted from traditional or operatic sources; a few from instrumental pieces or continental vocal compositions. Indeed, any music thought likely to have a wide appeal might form the grist of the parlor-song arranger.

These compositions were commonly referred to as *ballads* on the title-pages of the sheet music, in the advertisements of publishers and in the articles and books on music. Their creators were almost always described as *ballad* composers; their performers as *ballad* singers. The question of what the term *ballad* signified to nineteenth-century musicians is a bothersome one. Whenever the author speaks about parlor compositions and whenever he publishes an article on the subject, some member from the audience or readership asks to have the word explained. Consequently, an inquiry into the meaning of the word is necessary in order to dispel a little of the confusion.

When Francis James Child published the well-known *English and Scottish Popular Ballads* (1882-98), his criteria for inclusion were—to the extent that they were known—that a ballad be of ancient origin, collected from tradition and in the form of a narrative. The text was all important; the tune ignored for the most part. The folklorists coming after Child were chiefly interested in songs of unknown origin, transmitted by oral tradition and found in rural areas. They too defined the ballad as a narrative, and understood it to include some reference to theme, character and setting.[5] Most of them ignored the music also.

One recent and much-quoted definition of the ballad, derived "from the definitions given" by several scholars and "an analysis of many of the pieces in the Child collection and elsewhere" is given by G. Malcolm Laws, Jr. He concludes: "A ballad is a narrative folksong which dramatizes a memorable event."[6]

Some folklorists were musicians and collectors of tunes as well as texts. Yet they tended to define the ballad by its text. For example, Cecil Sharp, a noted collector of English and American folk songs, asserted that ballads are narrative songs sung in an impersonal manner. On the other hand, he discovered among the folk songs he collected a song type "far more emotional and passionate" in its utterance and "usually the record of a personal experience. . . very frequently of an amatory nature."[7] These were lyrical songs that told no story. Since the texts concerned feeling and neither hinted at narrative nor allowed for an emotionally detached rendition, Sharp would not label them as ballads.

Sharp did state the scholar's distinction between ballad and lyrical song was arbitrary and unrecognized by rural folk singers. Indeed, other collectors of folk songs have admitted that rural singers often sang sentimental parlor songs of the type forming the basis for this study rather than narrative works long in oral tradition whenever investigators asked them for ballads.[8]

Since most parlor songs are printed, non-narrative, lyrical compositions of urban origin and known authorship, they fail to conform to the scholar's definition of the traditional ballad. Moreover, many definitions of ballad from the first half of the nineteenth century do not fit the parlor song. Typical is one given by the otherwise unknown H.G. Pilkington in the *Musical Dictionary* (Boston, 1812), where ballad is defined as "A Brief, simple Tale, of three, four or more verses, set to a familiar air." In all probability Pilkington is referring to the broadside ballad, which G. Malcolm Laws described as a printed journalistic piece meant to be sung to an already extant melody.[9]

A somewhat similar definition is given by William S. Porter in his *Musical Cyclopedia* (Boston, 1834), a book prepared with considerable help from Lowell Mason. Porter adds to what Pilkington says that the words and melody are equally important because "with ordinary listeners this species of song is more generally felt and understood than any other."

Not until around 1870 is the ballad's description one that fits the parlor song. In his *Pronouncing Musical Dictionary,* published in Boston in 1875, the respected voice teacher William Ludden calls it "a short simple song of natural construction.... The word Ballad means, now, any unvaried simple song, each verse sung to the same melody."

Characteristics shared by all parlor *ballads* published as sheet music in early America are that they are easy to perform, strophic, and issued with keyboard accompaniment. Some are for voice and "harp or piano." Others have an alternate guitar accompaniment. The texts are in two or three stanzas generally, sometimes narrative but preponderantly lyrical.

Only a few pre-1860 compositions for solo voice have subtitles other than Song or Ballad. In contrast to parlor songs, these other pieces, subtitled Cavatina, Scena, Polacca, or Rondeau, almost invariably are not strophic songs and exhibit a more complex musical structure. In addition, they have more extended melodic lines, richer harmonic movement and more elaborate accompaniments. Often a profusion of melodic ornamentation and extended melismatic passages obscure the sense of the words.

Most non-ballad types of song performed in America came from English operas. A Cavatina usually appears as a short non-strophic operatic air; a Scena, a dramatic recitative and aria; a Polacca, a vocal show-piece in 3/4 time and normally in simple rondo form (A B A C A); a Rondeau, a work also in simple rondo form though not necessarily a show-piece or in 3/4 time. A song subtitled as a Canzonet or Serenade—the former generally defined as a short song, the latter as an evening song—is frequently strophic and of simple construction, therefore can be considered a parlor song.

To cite one song of the non-ballad type, John Braham's *No More by Sorrow* (New York, ca. 1803) is called a "Pollacca" on the first page. It is in rondo form, A B A C A, has a profusion of sixteenth-note melismas difficult for amateurs to sing, and a range of an eleventh, from e′ to a″.

Parlor ballads normally employ melodies of more limited range, made up of easily sung intervals, and in regular four-measure phrases. In most instances only the words of the first stanza underlie the music or less frequently those of the first two stanzas. Remaining stanzas, if any, are printed following the music. Simple keyboard accompaniments function mostly as supports for the melody. Harmonies are uncomplicated, particularly in songs composed by Americans during Period III, and comprise mainly the common chords—tonic, dominant, and subdominant. Quite a few British songs tend to be more complex harmonically than American ones. They often employ chords of the submediant and mediant, and contain modulations to related keys.

A closer look at some actual compositions reproduced in this volume's Musical Supplement should make matters clearer. **Flow Gently, Sweet Afton,*[10] words by Robert Burns and music by the American J.E. Spilman (Philadelphia, 1838), is a typical composition by a native composer. Its undemanding accompaniment is distinctly subordinate to the vocal melody. The A-major melody, regularly pausing every four measures, remains within the octave e′ to e″, except for f″ sharp. Aside from a single sharped fourth of the scale, the work is diatonic. The text is in two stanzas, the second printed following the music. The song provides a consummate illustration of a parlor ballad.

A somewhat different layout is seen in a few songs; two or more stanzas are printed one after the other, each with the same music. The publisher may have had the convenience of the singer in mind, or may have spread the song out so he could charge more for a copy. Isaac B. Woodbury's **Be Kind to the Loved Ones at Home* (Boston, 1847) has three stanzas printed in this fashion, with a fourth and final stanza printed at the end without music. Because the price of this piece is the prevailing 25 cents, one cannot conclude that the publisher always followed this format in order to charge more. On the other hand, songs exist with the music repeated for subsequent stanzas and for which a slightly higher price per copy is asked. Usually these are the works of British composers resident in the United States. For example, the New York publisher Hewitt and Jacques issued Charles Horn's **Near the Lake Where Drooped the Willow* (New York, 1839) with the music of stanza one reprinted for each of the following two stanzas. The price showing on the first page is 50 cents.

Parlor songs, especially the most popular ones, eschew melodic ornamentation and expression marks. **Flow Gently, Sweet Afton,* labelled *Andante,* has accents on two c″ sharps, and indicates one *forte* and one *piano*—that is all. **Be Kind to the Loved Ones at Home* is marked *Andante Espressivo.* But not a single dynamic or expressive indication occurs anywhere in the music. Both songs are characteristic of most compositions from all three periods.

Several nineteenth-century books on music and musicians, articles in musical periodicals and other writings confirm what has just been observed. In addition, their authors agree that a ballad's melody must sound natural and unforced. It should avoid passages added merely to dazzle the listener. Only in this manner, they claim, can a tune bring out the central sentiment of the text, usually the emotion of love, fear or pity. In order not to detract from this all-important function of melody, both harmony and accompaniment must remain plain and in the background.[11]

A characteristic comment on the parlor song is contained in an unsigned article on "Ballad Singing," in the *Southern Literary Gazette.* The article was reprinted in the New York *Musical Times,* 27 December 1851, p. 118. After stating that a singer's concern over the execution of ornamental and difficult passages kills expression and is more proper to the operatic aria than to the ballad, the writer continues: "Ballads are much oftener the theme of more natural human love and sorrow. A blind child's lament for the glories of the sky—the husband's tender mourning for one departed—the regretful thoughts of brighter and purer days—the half awakened consciousness of sincere affection—all this finds voice in a ballad, a voice that soonest reaches the heart. Its peculiarity is the investing one thought or subject with a finished expression of all that it can suggest."

Another important characteristic of parlor song is melodic recurrence as a means for heightened eloquence, structural unity, and ready comprehension. Valuable comment in this regard is furnished in a brief item entitled "Song Writing," published in the New York *Euterpeiad,* 15 May 1830, p. 17: "The most passionate of all music is, perhaps, that where a beautiful passage is repeated, and where the first subject is judiciously returned to, while it still vibrates on the ear, and is recent in the memory."

William S.B. Mathews, a native of New Hampshire and a respected writer on music in Period III, gives further detail on the matter of repetition. In his book *How to Understand Music,* the chapter on the parlor ballad stresses the importance of recurrent melodic phrases that are of "symmetrical balance" in order to reinforce a song's sentiment.[12] Such melodic repetition, Mathews maintains, strengthens unity of expression and is essential if the song is to be understood and enjoyed by "a common people."[13] For examples of symmetrical balance, he refers the reader to songs by Stephen Foster and George Root, citing the latter's **The Hazel Dell* and **Rosalie, the Prairie Flower* as "exemplary" compositions.

Both these pieces, like Foster's *Old Folks at Home* and *My Old Kentucky Home,* have melodies in regular four-measure phrases and cast in an A A^1 A A^1 B A^1 [or A^2] form. When the phrases in *The Hazel Dell* are divided in turn into two-measure half-phrases, the form becomes:

Phrases: A A^1 A A^1 B A^1.
Half-Phrases: ab ac ab ac de ac.

As one can see from the above, three levels of melodic repetition exist: that of the entire melody, of one or more melodic phrases, and of one or more half-phrases. Parlor songs from all three periods exhibit such repetition.

Unassuming works like those just described are designated as *parlor* compositions because their ultimate destinations were the parlors of amateur singers. Comments to this effect are often made by contemporary writers. This was, for instance, the conclusion of a

German emigrant, Francis Grund. After attending a public concert given by a ballad singer in Boston in the early 1830s, he wrote that her songs did not sound to best advantage in the hall, since they really were meant to be sung "in a private parlour and . . .[not] in a large concert room."[14]

Another commentator confirms Grund's conclusion. After hearing several performances by ballad singers, the unidentified writer in the Boston *Musical Magazine* of 20 July 1839, p. 238, states: "Several distinguished performers have given very pleasing and interesting concerts, among whom may be mentioned Madame Caradori Allan; Miss Shirreff, Wilson, and Seguin; Signor de Begnis, and Mr. Dempster. . . . Airs and songs suitable for parlor music are generally selected for these concerts. . . . Our amateurs will take these same songs, and after a few attempts to imitate the style and manner in which they have heard them sung, are apt to fall in with the opinions expressed by some of their injudicious friends, that they sing them as well as the artists they are trying to imitate."

Some of these parlor works are undoubtedly those designated as sung by one of these singers and found in several amateur music collections of the time. To cite a few instances, Madame Caradori Allen's name appears on the title-page of Alexander Lee's *I'm O'er Young to Marry Yet* (Philadelphia, ca. 1838), Miss Shirreff's name on William Clifton's *Will He Be True?* (New York, 1839), Mrs. Seguin's name on John Barton's *The Irish Mother's Lament* (New York, ca. 1835), and Mr. Dempster's name on one of his own compositions, *Can I Forget to Love Thee?* (Philadelphia, 1839).

A writer in the Buffalo *Advertiser* advises readers to seek relaxation even in difficult times by attending "musical entertainments of the highest order. . .[because] the general influence of these does not end with the mere listening for their performance. They go to the home circle, are chanted at our firesides, and the bright carol of children, or the more elaborate duet or quartet of our older sons and daughters will tend to soften the asperities of the coming winter."[15]

Corroboration that these songs were intended for singing in the home is found in the advertisements of music publishers who recommend their songs as suitable for "the home circle." Finally, two leading American composers, John Hewitt and George Root, state their aim was to compose works acceptable in as many households as possible. Root says in his autobiography that friends kept urging him to compose more ambitious pieces than *Hazel Dell*. His invariable reply was that he preferred to leave this field to Schubert and Franz. He himself wished to write elementary music for the "tens of thousands of people whose wants would not be supplied at all" if only the more complex songs were written.[16]

That this aim was realized is apparent in the thousands of parlor songs purchased as sheet music for singing in the home and still preserved in the bound collections that once belonged to nineteenth-century amateurs. By the end of the fifties parlor songs were found in parlors throughout settled America. Among the extant collections now at Houghton Library of Harvard University and at the Boston Public Library are several that once belonged to amateurs living in Louisiana, Iowa and Illinois. In *Life on the Mississippi,* Mark Twain observes that in the 1850s he had seen bound and unbound sheet music on and around the parlor piano in most mansions bordering the Mississippi River that he had visited. He names several parlor songs—*On a Lone Barren Isle; The Last Link Is Broken; She Wore a Wreath of Roses; Go, Forget Me; Hours There Were; Long, Long Ago; Days of Absence; A Life on the Ocean Wave; Bird at Sea;* and *The Silver Moon.* His list of songs includes compositions from all three periods.[17] These are the sorts of musical works with which this study concerns itself.

Notes

1. Most of the music cited can be found in one private collection now at Houghton Library, Harvard University, but without a shelf-number. The music once belonged to a Mrs. Wood, of Medford, Massachusetts.

2. For example, a privately bound collection of music, once belonging to Charles F. Shimmin, of Cambridge, Massachusetts, dated "Aug. 24, 1839," and now at the Boston Public Library (shelf number S5), contains songs by Shaw, Knight, Russell and Bayly. In it, also, are two Italian arias from Bellini's *La Sonnambula,* one French aria from Auber's *La Muette de Portici* (renamed *Masaniello* in England and America), and one German song by Henri Herz.

3. A typical collection from this period, now at Houghton Library and without shelf-number, once belonged to a resident of Illinois. Most of the contents are the most popular American songs of the time. A few songs are British.

4. The author has made a special study of several hundred private collections of parlor songs from these years.

5. MacEdward Leach, in *Funk and Wagnell's Standard Dictionary of Folklore, Mythology and Legend* s.v. "Ballad."

6. G. Malcolm Laws, Jr., *Native American Balladry,* rev. ed. (Philadelphia, 1969), p. 2.

7. Cecil Sharp, *English Folk Songs from the Southern Appalachians,* ed. Maud Karples (London, 1932), p. xii.

8. See Arthur Kyle Davis, Jr., *Traditional Ballads of Virginia* (1929; reprint ed., Charlottesville, VA., 1957), p. 36. Mr. Davis writes that collectors had to ask for "old songs" in order to encourage folk singers to produce the narrative folk ballads.

9. G. Malcolm Laws, Jr., *American Balladry from British Broadsides* (Philadelphia, 1957), pp. 2-3. See also, *Native American Balladry,* p. 5.

10. An asterisk (*) placed before a song title indicates that the entire composition may be found in the Musical Supplement at the end of the volume.

11. See, for example, the unsigned article, "Remarks on the Use and Abuse of Music," Boston *Euterpleiad,* 27 April, 1822, p. 19. During its thirty-four months existence (June 1820-March 1823), this periodical, edited by John Rowe Parker, published many articles on British and American song. See also, Henry C. Watson, "Preface to the American Edition," dated 2 October 1843, to George Hogarth's *Musical History, Biography, and Criticism* (New York, 1845).

12. William B. Mathews, *How to Understand Music* (Chicago, 1880), pp. 125-31.

13. A concern that the "common people" enjoy and understand the parlor song's words and music is shared by many of the music educators of Period III.

14. Francis J. Grund, *Aristocracy in America* (New York, 1959), p. 160. The book was first published in London, in 1839.

15. The article is reprinted in the New York *Musical Review,* 14 November 1857, p. 354.

16. George Root, *The Story of a Musical Life* (Cincinnati, 1891), p. 96.

17. Mark Twain, *Life on the Mississippi* (Minneapolis, 1967), pp. 267-69.

Chapter 2

The Parlor-Song Public

The early American parlor song, though enjoyed by the least affluent and educated Americans, depended for its existence on an urban middle class willing to pay admission to concerts and stage productions that featured it, and willing to buy significant quantities of its sheet-music reproductions for private performance in the home. Because it was written to have and did have an immediate and wide appeal, the parlor song must be considered a genre of popular music. Its creation and its performances were intended for no one in particular. Its introduction to the public was a speculation on the part of all those involved that large numbers of people would sponsor it. For this last reason, it was bound to reflect the preferences of a sizeable but generally indiscriminate audience.

The heavy purchase of a few songs, while most competing works experienced comparative neglect, served to designate what particular kinds of music the public desired and publishers found profitable to issue. Inevitably those one or two songs with extremely large followings became the bellwethers for the music industry and the exemplars that contemporary composers patterned their compositions after. What emerged was the articulation of a common aesthetic taste. Without question a widespread consensus existed on the nature of the music that people desired to hear. That this consensus centered on the popular parlor song, not on cultivated music of artistic intent, is readily established in the contemporary writings on music and in the contents of the surviving music collections. One revealing statement occurs in the 9 December 1854 *Dwight's Journal of Music,* p. 75, a periodical edited by John Sullivan Dwight, a man who disliked parlor music and praised German art song. This issue reproduces a report on popular music by an unidentified correspondent in Washington, D.C. The writer, who signs himself "De Profundis," laments that too many people living in the Washington area were still contaminated by what he considers an inordinate affection for parlor song, while "High Art" is neglected. If "De Profundis" shared the same musical tastes as Dwight, then "High Art" meant German chamber and symphonic music, opera and song. He would have considered Italian opera only a little better than parlor music.

The writer acknowledges the large number of Catholics living in the area have "more wealth than is usual with Catholic communities, with everything calculated to bring them in connection with the highest music." But he is shocked that even the old Maryland first families "have an obstinate fondness" for Russell's *The Maniac* and *Newfoundland Dog,* and for "Dempster's soul-and-eye filling pathos (see 'Blind Boy,' 'Irish Emigrant's Lament,' etc.), so the young Ladies from the Convent are wont to make us in turn feel the pangs of the individuals referred to."

Although Maryland's Catholic first families lacked an appreciation for "High Art," they were no different from many first families elsewhere in the early United States. Certainly their taste was also that of Charles Francis Shimmin, a prominent Boston lawyer. Shimmin has left a collection of sheet music, which he had bound into one volume shortly after the end of his freshman year at Harvard College, 24 August 1839. In Shimmin's volume are several parlor songs by William Dempster and Henry Russell, including Dempster's *Oh! Promise Me to Sing, Love* and *Can I Forget Thee?*, and Russell's *Woodman! Spare that Tree!* and *The Ivy Green.* In New Orleans, the wealthy Daniel Holmes purchased and sang the same Russell songs.[1] In Indiana, Maggie Duey owned a number of Russell works;[2] in Pittsburgh the young Stephen Foster, son of a prominent local citizen, wept when he sang the Dempster compositions and was deeply impressed with Russell's singing of his own ballads.[3] Without question Americans from all parts of the country had "an obstinate fondness" for the Dempster and Russell songs. The same can be said for the songs of other British ballad composers—Henry Bishop, Thomas Moore, William Nicholls Crouch, John Norton and Michael Balfe; and those of American composers—John Hewitt, Isaac B. Woodbury, George Root, Septimus Winner and Stephen Foster. The private music collections of American amateur musicians from all over the United States abound with their compositions.

Although they lived in a city reputed at mid-century to be receptive to "High Art," a goodly number of Bostonians failed to live up to the expectations of Dwight and other advocates for artistic music. Henry Lee Higginson, future founder of the Boston Symphony Orchestra, wrote in February 1853: "The Germanians brought out a new symphony of Beethoven last Saturday evening, the first time it has ever been performed in this country. Dwight, I believe, says it was very fine, beautiful, etc., but no doubt most of the audience thought it terribly dull."[4]

The point that the sponsors of "High Art" fail to make is that with the best will in the world, the general public could make little of the complex and lengthy artistic works which they heard only infrequently and, as often as not, performed by inadequately rehearsed musicians. Neither their childhood experiences nor the music teachers they relied on for their training had prepared them for music of a highly cultivated nature. Perforce the compositions of Beethoven made an alien sound in their ears.

For most Americans, simple songs with attractive melodies taxed their patience least. Within brief spans of time such works provided all the diversion they could desire. The sophistication necessary for enjoying long expanses of complicated music, either in an incomprehensible foreign language or without the guidance of words at all, was not theirs. Mark Twain expresses the common view of high art succinctly. Speaking of Wagner's operas, he states that one act he might enjoy, two left him "physically exhausted;" but "whenever I have ventured an entire opera the result has been the next thing to suicide."[5]

On the other hand, traditional narrative songs of any length and their rendition by rural singers were at times also rejected as dull. Occasionally one comes upon an incident such as that related by J.P. Kennedy, a writer on Virginia life in the first quarter of the nineteenth century. Kennedy says he once came upon an old "minstrel" in whose "excellent memory" was retained many ancient narrative songs. This elderly musician was playing his fiddle for a party of ladies and gentlemen. Soon the old man began to sing in a nasal and monotonous manner. The company quickly stopped him and requested something "sentimental" and "pitiful." Instead of the parlor songs they desired, he could only produce items from oral tradition like *The Gosport Tragedy* and *Jemmy and Nancy*.[6] Not wishing to hear this kind of music, they interrupted his singing and asked him to play fiddle tunes so they could dance.[7]

The Amateur Singers

From what circles did the American singers of parlor songs come? Many can be named because they left still-intact music collections, wrote about themselves, or achieved sufficient prominence to have others write about them. Some, like Charles Ammi Cutter, Harvard and Boston Athenaeum librarian and an "ardent lover of nature, music, and dancing,"[8] came from literary circles. Others, like Daniel Henry Holmes, the New Orleans lawyer, poet and musician, and Olivia Richardson, wife of Dr. William Lambert Richardson, obstetrician and member of Boston Lying-in Hospital, from professional circles.[9] Still others, like Edith Forbes

Perkins, whose father owned a fleet of ships (one of which was named after her) engaged in the China trade, and whose husband was president of the Chicago, Burlington and Quincy Railroad, from prominent business and financial circles.[10] And others, like Elizabeth Wooster Baldwin, daughter of Roger Sherman Baldwin, governor of Connecticut and later a United States senator, and like Eleanor Parke Custus, granddaughter of Martha Washington and brought up at Mount Vernon, from important political circles.[12]

In later times people from backgrounds like those just described would be found among those who enjoyed hearing symphonies and grand operas. In the pre-1860 United States they delighted mostly in performing for themselves and, on occasion, listening to professional musicians perform parlor music. Only rarely did any of them hear a symphony. And grand opera, for the most part, was a now-and-again affair.

The great majority of these amateur musicians traced their lineage to the British Isles. Not surprisingly, they shared a fondness for parlor songs with their peers across the Atlantic. In addition they belonged to the group that purchased and read American periodicals containing articles on parlor music, some of the articles reprints from English publications. Two of the earliest of these periodicals were the Boston *Euterpeiad* of the early 1820s, edited by John Rowe Parker, and the New York *Euterpeiad* of the early 1830s, edited by Charles Dingley. Along with local musical notices, reviews and some original articles written mainly by the editors, these publications featured excerpts from British books and periodicals on the lives of British parlor-song composers and singers. They also contained information on British song style and performance, and on London musical life centered on the parlor song. That amateur musicians subscribed to these American periodicals is established in their collections, which frequently include music originally issued as supplements to these publications.

The American purchasers of sheet music would also have been the ones attending the performances of visiting British singers. They brought scores of parlor songs composed in England into their homes, particularly during Periods I and II. It was not until Period III that they patronized the performances and purchased the works of American musicians.

As far as one can ascertain these amateur musicians not only had good educations but shared the inclination, the means and the training—limited as it might have been—to perform songs with keyboard accompaniment as the composers intended.

It is also true that Americans of small means and slight

Family Group. Reprinted with permission from the Corcoran Gallery of Art.

education enjoyed parlor songs. Regrettably, writing other than that of an essential and practical nature is an attribute of an educated and leisured class, certainly not of the poor. And whatever writing these less affluent Americans did has largely disappeared as being of slight consequence. Only a few accounts written usually by observers from the more affluent classes describe the relation of small farmers, laborers, etc., to the parlor song. Undoubtedly many "caught" the songs "by ear" and sang them without accompaniment. Some did accompany their singing with an inexpensive or homemade violin or guitar or whatever was handy. One or two fortunate singers may have owned or had access to a keyboard instrument.

A very early mention of the singing of a parlor song by someone in humble circumstances comes from one of Philip Vickers Fithian's journals. Fithian writes that he was traveling as an intinerant preacher at the wilderness edge of Pennsylvania in 1775. On 4 July he entered tiny Northumberland Town. Here: "Mrs. Scull entertained me with—Many good agreeable Songs. She moved my Heart towards my charming *Laura* when She sung the following,

Constancy

O lovely Delia, virtuous Fair,
Believe me now, my own Dear—
I'd not exchange my happy State
For all the Wealth of all the Great.

Later that same day, he spent time with a Mr. Barker and Mr. Freman, who "beat the Drum, & we had a Good Fifer, so that we spent the Evening in Martial Amusement."[13]

About fifteen years later Samuel Griswold Goodrich listened to the singing of a shoemaker in the Connecticut town of Ridgefield. His repertoire consisted of songs in current favor: "Amby Benedict, the circulating shoemaker, upon due notice, came with his bench, lapstone and awls, and converted some little room into a shop, till the household was duly shod. He was a merry fellow, and threw in lots of singing gratis. He played all the popular airs upon his lapstone—as hurdygurdies and hand-organs do now."[14]

References to members of the laboring classes singing parlor songs, never plentiful, are extremely rare before the nineteenth century. An indication that a sizeable number of them were doing so can be gathered from a report on music heard around the Philadelphia area about the year 1810. The writer claims he knows of many homes that have a piano, harpsichord, violin, flute or clarinet. What is more, he says, young men and women "from the children of the judge" down to those of "the huckster and the drummer" were studying music. With some sarcasm he continues: "Europeans, as they walk our streets, are often surprised with the flute rudely warbling 'Hail Columbia,' from an oyster cellar, or the piano forte thumped to a female voice screaming 'O Lady Fair!' from behind a heap of cheese, a basket of eggs, a flour barrel, or a puncheon of apple whiskey; and on these grounds we take it for granted that we are a very musical people."[15] The author dissociates himself from such "frivolity" as singing the favorite songs of his time. Instead, he prefers the music of Handel and Haydn. Yet this writer does testify to the increasing participation of Americans from varied walks of life in secular music.

Some twenty years later, mention of the less well circumstanced classes in connection with secular song becomes more plentiful. Foreign visitors, in particular, noted with astonishment how Americans from the humbler walks of life enjoyed singing the genteel parlor songs. They commented on the large numbers of small tradespeople who participated in contemporary musical life. These people did not hesitate to take their small savings and invest in a musical instrument. Children were given music lessons. Entire families attended concerts and the musical theater. In 1830 an English visitor to New York City writes of hearing a black woman sing two British parlor songs, Joseph Wade's *Love Was Once a Little Boy* and Thomas Haynes Bayly's *I'd Be a Butterfly,* outside his window. About the same time, another foreigner notes with tongue-in-cheek that even grocers have pianos, and ironmongers' wives are becoming patronesses of the arts.[16]

In the 1840s, accounts of laborers, factory workers and members of farm families who perform parlor songs increase greatly. Even girls working in the mills of Lowell, Massachusetts, describe themselves as having access to pianos and singing compositions like James Maeder's *The Silent Farewell* and John Norton's *Fanny Grey*. Moreover, these girls mention the families of small farmers and inhabitants of New England hamlets as entertaining themselves with hymns, folk songs and parlor works like Richard Leveridge's *Black-Eyed Susan* and James Hook's *The Lass of Richmond Hill,* at weddings, work "bees" and evening "sociables."[17] A characteristic shared by many parlor songs heard in rural areas is their age. Like the Leveridge and Hook works, they are often fifteen or more years old. Few are up-to-date compositions; that is to say ones published no more than five years prior to their rural performance. Owing to the primitive road system and the infrequent appearance, if at all, of professional singers, some remote villages might wait years to learn of a favorite song made popular in a New York theater.

Then in the fifties improved train service opened up vast stretches of the country to the culture emanating from the cities of the Northeast. At the same time the number of American troupes traveling through the American countryside increased dramatically, and a mail-order system for purchasing music grew in efficiency. On the eve of the American Civil War, rural residents were managing to become *au courant.* A few farm families tried to take on the trappings of gentility, according to one person identifying himself as "El Medico." Wherever he traveled in the country he found pianos, melodeons, guitars, flutes and violins. He offers no substantiation for his claim that " 'Nigger' melodies [minstrel songs] are dying out, and the more refined domestic ballads, breathing the moral sentiments, have usurped their place, with not unfrequently the more elaborate *canto* and *canzonetta* of the Italians."[18]

A surviving document does give details on what one rural song repertoire from this period was like. A manuscript songster from isolated Wyoming County in western New York, its contents dating from 1841 to 1856, shows one rustic family entertaining itself with ancient narrative, more recent broadside and parlor ballads. The parlor works are mostly American, three of them Daniel Johnson's *The Carrier Dove* (1836), H.S. Thompson's *Lilly Dale* (1852) and Stephen Foster's *Old Dog Tray* (1853).[19]

In recognition of the proliferating interest in parlor works among the least educated and sophisticated, the New York *Musical Review* of the 1850s began to distinguish between the more elaborate songs intended for the musically trained and the simplest songs, which were designated as "Music for the Millions." Its reviews carefully separate all new compositions into these two categories.[20] American composers who wrote articles for the *Review*, among them Woodbury and Root, began to advocate the writing of songs that could be enjoyed by the common people. By the end of Period III the democratization of the parlor song was complete. Its enthusiasts inhabited every American social class.

Amateur Singing, Private and Public

Youth was undeniably the time of least responsibilities and greatest leisure, at least for the middle class. It follows that the premarriage years were also the time for musical studies, if they were to be undertaken at all. Young men and women did study singing and acquire sufficient command of the keyboard to execute the easy accompaniments of the compositions they sang. One hastens to add that when amateur performers from the latter part of the eighteenth and first half of the nineteenth century are named, they are more often unmarried women under twenty-one years of age.

With adulthood and marriage, husbands spent long hours at work in factories, at offices and elsewhere. Wives spent equally long hours caring for the household and the children. This was true for most Americans, rich and poor alike. Hardly any opportunities for musical activities remained. Certainly the moments of leisure were scarce for Helen Skipworth Coles, wife of Tucker Coles, eighteenth-century owner of a plantation in Albemarle County, Virginia. A typical day's tasks left her so drained it was a wonder she turned to music at all. Her niece writes that her Aunt Helen commenced her domestic duties at sunrise, never stopping for a moment except to eat. Only at night could she think of "sitting down to her books and music."[21]

Similar accounts are given of life in the North. Susan Lesley states that at the beginning of the nineteenth century her mother was a girl in Northampton, Massachusetts, and devoted to music. But after marriage the carrying-out of her domestic tasks consumed most of her strength. Though music had always been "a great occupation and pleasure to her," after marriage "she had little time for practising and confined herself to playing for a half hour at twilight or after tea, the short time before the children went to bed."[22]

Americans too tired or old to amuse themselves continued to welcome the singing of others fresher and younger. Sarah Forbes Hughes says her elderly father, John Murray Forbes, the wealthy shipping magnate, still hungered after his "favorite songs, ballads and hymns." One of his principal delights was to receive visits from a Miss Emma Ware. He could then spend his time most agreeably, listening to her perform "old song after old song," which gave him "a pleasure beyond words."[23]

These adult song lovers are to be admired for their persistent pursuit of music in the face of difficulties: women fatigued by their endless chores choosing music instead of rest at day's end; men, even the most affluent, driving themselves for sixty or more hours a week then giving over their leisure hours to musical performances by sons and daughters; worn-out oldsters happy over every hour spent with song.

Given the difficult conditions that oftentimes prevailed, the extent to which music permeated the lives of early Americans is astonishing. We do know something about their attendance at public performances. We know far less about the circumstances which gave occasion to their singing at home. Of course, many men and women sang parlor songs for self-amusement when alone. This was the case for Nancy Shippen of Philadelphia, on 10 February 1785. At the end of the day she wrote into her journal: "Worked a little at my needle, read, sang, play'd upon the guittar, &c. &c."[24] Many years later another young woman living in a country parsonage near Worcester, Massachusetts, wrote in her journal: "Father, Mother, and Nellie have gone out to tea. Susie and Emma are singing. Maria is playing the greatest variety of rondos, waltzes, etc."[25] These are commonplace entries in young women's journals.

While most contemporary references are to women, every now and then men are described as the singers. One prominent American, John Randolph, the Virginia statesman, loved singing forthright works like Samuel Arnold's *Fresh and Strong* when he was at home. Randolph's voice is described as pleasant though untrained. Powhatan Bouldin writes that his father remembered Randolph once singing to himself at an odd hour: "I once stayed all night with Mr. Randolph at Roanoke, and for some reason which I do not remember I slept in the same room with him. Having gone to bed, Mr. Randolph, at a late hour of the night, roused me by setting his books to rights and singing:

> Fresh and strong the breeze is blowing,
> As your bark at anchor rides.[26]

These were years before the advent of player-pianos, phonographs, radios and television. People depended on their own resources for their routine diversions. For this reason family members met in the evening to sing for each other or together. Such gatherings were everyday occurrences. In 1832 a foreign visitor strolled around Boston's Frog Pond in the center of the city. He heard numerous "unknown fair singers" performing for their parents: "This park or walk is on three sides surrounded by houses. . . . The season was still very warm, (in August) and all the windows were open; in almost every mansion, it was customary to have music in the evening. These melodious sounds attracted a number of passers-by, and many a delightful evening have I spent in this way. Proceeding from house to house, I listened with rapture to very fine music and many excellent voices."[27]

To cite a specific family, when Oliver Wendell Holmes was a child, his parents, the Reverend and Mrs. Abiel Holmes, owned a piano they had purchased for $250. The family was in the habit of gathering evenings around the instrument to listen to Mrs. Holmes or one of the children sing parlor songs, among them those of

Thomas Moore.[28] The same was true of Henry Longfellow's childhood in Portland, Maine. His brother Samuel writes that their mother, Zilpah Longfellow, was passionately fond of music. She and her children frequently sang parlor works to her piano accompaniment. Among the Longfellow favorites were Ignaz Pleyel's *Henry's Cottage Maid,* John Clarke's *Brignal Banks,* and Thomas Moore's *The Last Rose of Summer* and *Oft in the Stilly Night.* Mother and children made "the house ring with gay music and laughter" during most evenings.[29]

From singing *en famille* to singing with and for guests is a short step. By far the greatest number of accounts describing amateur performances of parlor songs show them taking place during informal "at homes." This was true in all three periods and for every section of the country. Early in 1788 John Quincy Adams wrote that singing made up one of the principal diversions when he visited homes in Newburyport, Massachusetts.[30] On 21 October 1910, a visitor observed neighbors and travelers like himself at a home in remote New Connecticut, Ohio, contributing parlor songs for the recreation of the company. One song named is James Hook's *Muirland Willey.*[31] Parlor music entertained family and guests around 1820, in the Woodland plantation parlor of Eleanor Custis Lewis, granddaughter of Martha Washington; around 1828, in the Pittsburgh parlor of Stephen Foster's parents; and around 1830, in the Brookline, Massachusetts, parlor of Dr. John Pierce.[32]

An engaging description of amateur music making in a New England home was written by Edward Everett Hale in his recollections of James Russell Lowell soon after Lowell had graduated from Harvard College. The account is especially valuable since a volume of music once belonging to James Lowell's oldest sister Mary when she was a girl is now in Houghton Library. Because Mary had charge of her brother from his youngest years, he would certainly have heard some of the songs contained in the collection. He would also have listened to his other sister, Rebecca, whom Hale calls "the songstress of the home; with a sweet flexible voice she sang...childhood hymns, and afterwards the Scotch melodies and other popular music of the day."[33]

The term *Scotch* does not necessarily refer to music of Scottish folk origin. Often it appears as part of the subtitle of parlor songs written and composed in imitation of Scottish style, like Lady John Scott's *Annie Lawrie,* "a Scotch Ballad" (Boston, ca. 1850). The "other popular music of the day" for a home like that of the Lowells did include parlor songs. Substantiation for this claim can easily be found in Mary's volume of music, which contains a great deal of piano music, mostly waltzes, marches, quicksteps and rondos; five vocal pieces from continental Europe; two vocal duets; and almost twenty parlor songs, among them Michael Kelly's *The Woodman,* Charles Gilfert's *Allan a Dale,* and Charles Horn's *Farewell to My Harp.*

One or two of these songs may have been sung on the 1841 evening recalled by Hale, when James Lowell requested music from the friends who surrounded him. To Lowell's surprise one of the girls present sang one of Lowell's own poems "adapted to a lovely air."[34] As he listened his face registered "surprise, pleasure, tremulous feeling, and finally a look of delight." Hale continues by saying that in those days they spent many evenings singing and dancing—as they did that night. Then about ten o'clock they entered the dining room for a late supper and more entertainment: "Sometimes James Lowell would be called upon for one of his two songs, 'The Battle of the Nile,' or 'Baxter's Boys They Built a Mill'." Though he "had no voice and little ear," James would begin to sing. The entire company joined in one by one, "until in the end the whole circle would be on their feet, singing at the top of their voices." Then James called upon his father for his favorite song:

In a mouldring cave where
The wretched retreat,
Brittania sat wasted with care—
She wept for her Wolfe.[35]

Next came songs and glees. "Or M.W. would repeat 'Binnorie, on Binnorie,' or W.S. sing 'A Life on the Ocean Wave'."[36] Hale concludes with: "It was all nonsense, but delightful nonsense, the bubbling over of these gay young spirits."[37]

The evening Hale described may have been an unusual one and possibly embroidered with a detail or two from his own imagination. Nonetheless, what is significant about the narration is the prominent role Hale felt music had played in these fondly remembered evenings among friends.

Since most houses tended to be small and crowded together in the cities and towns, the stifling closeness of indoors during the summer was gladly exchanged for whatever breeze the outdoors afforded. Singing customarily provided amusement for the loungers on the front porch or steps. The great prevalence of this practise amongst urban dwellers from all walks of life came as a surprise to the author. These musical get-togethers were relaxed impromptu affairs.

In the eighteenth century, Anne Blair wrote of a Williamsburg, Virginia, evening when several ladies and gentlemen "stay'd the Evening with us, and the Coach was at the door to carry them Home by ten o'clock; but everyone appearing in good spirits, it was proposed to set at the Step's and Sing a few Song's which was no sooner said than done."[38] Similarly, W.E. Woodward describes New York City on warm summer evenings, when "it was the custom for everyone to sit on the stoop, and the street had a lively appearance with all the vivacious front-door parties, laughing and singing, and visiting one another."[39] And John Watson tells of a Philadelphia where boys occupied the porches, told stories and sang ballads.[40]

Even more surprising was the discovery that ceremonial parties and dinners were also eminently suitable occasions for singing parlor songs. During 1787-1788, when John Quincy Adams made his way from one Newburyport dinner party or dance to another, he heard the favorite songs of the day sung everywhere.[41] About ten years later George Channing listened to the song *Fresh and Strong* at a "stiff" Newport, Rhode Island, tea party, the singer "increasing the volume of sound to an incredible degree." Others at this formal party performed the Moore-Stevenson *Meeting of the Waters,* and Thomas Paine's *Adams and Liberty.*[42]

The Englishman D.W. Mitchell has left an informative description of a Richmond, Virginia, party held in 1850. One evening, he writes, he attended a "social frolic." Present were men and women of all ages, and from "the ranks" of bakers, machinists and farmers. At first they sat facing each other without conversation. Then someone spoke up: "Oh, Jenny, sit down at the piano and give us a song—something funny, never mind that cold." Jenny complied contrarily by singing the sentimental *Lament of the Irish Emigrant* of Dempster. "Very sweetly, too," Mitchell adds. Someone else proposed dancing. However, too many "church members" were present who would have disapproved. Therefore a "jogging along" was substituted. Couples formed a large circle around a young man seated at the piano. He began playing; the couples marched arm-in-arm around him, constantly singing, occasionally stopping to exchange partners.[43]

The author has come upon at least one man who took the singing at parties seriously, perhaps because the songstress was as much admired as the song she was asked to sing. Houghton Library has a badly torn copy of Henry Bishop's song *Trifler Forebear,* issued in Philadelphia about 1820. On the first page is written: "Dear Cliffords favorite—torn by him because I refused to play it at an Evening party, when there were *too many folks* standing around me to do it justice!" Was the raging Clifford a suitor?

Fortunately for the equanimity of polite society, young men had other means for showing their admiration of the ladies than the ill-tempered tearing of music. Throughout the years under study, a prominent pastime for bachelors was the night-time serenading of young ladies, with instrumental pieces and songs. While the author knew the custom was widely observed in Europe, his previous reading about early American life had not led him to expect it to occur with the frequency it did in a land more noted for its puritanism than for its frivolity.

One foreigner, John Finch, was astounded at the amount of serenading he witnessed in New York City in 1830. He suggested gallantly that "the beauty of the American ladies demands that every homage should be paid to their charms."[44] A second foreigner, D.W. Mitchell, after listening to a band of evening serenaders in Richmond, concluded: "This is a common practice in many parts of the States, every sort of music being employed, from the voice or guitar up to the German band...to perform before the houses of young ladies..."[45]

Since most comments on such activities are brief, one welcomes any information on what actually took place during an evening devoted to gallantry. Fortunately one observer, Carl Arfwedson, has left a detailed account of an evening's serenading in which he participated while visiting Boston in 1832. He was told by a young Boston man that an important local custom was the performance of nighttime serenades "for the edification of the fair sex." He was invited one evening to accompany a half-dozen young gentlemen on an after-dark musical progress through town. After supplying themselves with a guitar and a flute, and wrapping themselves in cloaks after "the Italian fashion," these Bostonians wandered down to the lower part of the city. They stopped before "the residence of one of the belles." Their serenading was commenced "under the window stated to belong to the bedchamber of the lady." A window slid open quietly. Thenceforth, "it may be easily imagined how sentimental were the tones which peirced the ears of the listening fair one.... The whole company, actors and audience, appeared, nevertheless, to part under visible feelings of melancholy...."[46]

During summertime young men enjoyed the company of the local belles at picnics and barbeques;[47] wintertime, on sleighing expeditions. These activities normally included dancing and the singing of parlor songs. Information on sleighing parties in the Pittsburgh of 1806 is provided by Thomas Ashe. He writes that as soon as sufficient snow had fallen, merry gentlemen hastened to engage sleighs and horses in order to "take out their favorite female friends." At night a large party of "twenty or thirty carioles" would set out by torch light for a "tavern several miles distant." Music accompanied them all the way to their destination. After arriving they began "the mazy dance." This in turn was "followed by supper, songs, catches, and glees."[48]

One feels Frances Wright was correct when she noted that the American young people "of both sexes here enjoy a freedom of intercourse unknown" in Europe. They "dance, sing, walk, and 'run in sleighs' together, by sunshine and moonshine, without the occurrence or even the apprehension of any impropriety."[49] She made these remarks after an 1819 stay in New York City.

Many Americans were inveterate singers on almost all occasions and levels of social intercourse. In 1788 a group of United States congressmen boarded a boat on Long Island Sound. They spent the day hunting birds, fishing, playing cards and singing.[50] On board packets sailing between New York and other coastal cities, barges on the Erie Canal and river boats on the Hudson, the passengers entertained each other with parlor songs.[51]

Indeed, travel and song went hand-in-hand. While traveling by coach, Americans sang. When stopping over for the night at an inn or hotel, they expected to find a piano to accompany their singing before retiring.[52] From the annual Fourth-of-July celebration to the weekly meeting of the ladies' sewing circle, the performances of parlor song were in order.[53]

The craving for parlor melodies was so strong that they were introduced into formal lectures and church services. Contrafacts substituting solemn or religious texts for the original sentimental ones were sung to the most popular of the the parlor tunes. In June 1839 James Boardman attended a New York public lecture on education among the laboring classes, given by Miss Frances Wright, and heard a choir sing "hymns in praise of science to the music of 'Away with melancholy,'—'Auld lang syne,' and 'Will you come to the bower I've shaded for you?,' " which he found ludicrous.[54] An upset writer, in *Dwight's Journal* denounces the "illiterate music" sung in American church services. He found them "out of place, and deleterious in their influence when used in the house of God, simply in consequence of their associations—I refer now, to such tunes as *Lilly Dale, Coming through the Rye, Nid, Nid, Noddin,* and all other secular melodies which are associated with certain secular works by a large majority of the community."[55]

On what occasions did amateurs sing before public audiences? First, one comes upon numerous descriptions of juveniles put on exhibit at schools, where they performed parlor pieces during receptions for parents and other visitors.[56] In addition, members of the music classes at girls' seminaries were expected, particularly in the wearisome winter months, to demonstrate their accomplishments before the local townspeople.[57] Furthermore, in

Rustic Dance after a Sleigh Ride. Reprinted with permission from the Museum of Fine Arts, Boston

Period III the attendees at singing-schools and music conventions, along with their teachers, gave concerts that included parlor songs. These public entertainments normally constituted the closing exercises of their music course. Typical of the music heard at these events were Bishop's *Home! Sweet Home!*, Russel's *The Spider and the Fly,* Wallace's *Scenes that Are Brightest,* and Rooke's *My Boyhood Home.*[58]

Although a town's musical association or church choir gave some concerts limited entirely to sacred music, the occasions were numerous when parlor compositions were also heard. Moreover, the audiences seem to have welcomed their performance. In 1851 the Presbyterian Church Choir of Canton, Michigan, gave a public presentation of songs like *I'm Fading Away, Granite Mountain State, Field of Monterey, We Are Almost There* and *The Ivy Green.* The reporter of this event saw no reason to describe it as exceptional or inappropriate for a church choir. Instead he points to the unanimous approval of the townspeople. His neighbors agreed the singing was done "with good effect and in excellent taste." The rendition of the songs "drew the silent tear more than once that evening."[59]

Some amateurs had voices of sufficient quality or training or both to permit their appearance on the concert or theater stage alongside professional musicians. For example when the British vocalist Mrs. Wood arrived in Boston to give a series of concerts, she required the assistance of another singer in the vocal duets. Charlotte Cushman, still a young girl, came forward to help and achieved a success that decided her on a stage career.[60]

The ladies and gentlemen who consented to appear in public usually asked that their names be excluded from advertisements and programs. Typical was the "Grand Concert of Vocal and Instrumental Music" given in Boston's Boylston Hall on Tuesday, 15 August 1820, "By the Professional Gentlemen of the Orchestra and Amateurs." The promised features of the performance were:

Part I

Sinfonia, "La Chasse,"		Pleyel,
Song, "Diana,"	Amateur	Shield,
Variations, Piano Forte	Mr. Eckhard	Eckhard,
Duet "Sweet is the Vale"	Miss Schaffer & an Amateur	Duchess of Devonshire,
Concerto, Clarionet	Mr. Hart	F.C. Schaffer,

Part II

Sinfonia .... Haydn,
Song .... Amateur,
Sonata,Pianoforte,—Mr. Eckhard, accompanied on the violin by Mr.Ostinelli .... Mozart,
Song, "Trumpet of Victory," Amateur .... Braham,
Minuetto.. Krommer,
Glee,................ Amateurs, accompanied on the Piano Forte by Dr. Jackson,
Finale,.. Full Orchestra.[61]

Nevertheless, such public appearances by amateurs were exceptional during the seventy years of this study. Most Americans confined their performances of secular songs to their homes. Quite true is the conclusion of an anonymous writer in the Boston *Musical Times:* "Here, music is an amusement of leisure hours, the occupation of social evenings; and only in comparatively rare instances do individuals voluntarily emerge from the refinement of private into the vortex of public life. Music ranks here mainly as an accomplishment, and the great majority of those possessing ample qualifications for becoming excellent vocalists would never dream of making music the business of their lives."[62]

The Functions of the Parlor Song

Explored were the questions of when and where the singing of parlor works took place. An accompanying question is why did amateurs purchase and sing these songs?

One reason not to be disparaged was the compelling force of fashion. Fashion propelled music lover and indifferent alike into collecting sheet music, binding it into volumes, and performing it at least occasionally before others. During the era under study, these occupations were the vogue for American and British ladies. Sometimes little personal involvement with the music seems to have been involved. In 1853 appeared a short story, "Idle Words," by Alice B. Neal. The author dislikes mindless young women who perform songs and remain indifferent to the beauty of the melody and verse. In the tale, two stylish ladies converse—Jenny, an unpleasant snob, and one of her acquaintances. Jenny abruptly interrupts her companion's conversation, asking: "O, are there any new songs? I meant to have written you to bring me some. I'm tired to death of all my old ones; Annie Lane catches everything I sing, and I always give up anything the minute it becomes common." To this, her friend replies: "Everybody has got ballad fever, since Catherine Hayes sang in Boston. You don't hear anything else but Kathleen Mavourneen, and The Harp That Once...." Swiftly, Jenny breaks in with: "What, those old things. Esther used to sing them as long ago as I can remember. It does worry me so, when Esther takes a musical fit. I won't go near the piano. I do believe she thinks she sings better than I do now, and she tries to be so young."[63]

Whenever a favorite professional singer made a tour of the United States, the pieces in his or her repertoire immediately became fashionable and were purchased and sung avidly by amateurs.[64] The very popular Welsh tenor Thomas Philipps toured America from 1818 through 1823. Several songs he composed and sang, like *The Hunter's Horn* and *This Blooming Rose,* drew large followings. He also introduced compositions by other composers, songs like Thomas Linley's *Ah, Sure a Pair Was Never Seen,* Thomas Moore's *Fanny Dearest,* and Henry Bishop's *Love Has Eyes.* All of these compositions were immediately sung in many American homes. They appear frequently in the extant collections from these years. Almost all the copies of these works are designated "as sung by Mr. Philipps."

Large numbers of Americans wished to appear fashionable, yet lived in towns rarely visited by professional singers. These men and women often felt confused by the number of songs available and the conflicting claims, printed on their title pages and elsewhere, that they were the compositions most favored by those with taste. As a convenience to such people, publishers issued by subscription (either in monthly, bimonthly, or quarterly installments) what they assured their subscribers was "a choice selection" of "favorite" and "fashionable" parlor songs and piano selections. An early musical publication issued by subscription was *The Musical Journal,* its first issue appearing in 1800. Benjamin Carr, its publisher, selected and edited the music.

By 1830 more and more publishers were making selections of the popular music of the day available by subscription. About this time another vogue began. Once a year, usually just before Christmas, a few firms put out elegantly bound musical annuals, sometimes consisting of the compositions issued by subscription during the preceding year, sometimes of new works. These volumes were meant to be given as gifts. There are several extant with a handsomely designed and printed introductory page, where the name of donor and donee can be entered.

During Period II. and III., two other sources provided women with fashionable music. Popular magazines like *Godey's Lady's*

Book included illustrations of the latest clothing styles, a variety of light reading matter and piano and vocal selections in their monthly issues. Also elaborate books meant for gift giving were offered. These contained poems, little items of advice to ladies, stories, color plates of dress styles and some parlor music.

A close second to fashion as a reason for purchasing and performing parlor music was the consideration that music was a necessary accomplishment and a mark of gentility. This was an especially important incentive for studying music for Americans unhappy over the rawness of their new civilization and sensitive to the criticisms of foreign visitors offended by the absence of manners and graces in American society. Thus, Susanna Rowson, writer, actress, teacher of women and well-known author in America around 1800, speaks with pity of a "Miss Withers" whose mother knew no difference between the education of a gentlewoman and that of a tradesman's or farmer's daughter. The girl was taught to cook, sew and keep house: "But to the fine arts she was a perfect stranger. Music, dancing, or drawing had no charms for her, nor had she the least idea of the pleasures resulting from a well-informed, elegantly cultivated mind."[65]

Even the dour John Adams, certainly no friend of frippery, conceded music "an agreeable Accomplishment." After meeting the "genteel and well bred" Francis Hopkinson, lawyer, poet and song composer, Adams mentions that he himself had neither the leisure nor the tranquility of mind to practice the "Elegant, and ingenious Arts of Painting, Sculpture, Statuary, Architecture, and Musick." He did, however, make certain his own children took up musical studies.[66]

Parents were persuaded into considerable expenditures for the sake of their children. Young people hastened to engage the services of voice and keyboard instructors. As a writer in the Boston *Euterpeiad* pointed out, "in the modern system of female education," a knowledge of music was considered "an indispensible requisite." For this reason, "the daughters of a large portion of the community, in the middle and upper ranks of life, think themselves neglected if they are not indulged with a piano-forte."[67]

The acquisition of musical skill could lead to marriage. An unidentified male once wrote down what he felt were the qualities of a fine wife. He mentions elegance, taste, gentle manners without "country awkwardness," and a cultivated mind. He continues: "She must love and cherish *Music* above all other arts and sciences; she must have an ear attuned in a particular manner, so she can distinguish one piece of music from another, when she hears it performed, and be a competent adept in musical sounds; she must have a voice which will charm the moon and stars, and when she sings her music must be such as will excite joy and grief, give pleasure and pain, and compose my disturbed thoughts after being out all night."[68]

Some achievement in music was useful to young men who wished to attract the women they admired. Lingering jealousy once caused John Randolph to speak disparagingly of a young man he once knew. This former acquaintance, Randolph told Theodore Dudley, "sang a good song, and was the envy of every foolish fellow, and the darling of every silly girl who knew him."[70]

A third and important reason for the existence of parlor songs was social enjoyment that went beyond mere amusement. It is true that one important musician and critic, Thomas Hastings,has suggested that too much parlor music had "the amusement of the multitudes" as its sole object for existence. He has no use for such superficiality.[71] However, his orientation was religious. He felt no sympathy for secular music that failed to convey a clear-cut moral message. What Hastings could not or would not see was that the performance of a parlor song with a winning melody and an inwardly directed verse gave intense pleasure to a significant number of Americans.

This was true for the families of some prominent Americans. On 23 October 1788, Francis Hopkinson wrote to Thomas Jefferson from Philadelphia: "I have amused myself with composing six easy and simple Songs for the Harpsichord, Words and music all my own. The music is now engraving. When finish'd I will do myself the Pleasure of sending a Copy to Miss Jefferson." Thomas Jefferson, who was in Paris with his family, wrote back on 13 March 1789 that a copy had been received: "Accept my thanks... and my daughter's for the book of songs. I will not tell you how much they pleased us nor how well the last of them [*The Trav'ler Benighted*] merits praise for its pathos, but relate a fact only, which is that while my elder daughter was playing it on the harpsichord, I happened to look towards the fire and saw the younger one all in tears. I asked her if she was sick? She said, 'no, but the tune was so mournful'."[72]

A contemporary of Jefferson, Elihu Hubbard Smith, a physician and one of the Hartford Wits, spoke of his passionate fondness for music. Above all, songs enchanted him most.[73]

Another physician, William Whiting, who practised medicine in Great Barrington, Massachusetts, once became furious when the local Congregational minister criticized his and his family's enjoyment of secular music. He was certain such intolerance showed little sensitivity to beauty and less to the genuine consolations afforded by song. He abandoned the

Congregationalists and joined the newly established Episcopalian congregation, for, "he could not admit, that, in the enjoyment of their melodies and harmonies, any inmate of his house could be found guilty of violating the precepts of true religion or sound morals. He felt no disgrace in being the head of 'the musical family' but, encircled by his happy group of wife and children, it was his great delight to have them all take part in a social enjoyment, which, beyond all others upon earth appeared to him to be a tuning of the soul for heaven."[74]

As a physician, Benjamin Rush advocated singing for the sake of one's physical and mental health. He claimed the activity strengthened the lungs and soothed "the cares of domestic life," much more than the mere playing of instrumental pieces. He added that he had noticed few people with the leisure necessary for instrumental practice. As a result too many keyboard instruments served only "as sideboards for their parlors."[75]

Music's therapeutic powers were well-recognized in eighteenth-century America. John Adams would have agreed with Rush's contention that singing helped ease domestic cares. Adams advanced a similar conclusion to Abigail before she became his wife. Abigail claimed to have a voice of poor quality. This, he decided, was a weak argument for not taking up musical study. He urged a reconsideration of her decision not to learn to sing: "You could never yet be prevail'd on to learn to sing. This I take very soberly to be an Imperfection of the most moment of any. An Ear for Music would be a source of much Pleasure, and a Voice and skill would be a private solitary Amusement, of great Value when no other could be had. You must have remarked an Example of this in Mrs. Cranch, who must in all probability have been deafened to Death with the Cries of her Betsy, if she had not drowned them on Musick of her own."[76]

A few years after their marriage, John Adams departed on a diplomatic mission to France. A desolate Abigail was left behind with the children. A parlor song she had her son Charles learn and sing to her helped assuage her gloom. She wrote to her husband that she found it impossible to describe how moved she was by a "Scotch song which was sung to me by a young lady in order to divert a Melancholy hour." The song had "all the power of a well wrought Tradidy [sic]." She told John that when she had her emotions under control, she begged the girl to teach the song to her son. Abigail ended her letter saying she was enclosing the song: "It has Beauties in it to me, which an indifferent person would not feel perhaps—

His very foot has Musick in't.

As he comes up the stairs.

How oft has my Heart danced to the sound of that Musick?

And shall I see his face again?
And shall I hear him speak?

Gracious Heaven hear and answer my daily petition 'by banishing all my Grief'."[77]

Telling the distant John Adams of hearing *There's Nae Luck About the House,* a love song to an absent husband, provided a nice touch to Mrs. Adam's letter. Indubitably what she wrote she meant. More significantly, she felt that the crystalization of her emotions was best expressed through a popular song of the day. It must be remembered that Abigail Adams was a woman with one of the keenest minds of her time. She was well read and had a sharp perception of the falsities in society. Yet, for her this parlor work struck no false note. Instead it mirrored her profoundest feelings. She detected nothing cloying or trite in its message or music.

The two couplets she quoted are from the fifth stanza of the lyric. The words were written either by Jean Adams (not related to the Adamses) or William Mickle, and were fitted to the air *Up and Waur at Them a' Willie:*

Sae true his heart, sae smooth his speech
His breath like cauler air,
His very foot has music in't
As he comes up the stair.
And will I see his face again,
And will I hear him speak?
I'm downright dizzy wi' the thought,
In troth I'm like to greet.
For there's nae luck about the house,
There's nae luck at a',
There's little pleasure in the house
When our gudeman's awa.[78]

A curious scene in which music is invoked for depression is described by Philip Vickers Fithian in his 1774 *Journal.* Fithian, a tutor to the children of Robert Carter, of Nominee Hall, Virginia, was present one July evening when Mrs. Carter was found to be very dispirited by her husband. Wishing to relieve his wife of her sadness, Robert Carter sent for his daughter Nancy. The girl was asked to sing for her mother. She proved recalcitrant. Slowly and silently she minced into the room, then fussed for several minutes over her guitar, finally singing *Water Parted from the Sea.*

Instead of thanking Nancy, Robert Carter scolded her for plucking her eyebrows. Fithian was then asked if he had ever studied singing. Two years, Fithian replied. Carter complained that he had been giving Nancy lessons, but she had proved lazy and would not study. "Sing the Funeral Hymn," Carter demanded as if to prove his point. Nancy, however, refused to comply: "Excuse me, Papa, I have lost the Verses."[79]

Water Parted from the Sea is a song from Thomas Arne's opera *Artaxerxes.* The piece, a favorite and widely sung one in eighteenth-century America, was not issued in sheet-music form by an American publisher until about 1796.

American singers valued most those compositions that stressed "the sentiments of the heart." Songs were also expected to illustrate the principles of social relationships that society found essential. An indispensable function of parlor song was the reflection and reinforcement of values shared by most Americans, values centered on concepts of propriety, morality and the idealization of emotion. All hints of sexuality were barred from most love songs. Marriage, home, parents and country were honored. Moderation in all things was advised. God was frequently invoked. The fate of the unwed girl who yielded to persuasion, the young man who abandoned his home or scorned his parents, and the soldier who deserted to the enemy was projected as abandonment, exile, insanity or violent death. Others may die—an innocent child, a loved sister, a beautiful maiden, a careworn mother, a heroic sailor—but heaven is their destination. Someone always remains behind to mourn their passing, extol their virtues and cherish their memory.

To music lovers the sentiments contained in the texts expressed tender and, at the same time, well-bred feelings. To people hearing these songs one hundred and fifty years later, an age where educated and sophisticated adults are less disposed to expose their emotions to public scrutiny, these sentiments incline toward sentimentality, and tender feelings verge on mawkishness—as in the following first stanza of *The Graves of a Household.* With words by the Englishwoman Felicia Hemans, the song became popular in the United States during the late forties, especially in the quartet arrangement sung by the Barker Family:

They grew in beauty side by side,
  They fill'd one home with glee;
Their graves are sever'd far and wide
  By mount and stream and sea.
The same fond mother bent at night
  O'er each fair sleeper's brow,
She had each folded flow'r in sight;

Where are these dreamers now?

The words, by a writer whose poetry was greatly admired in the early nineteenth century and who wrote the texts of many parlor songs, achieve what may be denominated as the typical tone of sentiment favored by Americans who purchased and enjoyed this kind of music.

According to Russel B. Nye, in his biography *George Bancroft,* Bancroft and his circle of friends required poetry to be committed to the advancement of morality. These men and women did not find a model to admire in the poetry of John Keats, which was too sensual for them, nor in the poetry of Lord Byron, which seemed too egotistical and uncontrolled. Instead, their highest praise went to Mrs. Hemans's poetry, because it "observed the boundries of virtue and always exhibited a moral."[80] Elizabeth Davis Bancroft and her husband George have left a collection of sheet music, now at Houghton Library, which contains parlor songs, all of them breathing virtue and morality.

Amongst the hundreds of surviving songs, only a few have texts with themes different from those mentioned. These usually express an aggressive patriotism or a mild comicalness.

Several contemporary writers have written about their concern over the quality of American democratic life. They are convinced that parlor songs can improve that quality since they teach moral precepts more effectively than other means. These writers approve the performance of these compositions in the home and recommend their cultivation by all of America's "free citizenry." Even Thomas Hastings, the New York musician ordinarily antipathetic to much of the secular music he heard about him concludes concerning the parlor song: "This species of composition, humble as it seems, should not be neglected in a republican country."[81] He does not mean to encourage songs on "trivial subjects," but "parlor music" intended to "promote moral principles, refined sentiments, and sympathetic emotions."[82]

Something is learned of how songs were expected to function in American society from a long essay on "Ballad," by John W. Moore, New Hampshire born musician and writer, who published an extremely ambitious *Complete Encyclopedia of Music* in 1854. Americans, Moore writes, "are eminently a working people." For them, songs could serve as a much needed means for relaxation, while at the same time introducing "refinement of taste" and a degree of "moral feeling." All people, he claims, are "susceptible to the influence of music."

Moore continues by saying that since music is the "language of the heart," it can encourage an "affinity for virtue" and for the purer and gentler emotions. All children are capable of musical study. In order to mold the character of the American democracy, the entire citizenry should study vocal music in the schools. Through song, Americans can be taught what elevates rather than what debases the mind. In this way music becomes "the handmaid of civilization." He ends the essay with these words: "Music is allied to the highest sentiments of man's moral nature—love of God, love of country, love of friends.... What tongue can tell the unutterable energies that reside in these three engines—church music, national airs, and finished melodies—as means for informing and enlarging the mighty hearts of a free people?"[83]

Although songs are found whose subjects Hastings and Moore might consider trivial, very few texts transgress the rather strictly delineated moral limits insisted upon by early American society. Most of them do strongly affirm the tenets of that society—the sanctity of its institutions, the love of home, God and country, the supremacy of conscience and duty, the necessity for moderation in thought, feeling and action, and the union of beauty with sentiment. These beliefs, given poetic expression and united to music, became what is called the parlor song, an instructive, entertaining and decorous diversion for the American family.

Notes

1. The Holmes music is in Houghton Library, though without shelf number.
2. Boston Athenaeum, shelf-number TR 9C685, vol. 1 and 2.
3. John Tasker Howard, *Stephen Foster, America's Troubadour* (New York, 1953), pp. 108,115.
4. Bliss Perry, *Life and Letters of Henry Lee Higginson,* I (Boston, 1921), 78.
5. *The Autobiography of Mark Twain,* ed. Charles Neider (New York, 1959), p. 59.
6. Both songs originated as British broadsides to traditional tunes, then entered aural tradition. See G. Malcolm Laws, Jr., *American Balladry from British Broadsides* (Philadelphia, 1957), pp. 57, 199, 268.
7. J.P. Kennedy, *Swallow Barn,* rev. ed. (New York, 1851), pp. 377-80. Kennedy, p. 10, stated that he was giving a faithful picture of the people and the life of the time.
8. Collection at Houghton Library, Mus. 403.3 and 475.1.
9. The Richardson collection is at Houghton, without shelf number.
10. Three volumes of her sheet music, without shelf number, are at Houghton.
11. The Baldwin music, without shelf number, is at Houghton.
12. Of the Custis music, six volumes are at Mount Vernon, two at Houghton.
13. Philip Vickers Fithian, *Journal, 1777-1786,* ed. Robert Greenhalgh Albion and Leonidas Dodson (Princeton, 1934), pp 47-49.
14. Samuel Griswold Goodrich, *Recollections of a Lifetime,* I (New York, 1856), 74.
15. "Mirror of Taste," Boston *Euterpeiad,* 2 February 1822, p. 199.
16. S.A. Ferrall, *A Ramble of Six Thousand Miles Through the United States of America* (London, 1832), p. 10; and Francis J. Grund, *Aristocracy in America* (New

York, 1959), p. 45.

17. See *The Lowell Offering,* March 1841, pp. 59-60; March 1845, pp. 51-52; April 1845, pp. 82-88; July 1845, pp. 145-149; December 1845, pp. 268-71. This periodical had as contributors and editors, women who labored in the textile mills of Lowell, Massachusetts.

18. New York *Musical Review,* 19 May 1858, p. 166.

19. Harold Thompson, *A Pioneer Songster* (Ithaca, N.Y., 1958). Lizette Woodworth Reese, in *A Victorian Village* (New York, 1929), pp. 279-284, states that in the tiny hamlet of Waverly, Maryland, in the 1850s her German-born mother had learned at singing school and sang hymns and secular songs; her father, a musical illiterate, sang one song, *Old Dog Tray.*

20. The 1855 issues of this periodical commence to make this distinction; see, for example, the issue of 29 December 1855, p. 436.

21. Parke Rouse, Jr., *Life in Colonial Virginia* (New York, 1968), p. 122.

22. Susan I. Lesley, *Recollections of My Mother* (Boston, 1886) p. 89.

23. John Murry Forbes, *Letters and Recollections,* ed. Sarah Forbes Hughes, I (Boston, 1900), p. 32.

24. *Nancy Shippen, Her Journal Book,* ed. Ethel Armes (New York, 1968), p. 228.

25. "Letters from a New England Village," ed. Ellen Chase, *The New England Quarterly,* II (1929), 145.

26. Powhatan Bouldin, *Home Reminiscences of John Randolph of Roanoke* (Richmond, Virginia, 1878), p. 11.

27. Carl David Arfwedson, *The United States and Canada in 1832, 1833, and 1834,* I (1834; reprint ed., New York,1969), 135.

28. Eleanor M. Tilton, *Amiable Autocrat, A Biography of Dr. Oliver Wendell Holmes* (New York, 1947), p. 14; Van Wyck Brooks, *The Flowering of New England* (New York, 1952), p. 29.

29. Samuel Longfellow *Life of Henry Wadsworth Longfellow,* I (Boston, 1886), 14.

30. See, for example, his diary entry for 2 January 1788; *Diary of John Quincy Adams, 1787-1789.* Proceedings of the Massachusetts Historical Society (November, 1902), pp. 363-64.

31. John Melish, *Travels Through the United States of America in the Years 1806 & 1807, and 1809. 1810, & 1811* (London, 1818), pp. 466-67.

32. Letter of Thomas Hill Hubbard to Mrs. Hubbard, 22 December 1817, in the Library of Alexandria, Virginia; letter of Eleanor Custis Lewis to Elizabeth Bordley Gibson, 22 May 1821, in the Mount Vernon Archives; Howard, p. 77; John Gould Curtis, *History of the Town of Brookline, Massachusetts* (Boston, 1933), p. 252.

33. Edward Everett Hale, *James Russell Lowell and His Friends* (New York, 1969), pp. 4, 11-12.

34. Adapting poems to extant airs was a frequent practice that, in several instances, produced some of the most popular songs of the day, including *Absence* and **Near the Lake Where Drooped the Willow.*

35. *The Battle of the Nile* was published by James Hewitt in New York, ca. 1804. *General Wolfe* is known to have appeared in print as early as March 1775, when the *Pennsylvania Magazine* published it as "A new song. . . Set to music by a gentleman of this country, the words by Atlanticus;" Oscar G. Sonneck, *A Bibliography of Early Secular Music,* rev. and ed. William Treat Upton (New York, 1964) s.v. "General Wolfe." The song became very popular and was often reprinted in late eighteenth-century and nineteenth-century songsters and songbooks. Its title is sometimes confused with that of another song, *Brave Wolfe,* which also found its way into many songsters and, at the same time, was transmitted through oral tradition. The first two lines of *Brave Wolfe* are:

Cheer up, ye young men all, let nothing fright you;
Though at your live's pursuits, let that delight you.
See G. Malcolm Laws, Jr., *Native American Balladry* (Philadelphia, 1964), pp. 13, 119.

36. A parlor song by Henry Russell, first published in 1838.

37. Hale, pp. 74-76.

38. Edmund S. Morgan, *Virginians at Home* (Williamsburg, Virginia, 1952), p. 92.

39. W.E. Woodward, *The Way Our People Lived* (New York, 1944), p. 105.

40. John F. Watson, *Annals of Philadelphia and Pennsylvania,*I (Philadelphia, 1845), 220.

41. See entries for 24 October, 27 December, 28 December, 1787, in the Adams *Diary,* pp. 357, 360-361.

42. George C. Channing, *Early Recollections of Newport, R.I.* (Newport, R.I., 1868), p. 170.

43. D.W. Mitchell, *Ten Years Residence in the United States* (London, 1862), pp. 91-94.

44. John Finch, *Travels in the United States and Canada* (London, 1833), p. 33.

45. Mitchell, p. 88.

46. Arfwedson, I, 150-52.

47. See, for example, the description of a Chicago picnic, in the New York *Musical Review,* 22 August 1857, p. 258.

48. Thomas Ashe, *Travels in America, Performed in 1806.* (London, 1808), p. 30.

49. [Frances Wright], *Views of Society and Manners in America* (London, 1821), p. 38.

50. Samuel Webb to Miss Hogeboom, 11 September 1788, *Correspondence and Journals of Samuel Blachley Webb*, ed. Worthington Chauncey Ford, III (New York, 1894), 115.

51. Melish, pp. 63-64; Caroline Gilman, *The Poetry of Travelling in the United States* (New York, 1838), p. 91; Louis Hall Tharp, *The Appletons of Beacon Hill* (Boston, 1973), p. 145.

52. See, for instance, Gilman, p. 105; Tharp, p. 151.

53. See the description of 4 July 1809, at St. Louis, in Ernst C. Krohn, *Missouri Music* (New York, 1971), p. 3; and that of an 1837 meeting of the Louisville "Ladies' Sewing Society," in Leonora Cranch Scott, *The Life and Letters of Christopher Pearse Cranch* (Boston, 1917), p. 37.

54. [James Boardman], *America, and the Americans,* By a Citizen of the World (London, 1833), pp. 62-63.

55. T.B.M., "Illiterate Music," *Dwight's Journal of Music,* 7 August 1858, p. 146.

56. New York *Musical Review* 4 January 1855, p. 14.

57. Ibid., 10 January 1857, p. 8.

58. *Dwight's Journal of Music*, 19 June 1852, p. 84; New York *Musical Review,* 2 March 1854, p. 74; 15 March 1855, pp. 91-92; Fall River *Key-Note*, January 1855, p. 2.

59. *American Musical Review*, 1 May 1851, p. 71. The performance took place 24 February 1851.

60. *Charlotte Cushman: Her Letters and Memories of Her Life,* ed. Emma Stebbins (Boston, 1879), pp. 20-22.

61. Boston *Euterpeiad*, 12 August 1820, p. 80. No song entitled *Diana,* composed by Shield is known; possibly the attribution is an error, a not infrequent occurrence during these years, and what was sung was probably the song *Diana,* composed by Shield's contemporary, James Hook, and issued in Boston about 1811. The song *The*

Trumpet Sounds a Victory was actually composed by Domenico Corri (Italian composer from 25 years of age a resident in England), and made famous through the singing of John Braham, in the English opera, *The Travellers*. The song was first printed in America about 1807.

62. "American Voices," Boston *Musical Times,* 24 March 1860, p. 36.

63. Alice B. Neal, "Idle Words," *Gleason's Pictorial Drawing-Room Companion,* 15 October 1853, p. 246.

64. For confirmation of this statement see Boston *Euterpeiad,* 8 April 1820, p. 7.

65. Susanna Rowson, *Mentoria,* II (Philadelphia, 1784), pp. 64-65.

66. John Adams to Abigail Adams, 7 July and 21 August 1776, *Adams Family Correspondence,* ed. L.H. Butterfield, II (Cambridge, Mass., 1963) 40, 104.

67. "John Bray," Boston *Euterpeiad,* 15 April 1820, p. 11.

68. "The Ladies' Friend," Boston *Minerviad,* 30 March 1822, p. 11.

69. Benjamin Rush to Lady Jane Wishart Belsches, 21 April 1784, *Letters of Benjamin Rush,* ed. L.H. Butterfield, I (Princeton, 1951), 328. *The Birks of Endermay* has a lyric written by Daniel Mallet, to the Scottish air *The Smiling Morn, the Breathing Spring.*

70. *John Randolph, Letters to a Young Relative* (Philadelphia, 1834), p. 26.

71. Thomas Hastings, *Dissertation on Musical Taste* (New York, 1853), p. 169.

72. *The Papers of Thomas Jefferson*, ed. Julian P. Boyd, XIV (Princeton, 1958), 33, 649.

73. The Diary of Elihu Hubbard Smith, 1771-1798, ed. James E. Cronin (Philadelphia, 1973), p. 18.

74. John Fredrick Schroeder, *Memoir of the Life and Character of Mrs. Mary Anna Boardman* (New Haven, 1849), p. 47.

75. David Freeman Hawke, *Benjamin Rush* (Indianapolis, 1971), pp. 333-334.

76. John Adams to Abigail Smith, 17 May 1764, *Adams Correspondence,* I, 45.

77. Abigail Adams to John Adams, 27 December 1778, *Adams Correspondence,* ed. L.H. Butterfield and Marc Friedlander, III (1973), 140.

78. The song can be found in the *Songster's Museum* (Northampton, Mass., 1803), pp. 80-82. The first known sheet-music issue of the song by an American publisher is that of George Willig, in Philadelphia, ca. 1815.

79. Entry of 6 July 1774, *Journals and letters of Philip Vickers Fithian, 1773-1774,* ed. Hunter Dickinson Farish (Williamsburg, Virginia, 1957), p. 132.

80. Russel B. Nye, *George Bancroft* (New York, 1964), pp. 48-49.

81. *Dissertation,* p. 190.

82. Ibid, p. 17.

83. John W. Moore, *Complete Encyclopedia of Music* (Boston, 1854), s.v. "Ballad."

Chapter 3

The Parlor Song In Music Education

The most frequent reference to parlor-song performance among amateurs occurs in connection with music education. It is therefore essential to give close scrutiny to this aspect of our early musical life. The majority of non-professional singers named in contemporary sources were adolescents between the ages of eight and twenty who were studying privately or in singing classes. Amateur musicians purchased most of their parlor songs during these years. Many bound music collections available for study today bear the names of unmarried women, sometimes followed by the name of a school. They contain works published within a time span of four to ten years, presumably the years of music study. Frequently the song's date of purchase is written on the upper right corner of the first page. Other valuable information is at times found. For example, in a Houghton volume that once belonged to Mary A. Moore, one finds written on the *verso* side of the cover the statement that in 1845 she was attending the Belchertown School in Massachusetts. On one of her pieces, she writes that she took her first music lesson at the age of twelve.

A lesser number of bound collections bear the names of men. Most of these also contain music purchased during adolescence.

One gets the clear impression that parents did not have to force lessons on their young. One excited boy proudly wrote on the page of one of his songs: "My very first song/Started study at the age of eleven." Another boy wrote: "At last! Had my first lesson today!" Girls told their friends how they looked forward to beginning their study of music. Youngsters were constantly comparing teachers, the songs they were assigned, and the progress they had made. Whenever possible they rushed to meet each other in order to demonstrate what they had learned. This kind of excitement over music study runs through the letters sent off to friends by the young Emily Dickinson.

Since music was considered a necessary component of a genteel education, parents allowed their daughters to commence study with a music teacher on a private basis, at a singing school or at a seminary, whenever they could afford it, and sometimes when they could not. Some educators thought the rush into music study was ridiculous for those whose commitment could be only slight. Why, they asked, should a girl take a few lessons then find that financial difficulties prevented her continuing? Moreover, if she came from a family unable to afford the services of servants, then the time necessary for practice would have to give way to the hundred-and-one household tasks requiring daily attention. Later, when she married, she was likely to find herself so preoccupied with raising children and catering to a husband that music would disappear from her life. In other words, these critics felt that only members of the wealthier classes, whose present and future promised some leisure, should take up music.

This kind of reservation was voiced more frequently before 1830, when music was considered an amiable refinement; much less after 1830, when Jacksonian democracy and the desire to encourage a broadly-based national culture caused educators to claim the right to a music education for all of their fellow citizens. However, at all times educators objected to the haphazard way some students underwent musical training and the inconsequence of a number of the compositions studied.

A pre 1830- point of view is expressed by a prominent educator of young ladies during the first years of the nineteenth century: "In the present refined age, if an industrious tradesman can afford to give his daughter five hundred pounds, it is immediately settled by Mamma, that Miss must be *genteelly* educated." So wrote Susanna Rowson. She adds that the learning of French, elegant needle work, singing and keyboard skills is usually wasted since a tradesman's daughter normally has "neither time nor opportunity" to make use of her accomplishments after marriage.[1]

At least one observer, James Boardman, felt advice like Rowson's was more ignored than honored. This English traveler asserts that music in the 1820s was "taught to all young misses, as young females in the sphere of society above the laboring classes are styled." This was his conclusion after surveying the musical practices in American towns like Rochester, New York (which numbered 13,000 inhabitants at that time).[2]

Contemporary writers state repeatedly that polite society considered the study of parlor songs essential to a girl's education. For example a statement in the Boston *Euterpeiad* of October 1822, p. 119, probably written by the editor, John Rowe Parker, sees music teachers following the "present mode of instruction" aimed at pleasing parents and pupils. It permits students to learn "principally the fashionable ballads of the hour," even from the beginning of their studies.

In their criticisms of the parlor song and its adherents, and in their disparagement of American taste, the advocates of sacred music and European art music testify to the popularity of the parlor genre among the middle class young. On page 51 of the New York *Euterpeiad,* 15 July 1830, for example, a Mr. Asaph, who disliked the drift of the secular songs of his time, complains: "No little weight ought to be attached to the fact that the present fashionable Songs, whose subjects are 'cupids-darts-love-butterflies-moths-doves,' etc., are placed before our young girls from the age of eight to eighteen." Since Asaph was the Biblical choir master in King David's time, the writer using this pseudonym may have been a church-choir director, or the editor, Charles Dingley. Five years later Dingley became editor of the *Family Minstrel,* in which capacity he concerned himself mainly with sacred music.

Another dimension to this criticism is revealed in an article on "Young Ladies' Musical Education," printed in the *Musical Reporter,* January 1841, pages 23-25. The writer deplores the quality of the parlor songs presented to girls for study. He says these questionable works include ballads of "sickly sentimentality" and songs of war or the sea that are too masculine for young women to sing. Cited as examples are two of the most popular songs of the day, Miss Browne's *The Captive Knight* and Neukomm's *The Sea.*

In defense of the Americans thus criticized, one can point to few educated persons aware of and desiring alternatives to parlor music. Most parents and their children knew only the popular songs that surrounded them. Sentimental compositions had inundated their senses during a large part of their lifetime. The only other music they had known was church hymns and the questionable ditties of the tavern. They desired something livelier than hymns and less vulgar than low-down tunes. Parlor songs were the perfect answer. Besides, many parlor melodies were genuinely beautiful. Grown-ups and their children insisted upon this music, which they understood and loved. Indeed, for many it was for the sake of performing parlor music that lessons were taken at all.

Evidence indicates at least a few teachers shared a strong preference for parlor music with their pupils. One such teacher, Powhatan Starke, was teaching the latest parlor music to the young ladies of Charlottesville, Virginia, in 1847. On off-hours he "joined in and enhanced every scheme for pleasure, and would finally spend half the night serenading us.... Four or five voices in unison would sing such songs as 'Oft in the Stilly Night,' 'The Last Rose of Summer,' 'Eileen Aroon,' 'Flow Gently, Sweet Afton,' and one voice render Rizzio's lovely song—'Queen of my soul whose starlit eyes/Are all the light I seek'."[3] So wrote one participant.

The writer was a girl of seventeen at the time and Mr. Starke's pupil. She concludes that, all in all, these months were a happy period for her, as she learned and performed parlor music and some campaign songs honoring Henry Clay. She also claims that such works were in constant demand at house-parties, therefore musts for music study.

By the end of Period II most educators had abandoned the position that musical training was only for children whose parents possessed ample means for providing them with a genteel education. Educators were increasingly leery of stands which seemed to contradict democratic principles by denying the arts to the decent but less affluent citizenry. These more up-to-date musicians presumed everyone possessed some trainable talent. They underlined the physical and psychological benefits to be derived from singing. What mattered, too, was not the high musical proficiency a student might attain but the possibility that through music a student's future could be directed along socially desirable pathways. A young man need not sound like a *tenore assoluto,* or a young woman like a *prima donna.* No deficiency in training or voice quality should deter anyone from making music, the educators decided.

Once a person knew how to sing, he or she could do so on a variety of occasions. Neither the possession of a piano, or the ability to play one was essential for enjoyment. For those with a modicum of skill, the inexpensive melodeon, a small reed organ, or the guitar could provide an instrumental accompaniment. For the remainder, songs could be performed and enjoyed without instrumental assistance. So long as some musical training was given the singer during youth, little or no musical practice and only a moment or two was needed to sing a simple song for one's own amusement or for the entertainment and edification of the home circle. The arguments for the musical education of the masses appear constantly after 1830 in the writings of influential educators and musicians like Lowell Mason, George Root and William Bradbury.

Throughout all three periods, agreement existed among voice teachers, including the most responsible, that instruction could begin at about eight years of age. This was recommended by the highly respected Lowell Mason.[4] A brief outline of the stages of learning advocated by teachers appears in an unsigned article of the New York *Musical Review,* 26 April 1855. The writer advises parents to start a child's voice instruction at eight years of age. If the youngster can reproduce simple melodies, then he can begin to study the accurate delivery of tones and words and commence acquiring taste and expression. At fifteen or sixteen years of age, the pupil's voice changes. Afterwards the student can aim at the full development of his vocal powers, so that by twenty years of age a professional quality is achieved. If no professional career is intended, then voice study to about eighteen years of age is sufficient for "all domestic and social purposes."

Private Instruction

Music studied under a private instructor was an extremely important part of the education of some young people. Yet, though they gained a high degree of competency, they rarely turned professional. This was true especially in the years before 1840. After 1840, Americans became bolder. Capable instrumentalists and singers began to brave the criticisms of their peers and soon numbers of them were plunging into the maelstrom of professional life.

One talented amateur for whom a professional life was inconceivable was Eleanor Parke Custis. She left eight volumes of music, six at Mount Vernon and two now at Houghton Library. Most of her compositions were purchased between 1789 and 1797 when she was 10 to 17 years of age. These were the years she lived with George and Martha Washington in New York and Philadelphia. During this time she studied keyboard playing and singing with four teachers: Alexander Reinagle, John Moller, Henry Capron and Filippo Trisobio.[5] Her musical progress was closely supervised by her grandmother, Martha Washington, who insisted on thoroughness in all of Eleanor's studies. The grandmother kept the girl practising her music for long hours—usually four or five a day. George Parke Custis, Eleanor's brother, says his sister sat "very long and very unwillingly at the harpsichord.... The poor girl would play and cry, and cry and play, for long hours, under the immediate eye of her grandmother, a rigid disciplinarian in all things."[6]

In the late 1790s Eleanor Custis won the reputation of being one of the most beautiful and accomplished women in the United States. Julian Ursyn Niemcewicz, a Polish visitor who stayed at Mount Vernon for a few days in June 1798, was overwhelmed by Eleanor's many virtues. He saw her as "one of those celestial figures that nature produces only rarely, that the inspiration of painters has sometimes divined and that one cannot see without ecstasy. Her sweetness is equal to her beauty, and this being, so perfect of form, possesses all the talents: she plays the harpsichord, sings, draws better than any women in America or even in Europe."[7]

While most young women studied music less intensively than

did Eleanor Custis, they did try to progress sufficiently to impress others with their gentility. Some of them apparently did make excellent impressions. Jean Pierre Brissot, a French visitor to Boston in 1788, was pleased with the amateur musical entertainment found in Boston homes. Carried away by the charms of the local young women, he commended their "forte-piano" playing and their singing: "This art [or music], it is true, is still only in its infancy, but the young girls who are learning to play are so sweet, so kind, and so modest that the pleasure they give you is far greater than any that proved proficiency could offer."[8]

To facilitate study, students purchased one of the many instruction manuals issued by British and American publishers. Significant early American publications of this type include Benjamin Carr's *Lessons and Exercises in Vocal Music* (Baltimore, ca. 1811), John Cole's *The Rudiments of Music, or An Introduction to the Art of Singing* (Baltimore, ca 1811), Thomas Hasting's *The Musical Reader, or Practical Lessons for the Voice* (Utica, 1817), Arthur Clifton's *New Vocal Instructor* (Philadelphia, 1820), and Thomas Philipps's *Elementary Practices for Singing* (Boston, 1822).

These instruction manuals are now found bound with copies of parlor songs in some of the extant collections. One that appears frequently is the fifteen-page *New Vocal Instructor* of Arthur Clifton, an English-born musician resident in Baltimore. Although he does not specifically mention parlor song in his instruction book, Clifton himself was principally a parlor-song composer, and he does say that his *Instructor* is aimed at the ten-to-fourteen year old student, male or female, soprano or tenor, who has already acquired a rudimentary musical kowledge, and who desires to study sacred and secular song in English. He states further that his publication gives rules "on the Art of Pronounciation, Articulation Emphasis, style [sic], and Taste." In order to convey the poet's theme, he advises: "It is necessary to study the subject that is to be sung. . .[so] the proper feeling and expression may be given."

To avoid monotony, one must learn to "modulate the voice so as to produce a rise and fall, or *crescendo* and *diminuendo* which gives the effect to Song, as light and shade does to Picture." Additionally, one must "give proper emphasis and expression to the words. Should the subject of a Song be lively, deliver the words in a short and animated manner. If plaintive, let the syllables be more extended, dwelling on the vowels longer and using more pathos and feeling. Let the countenance share in the expression of the subject, thus suiting 'the action to the word'."

In a superficial manner, Clifton explains and gives brief

exercises on the swell, major and minor scales, chromatic passages, melodic intervals, staccato singing, the execution of runs, ornaments, and cadenzas, breath control, rhythm and singing in general.

Instruction books like Clifton's were unsatisfactory in several important respects. No thought-out pedagogical system is apparent. The author tosses off vague ideas and leaves it to others to explain what he means. The musical examples seem models intended to guide the efforts of individual teachers, rather than carefully considered passages designed for maximum usefulness to the student. Clifton's music undoubtedly had to be supplemented with numerous additional exercises written into a student's blank book by his teacher.

No songs appear in Clifton's *Instructor,* possibly because he felt that the voice teachers themselves would wish to recommend the songs for their students. Another consideration might have been that as time passed any songs which might be included would become passe′, outmoding the entire publication and shortening its sales life. Regrettably Clifton failed to discuss or give instructions on "style," "taste," the interpretation of the text with "proper" expression, and the registering of feeling on the face. These are only mentioned in passing. Moreover, the exercises he provides are sufficiently demanding to necessitate a skilled teacher to supervise a pupil's training. This could explain why the *Instructor* is also found in the music collections of professional singers and teachers like A.F. Nichols and Benjamin F. Baker.[9]

Teachers made their availability known through advertisements in periodicals, like the typical one appearing in the Boston *Euterpeiad,* 1 April 1820, p. 4: "Miss Hewitt begs to inform her friends, that she teaches the Piano Forte, Harp, and Singing—Her terms may be known by applying at Mrs. Rowson's, Hollis Street, or at the Franklin Music Warehouse, No. 6 Milk-Street."

Many musicians taught privately at the academies for young ladies. One famous early school was established by Susanna Rowson, who is mentioned in the Hewitt advertisement. She inaugurated her Young Ladies' Academy in Boston, in the spring of 1799. The school later moved to Medford, then to Newton—towns close to Boston. She saw to it that her pupils had a pianoforte for practise. Three of the finest local musicians, Peter von Hagen and Mr. and Mrs. Gottlieb Graupner, provided keyboard and voice instruction. The music fees were $5. entrance and 75¢ a lesson, per quarter of a year.[10]

Only the affluent could meet expenses like these. For the less well-off, sending daughters to an academy and giving them music lessons was an on-again, off-again affair. As a Mrs. Harris, who operated a tavern in Georgia, explained to Adam Hodgson in 1820, whenever cotton went at 30¢ a pound, her business thrived. She could then manage her daughter's expenses of $300 for board and $50 for piano lessons at the nearby academy. (She fails to give the length of time covered by such payments.) Mrs. Harris also told Hodgson that cotton was at that moment at 15¢ a pound, business was off, and she "supposed her daughter must forget her music."[11]

In less rural areas of the country, those unable to pay for private lessons had an alternative—singing classes.

Singing Classes

Publications like the Clifton *Instructor* were intended for private teaching. Another type of instruction book, whose history dates back to the early eighteenth century, was available for class use in singing schools.[12] During Period I, Yankee singing masters and composers with slight formal training in music—musicians such as William Billings, Timothy Swan and Daniel Read[13]—issued such books. These usually opened with instructions for singing and some rudimentary musical theory. But they contained mainly sacred choruses with simple melodies harmonized in rather primitive fashion.

During the nineteenth century, this kind of publication spread into the south and west of the country, where similarly constituted "shape-note" books appeared.[14] The melodies in these books often originated in folk sources, though some did come from popular parlor songs.[15] The appearance of parlor-song tunes notwithstanding, no connection was established between such singing books and the amateur students and purchasers of parlor songs.

In contrast, a connection exists between these song lovers and the better-schooled music teachers conversant with contemporary musical theory, compositional practices and voice production in accord with accepted European standards. It was the *au courant* teacher who conducted the voice classes at nineteenth-century singing schools in the northern and northwestern parts of America, as well as those at seminaries, public schools and musical conventions.

None of the private collections contain compositions by the singing masters of the eighteenth century, nor any from "shape-note" books. They do contain works by the better-schooled voice teachers—hymns of Lowell Mason and William Bradbury, and songs of Oliver Shaw, Isaac Woodbury, George Root and Luther Emerson. What is more, several extant collections of parlor music

Little Parlor of Mt. Vernon. Reprinting with permission from The Mount Vernon Ladies Association, Mt. Vernon, Virginia.

once belonged to known teachers of voice classes.[16] Moreover, several prominent Americans, including Emily Dickinson and Henry Longfellow, did attend singing schools when they were young and did study and perform parlor music.[17]

Along with the growth in population, the burgeoning of urban centers and the increased secularization of American society, the proliferation of music classes where inexpensive singing lessons could be had was instrumental in causing the surge of interest in parlor song, from 1820 to 1860. A characteristic advertisement by a conductor of singing classes was inserted in the Boston *Euterpeiad,* 16 September 1820, p. 100. A Mr. Lyons announces the organization of a singing school for young ladies and gentlemen, to be held on Thursday and Saturday evenings. Five months earlier, a Mr. Eastman had advertised a singing school for Thursday and Saturday, from 3 to 6 o'clock, with twenty-six lessons constituting a quarter (three months of instruction). As an added inducement, Eastman promised to teach his pupils several songs by the then popular Providence, R.I., composer Oliver Shaw.[18]

An announcement of a singing school to be conducted by Eben Tourjee in Fall River, Massachusetts, provides us with the information that sheet music was used in class and also that controlling rowdy students was sometimes a problem, then as now. The new pupil, Tourjee warns, will be charged 37.5¢ for an instruction book. All students beginning their second session had to purchase sheet music for instruction and practice. Meetings would take place on Saturday afternoons. One hour would be devoted to beginners; another to advanced singers. Tourjee's final comment is: "Strict observance of the rules of the school will be expected of all. Some half a dozen grown boys seemed to attend last term more for the purpose of annoying others than getting any good to themselves. Such annoyance we are determined shall not continue."[19] Since this is one of the very rare instances of the mention of a discipline problem in the singing school, Tourjee's difficulties must be regarded as atypical and perhaps of his own making.

As with the classes of Lyon and Tourjee, most sessions were held twice weekly for three months, or once a week for six. Whatever the term's length, about 24 to 26 lessons were given. An unidentified writer in the New York *Pioneer,* possibly Isaac P. Woodbury, the editor, states that when only one lesson a week is given, as is common with most teachers, he would recommend 36 to 40 lessons a term, instead of 24.[20]

During Period III, several schools began to place great emphasis on musical training—offering courses in theory, performance and the literature of music. One such school, the Columbian Female Institute in Tennessee, is described in the 17 August 1838 issue of the Boston *Musical Gazette.* According to the author, one music "professor" and "four female music teachers" taught, and an organ, three harps, ten pianos and countless guitars were available for practice. All pupils were placed in either the elementary or advanced section of "Elements of Music." Classes met daily with the professor in order to study "the art of reading music." The Institute also offered class or private instruction in harmony, singing and instrumental playing. No detailed information appears on who gave most of the instruction or of what this instruction consisted. Nor is any indication given of the size of the student body or of the class.

Somewhat more detailed information exists on another school stressing music education, the Lyons Musical Academy of Lyons, New York. Founded in January 1854 by L.H. Sherwood, father of the pianist and composer William H. Sherwood, the Academy offered theoretical and practical instruction, especially to those desiring to become music teachers.[21]

An item in the New York *Musical Review* describes the Lyons academy as giving lessons in piano, organ, melodeon, guitar, violin, vocal music, voice cultivation, harmony and thorough-bass. Tuition for each term of thirteen weeks was $20. Board in the principal's house, three hours' use of the piano daily, washing and heat cost an extra $75 a term.[22] The tuition, in terms of dollar values prevailing in the late 1970s would have been about $450; the other expenses, $1700.[23]

Throughout the years under study, three hours of musical practice a day indicated a serious commitment to the art. Only those intending a professional career were expected to apply themselves so diligently. The daily practice for others, according to the editors of the New York *Musical World*, at least for seminary students, averaged about one hour; if music is given special attention, two or three hours daily. Two music lessons weekly, each lasting one hour, was the norm.[24]

The quality of the instruction manuals improved strikingly in the thirties and forties. The sketchy *Instructor* of Clifton was superseded by lengthier and more thorough educational handbooks. Courses of musical instruction were carefully systematized. The new music educators thought mainly in terms of class, not individual, lessons; in terms of students from modest backgrounds and with limited cultural advantages; and in terms of teachers who might feel diffident about their ability to instruct. The new type of manual was designed to anticipate the several difficulties that might arise in classroom situations.

The effort to make music education efficient was prodigious; the attempt to teach music to the general public, admirable. Whatever teaching success resulted was owing as much to the enthusiasm of the educators as to the lucidity of their manuals. Of course fortunes were made through the mass sale of these publications and of the compositions intended for use in the classroom. A few musicians made huge profits. Nevertheless, the primary motivation of the authors was not financial gain but the desire to reach out to their fellow citizens through music.

Possibly the best known instruction book among the lot was *The Manual of the Boston Academy of Music,* first published by Lowell Mason in Boston in 1836. Mason intended it for "singing schools," "common schools, and other seminaries of learning." He also planned the book as a step-by-step guide for parents who wished to teach their children, and for others wanting to teach themselves—although self-teaching presumed "some knowledge of music."[25] To complete the course of instruction, Mason wrote, required a minimum of "two or three years, two lessons being given in each week. . . about two years for the adult class." Members of the Juvenile Class might range from 8 to 16 years of age.

Like the Clifton *Instructor,* the Mason *Manual* contained instructions and exercises, but no vocal pieces intended for performance.[26] Unlike the *Instructor,* the *Manual* explained the instructions in careful and systematic detail. Exercises, except for those in parts, progressed from the simple to the complex, and were meant for unison singing by the entire class. Under "Sources of Information" (pp. 14-17), Mason pointed out that his methods derived from the teaching theories of Johann Heinrich Pestalozzi, a Swiss educator, as adapted for voice teaching in the classroom by German educators like Hans Georg Nageli.

Music, Mason insisted, should be taught "not as a mere sensual gratification, but as a sure means for improving the affections, and ennobling, purifying, and elevating the whole man." Instruction should be made available to everyone. When children grew into adults, the ability to sing would soothe "the cares of domestic life" and make for "social order and family happiness." In Mason's system the rote learning of music comes before the study of written notation, the familiar leading to the unfamiliar, and the practice and experience preceding theoretical study.[27]

Printed music books recommended for use with the *Manual,* specified by title, were to be purchased. The *Manual* itself was meant for the teacher, not the pupil, except for the self-teacher. Ordinarily the student was expected to copy precepts, examples and exercises from the blackboard into blank notebooks.[28]

Mason began with a few general observations, following them by an explanation of the teaching methods employed and the equipment needed. He then arrived at the main divisions of the book, set forth under the headings of "Rhythm," "Melody," and "Dynamics." Each division in turn was organized into a first, second and third "Course of Instruction." Mason claimed a "good class" could complete each course in thirty lessons. Toward the book's end were nine pages on the "Expression of Words in Connexion with Sound."

Mason criticized "the time usually allotted to singing schools" as "quite insufficient to learn much on any plan." He promised that something of value can be taught by such schools if they employed his recommendations, even in part. Experience proved, he added, that a "good class may pass through" a complete course "in about thirty lessons or evenings."

Since the printed music suggested by Mason—the Mason and Webb *Juvenile Singing School* for children's classes, and the *Boston Academy's Collection of Church Music* for adult classes—feature sacred works, the question arises if parlor songs were used in singing classes. Was Tourjee's use of sheet music in his classes unusual?

First, one surmises, though admittedly the evidence is mostly circumstantial, that the parlor songs belonging to young ladies and gentlemen known to have attended a school at the time of purchasing the music might well have been sung in unison in class. This would be true especially if a class were not then ready for part singing, and teacher and students were predisposed to parlor music. Or the songs might have been sung as solos by individuals. Without doubt, as George Root and others admitted, vocal music of this type could be and was used to sustain a class's interest. Furthermore, music publishers advertised many parlor songs as "suitable for schools." At the end of a copy of *My Trundle Bed,* music by John C. Baker (New York, 1860), for example, the publisher lists many songs of the "Home," "Heart," and "Sacred" variety as having "words suitable for schools." In the list are given such parlor titles as Emerson's *The Log Hut,* Howard's *Our Mother's Grave,* Webster's *Only Going Home* and Perkin's *The Orphan Wanderer.*

Most books written especially for singing classes contain parlor music, though normally in a part-song setting. Such a book as *The American Elementary Singing Book* of Elam Ives, Jr. (Hartford, 1832), for example, intended for children's or adult-beginners' classes[29], contains sentimental songs like *The Beggar Girl* and *The Orphan Nosegay Girl.*[30] Ives claimed that this was the tenth such book he had published in the last eight years,[31] which would date his first employment of popular songs of this type for class instruction back to around 1824.

The educators expected the amateur singer to use and enjoy the music contained in their volumes in both the singing class and the family circle. In *The Odeon* (Boston, 1837), George Webb and Lowell Mason, state that their book was compiled for "adult singing schools, or classes in vocal music, and also for families and social musical parties...[and consist chiefly of] songs, and other pieces which have obtained a decided popularity."[32] Several pieces are parlor songs with huge followings: Miss Browne's *The Captive Knight,* Thomas Haynes Bayly's *Isle of Beauty,* Thomas Moore's *'Tis the Last Rose of Summer,* Henry Bishop's *Home! Sweet Home!,* and George Kiallmark's *Araby's Daughter.* Increasingly from 1840 on, the music books for singing classes, which were compiled and arranged by the most respected music educators of the day, included popular songs, mostly those deeply sentimental.[33]

After Lowell Mason pioneered the introduction of music into the curriculum of public schools, in 1838, a host of other music manuals intended primarily for the same use came into existence. They too relied on parlor songs. One typical volume, Artemus N. Johnson's *The Young Minstrel* (Boston, 1843) was endorsed for public school use by several New England school principals for its "good instruction, good exercises, and good tunes."[34]

The songs were usually arranged for three or four voices, less frequently as solos with simplified piano accompaniment. George Root's *The Academy Vocalist* (New York, 1852), designed for every kind of private or public class, begins with 48 pages of elementary instructions, vocal exercises and solfeggios by Lowell Mason. Next, Root gives a selection of sacred and secular songs arranged in three parts with the melody in the top voice. Other such publications, such as E.L. White and T. Bissell's *Seminary Class Book* (Boston, 1852) include more secular than sacred works. One, Charles Jarvis's *The Young Folk's Glee-Book* (Philadelphia, 1854), is made up preponderantly of secular music, including "One Hundred Copyright Songs" arranged for SSTB part singing. Numerous widely known songs were reproduced—*Annie Laurie, Blue Juniata, Do They Miss Me at Home? Grave of Bonaparte* and *Lilly Dale,* for example.

It would appear, therefore, that singing classes did study parlor compositions, certainly in arrangements for three or four voices, and perhaps with the class singing the melody in unison to a piano accompaniment executed by the teacher. Since the sheet music was readily available and students might have wanted to make their own collections of parlor works, less need existed for including the solo voice-piano version in the music books for singing classes. Even today in public-school singing classes, popular music, though not found in the educational songbooks, is sung in grades four through eight. These songs are sung in the unison while the teacher plays the accompaniment from the sheet music.

Musical Conventions

Another means for voice study came with the rise of the musical convention. The convention enabled amateur singers, especially those in small towns and villages to receive at least a modicum of instruction at negligible cost. One of the first musical conventions, a meeting of choristers and music teachers, took place for two days in New Hampshire in 1829. During the thirties, annual conventions grew in popularity and spread throughout New England.[35] With Period III, conventions were held as far west as Iowa. Teachers like Mason, Root, Baker and Woodbury filled musical journals with announcements of proposed convention circuits and invited groups to engage their services.

In Period III convention membership consisted mainly of amateurs. "Social enjoyment" and "musical advancement" became twin benefits for those attending. Since most students and some teachers preferred secular as well as sacred music, almost certainly parlor songs were among the compositions studied. For example *Dwight's Journal* prints a report on a Boston convention in its 4 September 1852 issue. The report states that at the close of the instructional period, the singers gave a sacred concert on one night and a "Miscellaneous Concert" on the next. The latter's program consisted of solo secular songs, glees, operatic arias and one sentimental duet. It should be pointed out that in the first half of the century most "glees" were actually the popular songs of the day arranged as easy part songs.[36] Several other reports extant tell of musical conventions whose concluding concert featured parlor songs.[37]

In his *Handbook of American Music and Musicians,* F.O. Jones explains the instruction at musical conventions as a study of notation, sight reading and voice production. Glees and choral works were practised mainly but solo performances were also encouraged. Most conventions, Jones said, lasted around four days. Morning, afternoon and evening sessions were held daily, each lasting two hours. A "first-class conductor" was generally paid $125 and expenses.[38]

It could be argued that the brevity of the convention precluded any serious and thorough instruction. Little of consequence, a critic might suggest, could be accomplished in four days. To a certain extent perhaps the brevity of time spent did impede extended instruction but a short period of instruction was better than none at all. Besides, in a period of five years a singer would have attended several conventions in his own and in surrounding towns. Thus musical knowledge would improve cumulatively. With each new convention the singer learned additional compositions that otherwise might have remained unknown to him. On balance the convention's benefits outweighed its weaknesses.

Further enlightenment on these conventions is afforded by William Bradbury. In "Organizing Musical Conventions," Bradbury stated that his usual fee for a convention, held within 200 to 300 miles, was $100. He felt that 100 to 500 singers were a desirable number, and that $1.00 to $1.50 was a suggested charge to participants.[39] When participants are few and all at a similar level of accomplishment, one teacher, he felt, could carry out the instruction. But when participants are numerous and unequal in ability, the conductor should bring one or more assistants with him. A great part of the expenses could be defrayed by selling tickets to the concerts given at the convention's close.[40]

For the most part these conventions seem to have stressed sacred choral singing. However, if two concerts were given at the end of a convention the second featured secular vocal works, including parlor songs. About three-fourths of the convention's time had to be devoted to preparing for these concerts.[41] It follows, then, that about forty percent of the sessions had to be spent learning secular music for presentation at the "Miscellaneous" second concert.

Bradbury recommended a collection like *The New York Glee and Chorus Book* or *The Metropolitan Glee Book,* if members wished to give a concert of secular music. Bradbury's *New York Glee and Chorus Book* (Boston, 1855) was claimed to be "adapted especially to Musical Conventions and Associations and Advanced Singing Classes." It contains only two pages of exercises and one of solfeggios, and its contents consist almost entirely of parlor songs arranged in SATB parts.

But whether secular music was studied or not, the voice training a member of a singing-school class or musical convention acquired would certainly have been applied to the singing of secular compositions. It must be concluded from the proliferation and vast sale of books containing parlor songs that such publications were in demand for every type of voice class.

From what Nathaniel Gould, a highly respected singing master from 1799 to 1843, wrote in his *History of Church Music* (Boston,

1853), the considerable incidence of popular songs in these books was owing in large measure to the insistence of the amateurs who attended the instructional classes. Because of this insistence concerts and "exhibitions" by sabbath music schools, sacred choral societies and members of musical conventions "are now rarely performed without the use of some words or music... never intended [for]... the service of God."[42]

Contemporary musicians gave several other reasons why popular songs found their way into these music books and instructional sessions. Three, advanced by the teachers themselves, concern the possible sacrilege that might result from using sacred music for instruction, the student's need for relief from the necessarily dry exercises and the probability that lessons built around well-liked songs would be remembered. For instance, Joseph and Horace Bird's *Singing School Companion* (Boston, 1852) reproduces numerous secular pieces for a book destined for use in "Singing Common Schools, Social Assemblies, Choir Practice, and Religious Worship." The compilers justify their including popular music amongst the sacred by claiming: "The singing-school [is]... no more a religious school than is the common school." Their book attempts to meet "the desire of a large and respectable body of singers, who regard the use of sacred words for the mere purpose of learning to sing as irreverent." Secular songs are "of a more light and airy description than sacred," therefore more likely to be learned swiftly, remembered, and sung during the hours away from class, "thus securing... an *extraordinary* amount of practice."[43]

Amateurs greatly valued the opportunities for sociality afforded by singing-school classes. One must recall that these were times of few public amusements, particularly in the smaller communities. What better way to enjoy the company of acquaintances and to meet new people than through learning and singing the songs currently popular? Irving Lowens has provided an example of fraternization at a 1782 singing school by quoting a Yale student's letter which describes the student as "almost sick of the World" but not of his music class, for he can indulge himself "a little in some of the Carnel Delights of the Flesh, such as kissing, squeezing, &c., &c."[44]

A little over seventy years later another person wrote of the pleasures enjoyed by attending singing-school during the wintertime. He recounts enthusiastically the evening sleigh ride to the meeting place and the gaiety of the young people as bells jingle, whips crack, and runners glide swiftly over the snow. "Then comes the joyous greeting of other parties, the relation of adventures, [and] ... the gathering of rosy cheeks and bright eyes around the stove."

The teacher calls out: "Please to come to order, ladies and gentlemen." All hurry to their seats. Solfeggio exercises warm up their voices. Next comes "the pleasing glee; and so we go with melody on our mouths and harmony in our hearts." The class ends; another merry sleigh ride home; and "we go to bed wishing next 'singing-school night' would come."[45] This was a younger crowd and, obviously, not as carnally inclined as the Yale student was.

In conclusion, several important singing masters considered secular music in variety as "almost indispensable" for effective teaching at singing classes of all kinds. They were sufficiently astute to recognize the appetite and demand for popular songs had grown strong among the amateurs who came. At the countless musical conventions that Nathaniel Gould observed or conducted, he noticed that whenever "the books lie promiscuously together, and are used alternately every few hours [then] . . . the longing eyes and evidently itching ears of a majority [betray the desire]. . . to use the book that has written on the outside, 'Songs, Duets, Madrigals, etc.,'. . . while those marked 'Church Music' will be. . . sung apparently with little interest."[46] Since Gould was widely regarded by his contemporaries to be the dean of singing masters, his statement must carry considerable weight. His testimony, and the many other comments that appear in this chapter, point to the parlor song as permeating almost every phase of amateur musical life in the early years of the United States.

Notes

1. "Essay on Female Education," In Susanna Rowson, *Mentoria,* II (Philadelphia, 1799), 86-91.

2. [James Boardman], *America, and the Americans* (London, 1833), p. 131.

3. Mrs. Roger A. Pryor, *Reminiscences of a Long Life* (New York, 1909), pp. 79-83.

4. "Advertisement," Lowell Mason, *Manual of the Boston Academy of Music* (Boston, 1830).

5. Verified from the "Household Accounts" of George Washington, in the Mount Vernon Archives.

6. Rufus Willmot Griswold, *The Republican Court* (New York, 1855), pp. 313-14; George Washington Parke Custis, *Recollections and Private Memoirs of Washington* (New York, 1860), p. 408*n.*

7. Julian Ursyn Niemcewicz, *Under Their Vine and Fig Tree,* trans.Metchie J. Budka, Collections of the New Jersey Historical Society at Newark, XIV (Elizabeth, N.J., 1965), 97.

8. Jean Pierre Brissot de Warville, *New Travels in the United States of America,* trans. Mara Soceanu Vamos and Durand Echeverria (Cambridge, 1964). p. 85.

9. The music is in the Boston Public Library, shelf numbers S 31 and Sp 51 respectively.

10. Elias Nason, *A Memoir of Mrs. Susanna Rowson (Albany, 1870),* pp. 98, 102.

11. Adam Hodgson, *Letters from North America,* I (London, 1824), 107.

12. John Tufts, *An Introduction to the Singing of Psalm-Tunes* (Boston, ca. 1721), and Thomas Walter, *The Grounds and Rules of Musick Explained* (Boston, 1721). No extant copy of the first edition of Tufts has yet been uncovered. Houghton Library has a copy of the tenth edition, dated 1738; Irving Lowens, in *Music and Musicians in Early America* (New York, 1964), p. 40, writes that the fifth edition is the earliest he has seen; Theodore M. Finney, in "The Third Edition of Tuft's Introduction to the Art of Singing Psalm-Tunes," *Journal of Research in Music Education,* XIV (1966) 163-70, writes of the discovery of the third edition.

13. An early and valuable history of this period is George Hood, *History of Music in New England* (Boston, 1846).

14. See George Pullen Jackson, *White Spirituals in the Southern Uplands* (Chapel Hill, 1933). Notes were given different shapes depending on their function. At first a four-note shape notation, later, in some books, a seven-note shape notation was employed.

15. Jackson, pp. 164-85.

16. For example, Boston Public Library, shelf-numbers Sp 39, 51, and 53, designate volumes that once belonged to Benjamin F. Baker, who taught privately and also conducted voice classes.

17. Emily Dickinson, *Letters,* ed. Mabel Loomis Todd (New York, 1931), pp. 3-4; Lawrence Thompson, *Young Longfellow* (New York, 1938), p. 17.

18. Boston *Euterpeiad,* 22 April 1820, p. 16.

19. Fall River *Key-Note,* February 1855, p. 4.

20. New York *Musical Review,* 1 November 1856, p. 21.

21. *A Handbook of American Music and Musicians,* ed. F.O. Jones (Canaseraga, New York, 1886), s. v. "Lyons Musical Academy."

22. New York *Musical Review,* 15 November 1856, p. 361.

23. These and other estimates are based on the summary of nineteenth-century wage and price trends given in Stanley Lebergott, "Wage Trends, 1800-1900," *Trends in the American Economy in the Nineteenth Century,* Studies in Income and Wealth, XXIV (Princeton, 1960), 462, 493.

24. New York *Musical World,* 12 November 1853, p. 85.

25. The "Advertisement" by Mason, and the "Forward" by George W. Gordon are both dated 1841; the copyright, however, was entered in 1836. By 1845, the *Manual* had already gone through five editions.

26. The *Manual* does contain a few rounds and brief musical examples with words.

27. Mason taught at the Boston Academy of Music. He also organized free juvenile classes at Boston's Bowdoin Street Church. By 1833, he had become so successful as a teacher that he was allowed to begin music classes in two private schools, the Mount Vernon and the Monitorial Schools. In 1837, he was permitted to start music classes in a Boston public school, the Hawes School. The next year he and several influential Bostonians convinced the Boston School Committee that music education should be introduced into all its public schools. Following Boston's example, school music commenced in Buffalo in 1843, Pittsburgh in 1844, Chicago in 1845 and San Francisco in 1851. See Arthur Rich, *Lowell Mason* (Chapel Hill, 1946); also Francis Grant, "Mary Cushing Webster: Pioneer Music Educator,"*Journal of Research in Music Education,* XIV (1966), 114; and Miriam B. Kapfer, "Early Public School Music," *Journal of Research in Music Education*, XV (1967), 191-200.

28. *Manual,* pp. 33-34.

29. See p. 3. Elam Ives, Jr., a recognized voice teacher, was the director of the Philadelphia Musical Seminary at this time.

30. See pp. 57-58. *The Beggar Girl,* music by John Percy, was first published in America in sheet-music form in New York, around 1802; *The Orphan Nosegay Girl,*

words by Mrs. Susanna Rowson, at Boston, around 1805.

31. On p. 4.

32. Preface, p. iii.

33. A few examples of such books are Benjamin F. Baker, *Baker's American School Music-Book* (Boston, 1845) and *Baker's Elementary Music Book* (Boston, 1847); Isaac B. Woodbury, *Woodbury's Youths' Song Book,* rev. ed. (New York, 1847 and *The Singing School* (New York, 1856); Edward L. White and John E. Gould, *The Wreath of School Songs* (Boston, 1847); Artemus N. Johnson and Joseph Osgood, *The Normal Song Book or Music Reader* (Boston, 1855); George Root, *The Musical Album* (New York, 1855); and T. Bissell, *The American Musical Class Book* (Boston, 1859).

34. See p. 3. Some of the songs are *Home! Sweet Home!, Oft in the Stilly Night,* and *There's Nothing True but Heaven.*

35. John W. Moore, *Complete Encyclopedia of Music* (Boston, 1854) s.v. "Musical Conventions."

36. See "A Word about Simple Music," New York *Musical Review,* 1 March 1855, p. 77.

37. New York *Musical Review,* 15 March 1855, pp. 91-92.

38. Jones, *Handbook* s.v. "Conventions, Musical."

39. New York *Musical Review,* 14 July 1855, p. 231.

40. See the statement by Isaac B. Woodbury in the New York *Musical Pioneer,* 1 March 1856, p. 87.

41. Op. cit., note 39.

42. His comments on this use of popular music are on pp. 192-93.

43. Joseph and Horace Bird, p. 2. Similar reasons are given in *The Oriental Glee and Anthem Book,* p. 2, and A.N. Johnson's *Carmina Meloda* (Boston, 1855), p. iii. See also, Boston *Euterpeiad,* 22 October 1822, p. 119; Isaac B. Woodbury, "Questions Answered," New York *Musical Pioneer*, 1 May 1856, p. 119. The two pages 119 are coincidental.

Recently panelists on the Education Commission for the States were quoted as stating that music teachers were failing to educate the young, and that not Bach or Brahms but "the hit songs of the moment" should be used to encourage musical learning; William A. Henry 3rd, "Off Beat," Boston *Evening Globe,* 8 March 1974, p. 12.

44. Lowens, p. 282.

45. "The Right Weather for Singing Schools," New York *Musical Review,* 19 January 1854, p. 23.

46. Gould, *History,* p. 192.

Chapter 4

Ballad Singers And Their Performances

Songs introduced to the public only through the medium of sheet music would have experienced meagre sales. Publishers depended on professional singers to acquaint the American amateur musician with the music they issued. Indeed, publishers were inclined normally to put out only those new songs that the singers were introducing to their audiences. Title pages proclaim song after song as in the repertoire of one or more popular vocalists, or as from a favorite musical show, or both. The few compositions without this sort of boost are almost invariably the creations of amateurs and intended for self gratification rather than profit.

In Periods I and II, the professional singers named were usually British. They knew and presumably preferred their own native musical productions. It is no wonder any sampling of the music popularized in America during these years establishes it as mostly British in origin. Not until after 1840 and the acceptance of the American-born singer did audiences in the United States hear a great deal of music composed by American citizens.

Professional singers performed parlor songs at the theaters and concert halls during the fall, winter and spring months, and at outdoor pleasure gardens during the summer months. In the theater, performers often sang these compositions as the principal components of English and American light operas. One early example of such an opera is William Shield's *Rosina,* designated by the composer as a comic opera in two acts. This music-stage work became popular in the years immediately following American independence. Some of its songs, issued in the late 1780s and the 1790s, are *Whilst with Village Maids I Stray, When William at Eve, When Bidden to the Wake or Fair, Sweet Transports, The Moon Returns, Light as Thistle Down Moving, By This Fountain's Flow'ring Side,* and *The Bud of the Rose.*

Songs also were introduced between and during the acts of spoken drama, whether tragedy or comedy. To cite an instance where songs by Americans were featured, a performance of *Uncle Tom's Cabin* in Pittsburgh, on 17 November 1853, had the actors singing the following pieces:

Song and Breakdown .... Topsy, by Mrs. Brickford
Song, Old Folks at Home .... Uncle Tom, Mr. Rodgers
Song, My Old Kentucky Home .... Topsy
Song, Massas in the Cold Ground .... Slaves
Song, Uncle Tom's Religion .... Uncle Tom
Song, Lilly Dale .... Emeline, Mrs. M'Millan
Quartette, Wakes Isles of the South.[1]

The popular songs of the day even found their way into the continental operas staged in America. Charles Durang says interpolations of this kind formed a curious feature of an 1824 Philadelphia performance of Rossini's *The Barber of Seville.* A Mr. Pearman, as Count Almaviva, introduced "a new ballad composed by himself, called 'A Garden Formed by Nature Wild'." He then sang by request Bishop's *Description of a Play,* "which certainly did not belong to Rossini's music," Horn's *'Tis Love in the Heart,* and Bishop's *Oh! Maiden Fair,* a composition based on an adaptation of a Paisiello tune.[2]

Parlor songs formed the main staple of the concert repertoire performed by vocalists in every part of settled America. This is made clear in the concert programs that appeared in newspapers and periodicals throughout the years under study. Any town promising a decent audience for a night and a large enclosed space was likely to receive a visit from one or more of these professional singers. A local resident or two with musical ability might assist the visitors. Often local musicians sold tickets for their own concerts. George Upton writes of a Chicago performance typical of most: "The programme of a concert given at the City Saloon, August 18, 1841, by John A. Still, contains some of the ballads which were favorites at that time, among them 'Here's a Health to Thee, Mary,' 'The Charm has Departed,' 'My Bark is on the Billow,' 'Poor Bessie,' 'Near the Lake where Drooped the Willow,' 'Gentle Zitella,' 'The Fairy Tempter,' and others."[3]

Some cities were fortunate to have a type of summer entertainment featuring parlor ballads which offered those attending a welcome relief from heat and close living—the pleasure garden and its musical presentations. In imitation of London's Vauxhall and Ranelagh Gardens, similar outdoor gathering places opened for business in or near the large urban centers. Americans from the upper and middle class who desired relaxation could set off on "evening excursions" to "petite Vauxhalls, where beauty, music, coloured lamps, and ice-creams are the never-failing attractions.[4]

Patrons required music they might only half listen to. Melodies had to be easily grasped over the rustle of vegetation, murmur of conversations and clinking of glasses and dishes. Since parlor songs contained music in a style familiar to everyone and relied on a simply constructed and attractive tune for their effect, they were much in evidence at these plein-air entertainments. The following program of a 1 June 1799 evening at New York's Ranelagh Garden demonstrates the wholesale reliance on parlor ballads on such occasions:

Hook	"Alone by the Light of the Moon"	Mr. Perkins
Hook	"Sweet Nan of Hampton Green	Mrs. M'Donald
Shield	"The Highland Laddie"	Mrs. Oldmixon
Shield	"Nong Tong Pow"	Mr. Jefferson
Shield	"On the Lake of Killarney	Mrs. Seymour
Shield	"From Scenes of Love"	Mr. Perkins
Hook	"The Wedding Day"	Mrs. M'Donald
Arne	"The Soldier Tir'd of War's Alarms"	Mrs. Oldmixon
Arne	"The Waiter"	Mr. Jefferson
Arne	"The Sailor Boy"	Mrs. Seymour[5]

Perhaps the most famous of these recreational centers was Niblo's in New York City, a combination of pleasure garden and building where concerts and operas were presented. This popular entertainment spot opened 18 May 1829. Thomas Goodwin describes it as follows: "In the rear of the Niblo and [James Fenimore] Cooper residences, between them and Crosby Street, and extending down to Prince Street, was a large open space, which was beautifully laid out as a garden. It was ornamented with trees, shrubbery, and flowers, and the whole space was conveniently intersected by walks, and dotted with arbors, in which were seats and tables for serving light refreshments. The building was known as 'Niblo's Saloon,' and the open space as Niblo's Garden, and they at once became favorite places of resort." The principal ballad singers of the time invariably appeared at this "first-class concert place."[6]

However much a few persons with highly cultivated tastes wished it otherwise, Americans showed an addiction to these ballad singers and their songs. In contrast, an insignificant portion of the public sponsored the sophisticated art music from the European continent. Of the twenty years or so before 1840 in Boston, John Sullivan Dwight has written a summary easily applicable to other American cities. "Concerts," he writes, were "far from classical;" symphonies and chamber-music compositions rarely heard. The operas performed were normally of the light English variety, not Italian, French or German. "Very popular...were the English ballad-singers,—Wilson with his Scotch songs; Russell with his *Maniac* and *Life on the Ocean Wave;* Dempster with his sentimental Tennyson's *May Queen;* and Mr. J.P. Knight, whose programmes were more classical and made appeal to better taste."[7]

Nor did the musical taste of the next twenty years, 1840 to 1860, take much of a turn in the direction Dwight desired. While Beethoven and Mendelssohn had more performances, their compositions were usually inadequately performed by the makeshifty orchestras and ephemeral chamber ensembles (only one or two lasted longer than a few years) attempting them. The fine Germania and Jullien orchestras and the praiseworthy Mendelssohn Quintette Club were exceptions to prove the rule. And even they had to play a great deal of music of a popular nature.

Beginning in Period II, American singers are named along with the British. Soon they dominated the concert stage. Still no art songs were heard. Parlor and minstrel songs were their forte. Walt Whitman writes: "Yes, there were in New York and Brooklyn some fine nontechnical singing performances, concerts, such as the Hutchinson band, three brothers, and their sister, the red-cheek'd New England carnation, sweet Abby; sometimes plaintive and balladic—sometimes anti-slavery, anti-calomel, and comic. There were concerts by Tempelton, Russell, Dempster, the old Alleghanian band, and many others. Then we had lots of 'negro minstrels,' with capital character songs and voices.... Every theatre had some superior voice, and it was common to give a favorite song between the acts."[8]

Fine singing was heard elsewhere, too. In the 1820s, towns as far west as St. Louis were enjoying an assortment of concert and theater presentations. By 1826, Mobile, Alabama, with a population of 5,000, of whom 4,000 were white, had its own theater building.[9] During the 1840s and 50s, countless troupes of ballad, and others of Ethiopian, singers traveled to remote parts of the country.[10] All these performers sang parlor songs. Even Italian-opera singers when on tour found the singing of at least one or two popular favorites necessary to attract an audience. Such was the case at a concert given in Zanesville, Ohio. Ole Bull (the concert violinist) and Strakosch, assisted by Appolonie Bertucca Maretzek and Amalia Patti, all under the direction of Max Maretzek, did entertain the local populace with the expected operatic arias and instrumental selections. However, to insure success the entertainment also included a "duet concertanto" based on melodies from parlor songs like *Lilly Dale,* and a vocal rendition of *My Old Kentucky Home*—a song in the repertoire of almost every touring opera singer in the 50s.[11] For similar reasons the violinist Ole Bull toured "the principal towns of New England" three years later, with George Harrison and Mr. H. Horncastle, two ballad singers, as collaborators.[12]

The British Ballad Singers in America

Some British singers came to America on a speculation; others, under contract to one of the several theaters in the larger cities; and still others at the behest of entrepreneurs sensing money was to be made on the concert circuit. These musicians all had something pleasing to offer an audience which insisted upon experiencing the total ambiance of a song performance: a handsome face, an attractive figure, expressively flexible features, dramatic gesticulations and tones replete with engaging sentiment or coaxing playfulness. Americans found ridiculous the two-hundred pound vocalist pretending she was a starving match girl, the wooden-faced performer claiming she was burning to death and the roulading prima donna pretending she was a naive country girl.

Again and again, music lovers and critics wrote down their requirements of and reservations about the music and musicians of their day—in books, letters and periodicals. They said they wanted to feel overwhelmed by more than just the art of the virtuosic singer or the skill of the master composer. To the American music lover, a song performance had to convey more than an aesthetic experience centered on music. It also had to be a human experience portrayed both aurally and visually. If the audience felt acutely the emotions projected by song and singer, then the composition was wholly satisfying and the singer praiseworthy.

That thinking was far removed from that among some twentieth-century writers on music. The early American's sense of fitness caused him to repudiate worship of the artist and genuflection before a proclaimed masterpiece. Music existed to be enjoyed or rejected as one wished. He would have been amused to hear of works written for an enlightened future generation to appreciate. Such arrogance on the part of a composer was considered insufferable and utter nonsense. Any artist had to communicate with his own generation or not at all. Nor could the singer think one sang to display a precisely-honed and flawless voice which had mastered every trill, shake, run and cadential flourish. The art of the ballad singer did not reside there.

The usual vocalists who came to America, though they sang modest parlor songs, had undergone a great deal more musical training than was customary for American singers. A few of these vocalists had received a thorough grounding in musical theory and composition. Most had studied singing for several years under fine European teachers. For example, John Braham, one of the most admired of all the British singers to tour America, had studied voice under prominent teachers in England and Italy, had enormous control over his sound projection, and was equally comfortable in Italian and English opera.[13] Another admired singer in America, Arthur Seguin, had taught at the London Academy of Music. In an article appearing in the New York *Tribune,* 15 December 1852, just after Seguin's death, the unidentified writer stated: "It was on the 3rd of February, 1831, that he [Arthur Seguin] made his *debut* in the character of Polyphemus, in Handel's *'Acis and Galatea.'* Mr. Seguin became a popular favorite and enjoyed profitable engagements at the [London] Italian Opera House, and the theatres of Covent Garden and Drury-Lane. He came to this country in 1838, and made his first appearance on the American stage at the old National Theatre, in this city, on the 15th of October.... He subsequently visited professionally the principal cities of the United States, and maintained an excellent reputation as a bass singer and comic actor."[14] Mrs. Sequin was also an excellent singer as well as fine pianist. She appeared in opera,oratorio, and concert.[15] The opera referred to was, of course, of the English type and plentifully supplied with strophic songs.

From the British singers, Americans learned what was currently popular in London. When the Seguins mounted a favorite London opera, Michael Balfe's *The Bohemian Girl,* in 1846 Boston, "gems of this opera were soon the rage in saloons, and ground upon organs, or hummed in the streets. 'I dreamt that I dwelt in marble halls,' absolutely possessed, as with an enchanter's spell, the female population of this vicinity, and that was *the* all-engrossing idea of amateur singers. In a large party given during this excitement, request was made for a song, and the ladies present being interrogated as to their repertoire, each and all responded 'I dreamt'."[16]

The ballad singer took care to sample the pulse of the musical public regularly. Nothing displeasing to concert-goers continued long in the repertoire. On the other hand, whatever composition had the ear of the paying audience was certain to have a constant airing. The singer came prepared to give an audience what it wanted. The celebrated Charles Incledon, for example, visited America in 1817 and appeared nightly in English-opera productions. On numerous occasions he sang by request "some favorite air which was not on the bill, such as 'Tom Starboard,' (composed by himself), 'The Bay of Biscay,' and 'Black Ey'd Susan.' These he gave nearly every evening, such was their intense popularity."[17]

For public performances, the accompaniment to these songs was normally provided by a small orchestra made up of local instrumentalists. Because orchestras were often unavailable when a singer went on tour, a piano might supply the accompaniment. Only rarely was a harp or guitar used.

With the beginning of Period II, an increasing number of British singers were interested primarily in concertizing, and not in operatic appearances. Though they did perform songs from stage works, a large part of their repertoire, like the *Irish Melodies* of Thomas Moore, was not originally from opera. Many compositions were by the singers themselves. Two ballad singers, William Dempster and Henry Russell, composed several of the most popular works of the early nineteenth century while they were in America. Favorite works for years were Dempster's *The Blind Boy* (1842) and Russell's *The Old Arm Chair* (1840).

Wherever they appeared, these singers drew huge crowds. The Musical Fund Society of Philadelphia, in 1847, wished to raise money to enlarge its concert hall. A bazaar was held, and William Dempster was invited to sing. He drew "throngs of delighted listeners" and helped the Society earn the money denied it when it sponsored more artistically-oriented concerts, performed by the Musical Fund Orchestra. Ballads—not Beethoven—provided the desired building funds.[18]

A Scottish or Irish musician sometimes featured songs based on the musical styles of his or her homeland, as did Samuel Lover in the Irish Evenings he gave during the 1840s. One incentive for doing so was the strong support one could expect from countrymen. The Irish singer William Webster appeared in America around 1807 and was admired for his voice and skillful singing. A major part of his support came from the American Irish, who "formed a numerous and highly respectable portion of the fashionable auditory."[19]

Everything said notwithstanding, some British singers made financially unrewarding tours of America. Henry Phillips, for example, though an English musician of excellent reputation at home, failed to attract any large American following during his visit in 1844. The economically difficult times may have been the explanation. A second reason may have been his anti-democratic views, which Americans perhaps sensed. He states in his *Recollections*: "My great horror always was, that a song should become so popular as to be sung in the streets." Once he heard a butcher boy singing one of his songs, Neukomm's *The Sea*. He confessed: "At the moment I was uncharitable enough to wish he had been at the bottom of it."[20]

As every historian conversant with the temper of this society knows, the pre-1860s American displayed extreme sensitivity to criticisms of his democratic way of life, particularly when they were advanced by foreign visitors. Some British actors and singers, because of their real or imagined insults, were boycotted during their American stay. Henry Phillips may have been dealt with likewise by at least some music lovers.

He offered two explanations for his lack of success: one, that he charged too much ($1.00); and,two, that he sang compositions from English operas with which the public was already surfeited, having heard them "fifty times before."[21]

Whether they offended Americans or not, many British ballad singers were popular only for a short time after their first arrival. The curiosity of American audiences satisfied, attendance dropped off. This happened to the capable Miss Clara Fisher, later Mrs. Maeder, who made her first American appearance in 1827. Fourteen years later a group of fashionable ladies cognizant of her merits and concerned over her lack of earnings organized a benefit concert on her behalf.[22] Significantly, the greatest drop-off in attendance at performances by British musicians coincides with the increase in the number of Americans coming before the public. These charged less for admission, displayed a more democratic temper and featured American-composed songs easier to sing and understand than British ones.

Prior to the 1830s the less affluent had no choice. If they desired professional entertainment, only British musicians offered it. In 1814 Wyer Trumbull, a Salem, Massachusetts, music lover of limited financial means, was in the habit of purchasing concert tickets from 50¢ to $1. for performances by British singers. Yet he made a salary of no more than $3.25 to $4 a week as a store assistant.[23] In the 1820s the German traveler Bernhard reported seeing sailors and Kentucky men at a New Orleans theater that was presenting an English version of Weber's *Der Freischutz.*[24] At a Philadelphia performance of the English musical *Rob Roy,* James Boardman saw "tradesmen and mechanics, fresh from their counters of their workshops...with their merry wives and daughters."[25]

Americans began to take serious notice of native entertainers in the 1830s. During the 1840s American family singers and minstrel troupes drew larger and larger crowds away from British musicians. In the 1850s they dominated the concert scene.[26]

The American Ballad Singers

The first native-born professional vocalists had to compete with singers from London by performing British songs almost exclusively at their concerts. One of the better known of the earliest American singers was Mrs. French, pupil of Benjamin Carr and wife of a Philadelphia merchant[27]. As with most American ballad singers, her forte was the song recital, not the stage presentation of English opera. From 1819 through 1820 she gave several performances in Boston, where she was well received. Her piano accompanist for these appearances, Sophia Hewitt, had a considerable local reputation as a keyboard performer and teacher. The charge for admission was $1. Concerts began at 7:30 p.m. She sang British songs almost exclusively. Mrs. French's program for a concert given on September 9, 1820 was:

"Believe me if all those" .... Moore
"Soldier's Bride" .... Irish air
"Auld Robin Gray," with a recitative .... Scotch air
"Be Mind tender Passion" .... Storace
"Dulce Dominum" .... Braham
"Oh, say not Woman's heart is bought," by desire .... Whitaker
"Echo, far away," (by particular request) .... Reeve
"Low hear the gentle lark" .... Bishop[28]

Most of the American singers coming after Mrs. French spurned her British repertoire and lacked her musical training. Quite a few had no training at all. For example, the Hutchinson Family, the most famous American troupe of the forties and fifties, was described as not highly trained but "a family of natural musicians."[29]

It was no coincidence that the effective start of the American singer and composer came with the election of Andrew Jackson to the Presidency in 1828 and the advent of Jacksonian democracy. The thirties and forties were decades when American society became acutely aware of the cleavage between a small incipient aristocracy based on wealth and an immense mass of less advantaged citizens demanding political, economic and social equality. The battles were fought at the ballot box and before the doors of Biddle's Bank of the United States. The conflict spilled over into the theater, concert hall and parlor. This aristocracy-manque was perceived by the American majority as scorning all manifestations of democratic culture and intent on aping the tastes and manners of British nobility. Rich New Yorkers had to have their Italian opera; others of comparable affluence, their imported actors, dancers and musicians. Nothing American seemed good enough for them.

Newspapers and musical periodicals sometimes printed protests about the exorbitant fees paid Italian opera singers, the high admission prices insisted upon by British ballad singers, and the attitudes of superiority displayed by foreign musicians. One or two angry American editors reprinted European articles that sneered at American taste, culture, literature, art and music.

The steadily growing number of American professional singers was aware of the burgeoning indignation. At first they appeared as individuals, later as troupes of musicians. The greatest impetus to the formation of native musical troupes came in 1839 when the Tyrolese Rainer Family first appeared in the United States. These Alpine singers won a huge following because of the pleasing way they sang uncomplicated Austrian songs, in close harmony and with clear enunciation.[30] Not a little of their success could be attributed to the American perception of them as representatives of the simple-living "folk" who dwelt in a rural Europe untainted by anti-democratic notions.

In imitation of these Tyrolese singers and in hopes of achieving some of their success, American troupes started to travel the country. They too tried to sing in close harmony and with careful enunciation—the latter always considered as essential to ballad singing. Some troupes even claimed a mountain origin. Besides the Hutchinsons, widely known were the Bakers, Ordway's Aeolians, the Alleghanians, the Gibsons, Father Kemp's Old Folks and Ossian's Bards.

They sang parlor compositions, from the comic to the melodramatic and highly sentimental. Traditional airs, sacred vocal pieces, simple but eloquent ballads, and homophonic part songs were their stock-in-trade. In the 1850s minstrel troupes singing in black-face also introduced native parlor songs into their programs. Mark Twain observed: "The minstrel troupes had good voices and both their solos and their choruses were a delight to me as long as the negro show continued in existence. In the beginning the songs were rudely comic. . . but a little later sentimental songs were introduced, such as 'The Blue Juniata,' 'Sweet Ellen Bayne,' 'Nelly Bly,' 'A Life on the Ocean Wave,' 'The Larboard Watch,' etc."[31]

Unlike the more formal and conventional British, these American performers felt no inhibitions about advertising themselves in novel fashion. The Hutchinson Family's method was to hire a hall in a town and have a local person distribute posters of the coming concert for display at strategic places. When they themselves arrived, they entered the town on foot and attracted attention by singing one or more of their songs as they traversed the town's main street. Once, in Kennebunk, Maine, Jesse Hutchinson ran up and down the streets ringing a bell and shouting out the proposed program for the evening concert.[32] Another company,

Father Kemp's Old Folks, liked to stage a colorful musical parade when they entered a town. Their old-fashioned clothing ("scare crow hats," "immense bonnets," "short-waisted frocks and great coats") and their vivid personification of Yankee characters, complete with comic drawl, helped attract large crowds.[33] British musicians and some proper Americans sensitive to foreign criticisms of American vulgarity considered such antics shocking and the Old Folks as little better than mountebanks.

One certain way to win audiences away from British singers was to charge less. While the usual charge to concerts given by foreigners was $1 to $2, the highest admission price to concerts by Americans was 50¢. Many times it was as low as 12 1/2¢. Asa Hutchinson said his family kept prices low because they did not wish to "keep away all the poor and laboring classes who have souls pure as the Monied Class and who enjoy music as much, and. . .[are] profited by its good influences as much if not more.[34]

Although a few American performers sang to piano accompaniment, others employed a small, easily transportable organ called a melodeon. The Rogers Family, for example, "sweet singers" and "entirely free from mannerism and affectation," sang to one.[35] In Hudson, New York, a blind "professor" sang *Rocked in the Cradle of the Deep,* among other pieces, with the "melodeon representing the waves of the ocean dancing and foaming."[36] The noted Hutchinsons took a small melodeon with them whenever they traveled. They also accompanied their singing with violin, guitar and harp.[37]

The lithographic pictures on the title pages of songs depict several of the American groups and their instruments. The violin, guitar and cello are most often seen; occasionally another instrument is presented. A typical cover, that of *Bonny Blue Eyes* (Boston, 1849), shows the Gibson Family, three men and a woman, holding a violin, cello, harp and guitar. Keyboard instruments are rarely pictured. We know the melodeon was employed at concerts. On the other hand, the piano was not nearly as ubiquitous an accompaniment instrument for native singers as for Europeans. Not only is it absent from the lithographs, but also is infrequently mentioned in contemporary descriptions of Period-III performances. The piano was not as transportable as other instruments were. At the same time it was either unavailable or in disrepair in many of the smaller towns the singers visited. (These were settlements rarely visited by European performers.) Another consideration was the benefit gained by identifying each member of a troupe with a specific instrument. The heightened recognition was invaluable in attracting audiences to future concerts and selling the published songs.

The native singers perceived themselves as allied to the common mass of Americans. In their song *The Old Granite State* (New York, 1843), the Hutchinsons stated that they wish to be numbered with the "good, old fashioned singers," whose motto is liberty. They are despisers of tyrants and champions of the downtrodden. When Jesse Hutchinson died at forty years of age, a writer summed him up as "a genius in his way. Gentlehearted, artless, and honest, he wrote and sang his songs preaching brotherhood and peace wherever he went."[38]

Without doubt the Hutchinsons were more extreme than most of their colleagues in advocating causes like emancipation for slaves and equal rights for women. Nevertheless all native troupes shared a willingness to appear before audiences from any class. None thought himself an artist separate from and above the ordinary citizens, from whose ranks he had come. In 1842 the Hutchinsons sang for an audience of about 500 at the Female Academy of Albany, New York. The auditors, largely from the middle class, listened to parlor songs like *The Cot Where I Was Born, The Grave of Bonaparte, The Lament of the Irish Emigrant, The Indian Hunter* and *The Maniac*. They appeared in Washington in 1844, before a select group that included President Tyler, John Quincy Adams and Levi Woodbury. Three years later they sang *My Mother's Bible* and *There's a Good Time Coming, Boys* to the inmates of Sing Sing Prison.[39] Other companies appeared before California miners, Illinois farmers and New York factory workers. Unlike the English singer Henry Phillips, they were delighted when their songs became so popular everyone sang them in the streets.

The Art of the Ballad Singer

The most important objective of the ballad singer, whether British or American, was to arouse emotions. All of a performer's skills aimed at this goal. Some writers explain and defend this excitation as an efficacious way to teach morality; others claim it an innocent exercising of the sensibilities. For example, an article, "The Use and Abuse of Music," published in the Boston *Euterpeiad* is instructive. A Mr. "Chiron" writes: "Music is to be understood as a powerful assistant to sentimental expression (I speak here of vocal music) which, by the power of its charms, enforces our attention to some natural passion of mankind." He speaks of how listeners are thus "strongly impressed with the ideas of love, fear, pity, or some other natural affection." At all times, he insists, music must be "an assistant to sentimental expression." Italian opera is "a ridiculous performance" to him, since "every passion is treated alike." The aria is designed merely to show off the performer's voice; it "can never delight or make us better."[40] Right or wrong, this was a common judgment of Italian operatic music, especially in Periods I and II.

American writers insisted that the performer has to create an impression of actually experiencing the song's sentiments if he wishes to communicate on a deeply personal level. For this reason the important parlor-song composer and singer George Root suggested that a part of the ballad singer's art was the ability "to assume emotions he does not really feel," so long as these emotions were "healthy and good." While he performs, "the singer should treat respectfully the emotion he excites."[41] In this way an intimate rapport between singer and listener is established.

An instance of the rapport possible between a fine performer and an audience was printed in the 1852 Sacramento *Daily Advertiser*. A review evaluates the singing of the Alleghanians, and of one member in particular, Miss Goodenow, at a California concert: "The exquisite song of 'Kathleen Mavourneen' was sung by Miss Goodenow with all the fervor and passion which belong to the Irish character; there was a pathos in her melodious strains which naturally and irresistibly called forth the deepest emotions of the heart, and the effect of this was visible in the moistened eyes of many unaccustomed to tears."[42]

The expert ballad singer could deliberately excite emotions absent from the written music. This, Clara Fisher did on one occasion when she sang "what was intended to be a ludicrous appeal to sympathy with such wonderful truthfulness of suffering, that a majority of the audience were overcome with tears."[43]

The primacy of the affections understood, it follows that in summing up a singer's desirable attributes, one usually concluded "high musical attainments" were "not so essential as expression, feeling, and vivacity." This advice Francis Courtney received just as he left for London to recruit new members for a Philadelphia theatrical company.[44]

Every now and then mention is made of a highly regarded singer who possessed neither an exquisite natural voice, nor a carefully developed vocal technique. The magic of such a performer resided in a musical presentation of utmost conviction which transcended these limitations. As a case-in-point, Miss Horton, one of the better ballad singers, "was remarkable neither for the quality of her voice, nor for the skill of her execution."[45] Inadequate as a prima donna in Italian opera, she nevertheless achieved fame as an interpreter of the sentiment in George Morris's ballads.[46]

One known performer continued to sing successfully after she had no voice at all. A friend wrote a description of the Boston actress and singer Charlotte Cushman at the time of her residence in England in the 1840s that illustrates the complete artistry of her ballad interpretations despite her voice's deterioration. Charlotte Cushman, we are told, no longer commanded "the upper notes of her voice," but her control over musical declamation remained strong. Her singing of *We Were Two Daughters of One Race* and *They Tell Me Thou'rt the Favored Guest* was "full not only of dramatic genius, but of pathos, sweetness, and vigor. Nor was it less remarkable as a work of art, because the artist was, by consummate skill and knowledge, conquering the imperfections of an organ already almost destroyed." The emotional intensity in her performance "riveted" the "audience's attention."[47]

Admired performers were rarely vocal acrobats. More often they were masters of "sweet" and "chaste" expression.[48] The sweet singer gave a delicate and warm coloring to a carefully delineated melody, thereby arousing pleasant sensations in the listener. The chaste singer performed naturally and simply, eschewing unnecessary melodic ornamentation and mannerisms that diverted the listener's attention from song to singer. An expert vocalist was Thomas Philipps. Americans considered his voice unrivaled for sweetness. They praised him for articulating distinctly and singing with more feeling and expressiveness than was the norm among ballad singers of his generation.[49]

In a series of lectures on the art of ballad singing he delivered in Boston, Philipps states: "A common voice may be drilled into regularity of tone, and a degree of sweetness, by persevering and attentive practice.... It does not admit of a question, that the power of the performer consists chiefly in accommodating the musical to the sentimental accent and emphasis, in giving the style all its varieties of light and shade, with the staccatos and sostenutos, to conform and to enforce the sentiments, and in studying elocution with minute attention."[50]

In short, to follow the directions given on the music page was insufficient. The singer's contributions were crucial in determining a song's success. The performer had to employ all his talents to conjure up an ambience that would stimulate the listener's imagination and engage his feelings.

The Parlor Song in Performance

Contemporary writers on the parlor song concluded unanimously that melody was all important and had to have sufficient integrity to be able to exist "without accompaniment, or any other collateral assistance." Accompaniments had to be "of the most simple and retiring kind," and "just enough to support and set off the melody without obscuring and impeding it."[51] Any accompaniment that overpowered the voice or diverted attention from the singer was "felt as an intrusion," therefore unacceptable.[52]

Almost all written accompaniments to parlor melodies contain little musical material of any consequence. They are invariably light, unobtrusive, and easy to execute. One explanation for their facileness is that mostly out of necessity, perhaps also to give a united expression to vocal melody and keyboard accompaniment, the singer with any pianistic ability was normally his own accompanist. Whether performing at public concerts or private musicales, the professional singers were mentioned from time to time as accompanying themselves. The English woman Louisa Pyne did so constantly during her American concert tours.[53] The singer-composer Henry Russell writes in his autobiography, *Cheer! Boys, Cheer!* (London, 1895), of how he always accompanied his own singing when he toured America.

One can be reasonably certain the amateur vocalists usually accompanied themselves. Most of them played the piano, evidenced by the mixture of songs and solo piano pieces in their music collections. Piano fingerings are found both on the solo keyboard compositions and on the accompaniment parts to the songs. Since they were unlikely to have purchased songs merely to accompany others, in all probability they did accompany themselves. Playing to accompany one's self, however, would not preclude their also playing the piano for other singers, or others doing the same for them.

On songs once owned by amateurs, one occasionally finds piano fingerings added above the vocal melody. One explanation for this, verifiable in contemporary accounts, is that by ignoring the piano-treble part and playing instead the vocal-melody line against the bass part, amateurs provided themselves with easily performable piano works.

A second explanation can also be offered. Among the songs dating from the 1820s that once belonged to Mary Nichols of Cooperstown, New York,[54] are pieces with piano fingerings written in pencil over the vocal melody and over the piano-treble part as well. Apparently, the singer first studied the song by playing the bass part with the left hand and the melody with the right. Once learned, the vocal line could then be sung while both the treble and bass parts of the accompaniment were played on the piano. Since music belonging to other amateurs shows the dual fingering, this mode of study must have been commonly employed.

When piano technique proved inadequate or singing remained insecure, the vocalist never did learn the piano-treble part. Irked by the omission, a Mr. "Chiron" wrote some "Remarks on the Use and Abuse of Music." He wants more music students to learn the vocal melody "by inspection" and not by "the artificial manner of spelling a song" out on the keyboard. He asks singers to use the piano to execute only the accompaniment, "never to play the song part, as is generally done."[55]

Oftentimes the professional singer or the song composer himself altered the published accompaniment. Some of the more difficult accompaniments were modified to make them performable by professional musicians with modest pianistic ability. George Root admits that he did this when he was a young man in order to perform certain Russell songs that required more technique than he commanded. If accompaniments were too difficult or pitch too high, Root altered the compositions to suit his own abilities.[56] A famous figure in the parlor-song world, Thomas Moore, regularly ignored the published keyboard parts to his own songs. Several acquaintances recollect that he customarily sang his *Irish Melodies* and other of his songs to accompaniments differing from the published versions.[57]

The free alteration of a song's key, mentioned by Root, was widely recognized. On the first page of John Baker's *My Boyhood Days* (Boston, 1849) is printed: "This Solo may be transposed to either a higher or lower key, as the taste and voice of the performer may require—the Author prefers G for a low Basso." Again, William Hall, a New York publisher, issued a piano-score version of William Vincent Wallace's English opera *Lurline,* in 1859. On the second page is the statement that the edition is a "Singer's Copy in the Original Keys;" later in the year, "all the songs, Ballads, Duets, etc. . . . will be transposed and published for parlor use." One agrees with Sims Reeves, an important English singer of the time, that all ballads "could be sung by anybody and in any key."[58]

Frequently the melody had to be altered to fit subsequent stanzas. In this regard, the editors of *The Singer's Companion,* a songbook containing about two-hundred popular songs, advise the amateur singer not to regard the notes of a tune as "fixed facts." The notes should be altered at will to accommodate the words of "succeeding verses." The performer is encouraged to "give time, emphasis, etc., in a manner most easy and natural, and best calculated to produce effect, no matter whether the music is written in that particular way or not."[59]

More than the necessary adaptation of notes to fit new verses is suggested in the last sentence. The permissibility of a "wholly arbitrary" change in melody and the encouragement of an execution "best calculated to produce effect," even if not indicated in the music, implies that a song may be altered not only to adjust the music to new words but to make the interpretation vivid to listeners. Little reliable evidence is extant on the nature of such alterations.

On the other hand, evidence exists concerning another kind of alteration practised by some professional British singers touring America in Period II—the addition of vocal embellishments to the original melodies, as in *Like the Gloom of Night Retiring* (Philadelphia, ca. 1819), "with vocal embellishments as sung...by Mrs. French," and *Cease Your Funning* (Philadelphia, ca. 1820), "with Madame Catalini's variations. As sung by Mrs. French." The editors of *The Singer's Companion* did not mean to encourage this type of alteration, since it failed to "give time, emphasis, pause, etc., in a manner most easy and natural."

Most lovers of parlor songs detested the meaningless florid "divisions" with which some singers, especially those with Italian training, encumbered even the simplest melodies. John Rowe Parker, editor of the Boston *Euterpeiad,* attended a concert of Madame Catalini and came away disappointed, despite her fine voice and amazing control over rapidly executed ornaments. He complained he heard "a tissue of embroidery" that obliterated all sentiment. He and the listeners around him bemoaned her lack of a musical soul and her uniform manner of performance for songs which demanded different emotional interpretations.[60]

Similar complaints about singers came from several other writers. Disgusted with bravurists, Thomas Hastings protested over their complete disregard of sentiment. He complained of how the simplest Scottish airs were sometimes disfigured, "just as if glides, and trills, and flourishes, and ad-libitums of every description from the Italian school were perfectly in keeping with Scottish tenderness and simplicity."[61]

An admonitory story about John Sinclair is told by Joseph Ireland. For seven years Sinclair was held in the highest esteem for his ballad singing. He then studied voice under Italian teachers in France and Italy. When he reappeared before audiences, his popularity entered a precipitous decline. Critics said he had lost the simplicity of his earlier style, "and those who had formerly delighted in his manly rendering of their national ballads were now annoyed by his incessant introduction of elaborate embellishments."[62]

Catherine Hayes succeeded where Sinclair failed. She won admiration as a true ballad singer, "that most difficult of musical specialties, wherein art and natural expression are curiously blended, and the highest cultivation of the voice concealed under a style of phrasing, simple and unstudied."[63] Most Americans who attended concerts given by ballad singers would have concurred with an opinion printed in *Dwight's Journal,* that less real cultivation and command of the vocal organs is required to sing a few roulades than to produce the "long sustained notes, the light and shade of execution, and the clear articulation of words required by the ballad."[64]

Even though American composers are usually silent on the subject, British composers whose parlor songs were extremely popular in America do encourage the singer to alter the delivery of a song to suit the implications of the text. For instance, *The Valley Lay Smiling Before Me,* by Thomas Moore, carries the admonition: "In moderate time and According to the feeling of each verse."[65] Thomas Haynes Bayly's *I'd Be a Butterfly* starts "Allegretto ma non Troppo Presto," but in the third verse changes to "Slow and Expressive."[66] Presumably, American singers acted on this kind of advice and applied similar precepts to the interpretation of American songs which were the stylistic counterparts of the British compositions, especially in Periods I and II.

Despite the evident concern over expression, a majority of printed parlor works carry few and sometimes no dynamic marks, expressive symbols, and verbal directions for the interpretation of the music.[67] Their absence is attributable to the composer's feeling that the interpretation of his song was within the province of the singer. One can also suggest that a common interpretative style existed, shared by singers of the time, whether professional or amateur. The composer provides a musical blueprint; the performer introduces every subtlety of emotion into the voice in order to make words and melody convincing. The singer is free to ignore the few directions given in the sheet music; he must remain true to his own "natural" expression, rather than to "the crescendos and diminuendos laid down upon the music sheet."[68]

A letter from "A.B." to "S.P.M.", printed in the Boston *Euterpeiad,* is on the teaching of song. At the same time, the writer gives valuable hints on how a singer might interpret a composition. A.B. stresses the need to study various brief passages "as exercises in *expressive* execution." Pupils must learn to sing the same melody according to the changing meaning of the words. Notes are sustained for almost their entire length for words of supplication: "The movement becomes slow, and the accent and emphasis (always distinctly and strongly marked with due reference to the language) are here little different from the gradual *swells and diminishes united.*" For cheerful subjects, the speed quickens, notes are not held their full value, and accentuation is sharper. "The plain narrative or didactic style" also requires a quickened movement, with the sounds verging on *staccato* and pronunciation on recitative. Words must be pronounced distinctly. Intonation must be precise.[69]

That the singer has latitude in tempo is made clear in the advice Isaac B. Woodbury, editor of the New York *Musical Pioneer,* gave to several amateur singers. They wrote to him in 1856 requesting information on how to perform a particular song whose title is not given. They state the piece carries no tempo indication and has a time signature of 2/4 in one edition, 2/2 in another. Woodbury replied that any number of tempos are correct for any given song; the rate of speed is subject to each performer's interpretative and expressive requirements.[70]

The freedom allowed the singer, nonetheless, involved certain responsibilities. In summary, they were to articulate words distinctly, to employ only those gestures that made the song more meaningful, and to vary the facial expression to suit the sentiment. Through a sympathetic delivery, the singer endeavored to aid expression; through accurate intonation, to clarify articulation; and through a few carefully chosen ornaments, to intensify feeling. The evaluation of a ballad singer's performance normally involved all of these considerations. For example, they are mentioned in an appreciative review of Thomas Philipps's singing, printed in the Boston *Euterpeiad* and possibly written by the editor, John Rowe Parker. The writer praises Philipps's "clear articulation," "ornaments. . . introduced with. . . propriety," and "general gesticulations. . . by which every note of music and every syllable of the air is completely and perfectly exemplified."[71]

The famous Hutchinsons claimed an enunciation that readily communicated the song's meaning to audiences. They took care not to slur final consonants or run words together. When they sang a part-song arrangement of a parlor composition, the parts normally were TTBB, with Abby Hutchinson's contralto voice pressed into service as first tenor. On these occasions they tried to blend so precisely that an audience found it impossible to distinguish between the four voices.[72]

During all three periods, a minimum requirement for the professional singer, and probably the amateur as well, was to register the varied emotions of the text on the face. Without doubt this is uppermost in the mind of an unidentified writer in the New Haven *Literary Emporium.* He praises the singing of Elam Ives, parlor-song composer and voice teacher then living in Philadelphia, and his students at a concert they gave in New Haven. Especially high praise is awarded Ives's "principal treble singer" for convincingly altering her face and tones to match the sentiments expressed.[73]

The successful registering of the lyric's meanings on the face comes in for praise in account after account of a singer's performance. Clara Fisher's talent in this area gave a tremendous impact to her performances. She is said to have not only sung but acted her songs. Her face mirrored every sentiment, humor, and feeling contained in the verse.[74]

Expressive gesticulation, already mentioned as characteristic of Thomas Philipps's manner, was used by singers in a limited fashion if accompanying themselves, freely if accompanied by others. No detailed description was discovered of how they went about their arm movements. Perhaps an analogy can be drawn from the gesticulations employed by reciters of poetry. John Neal, of Portland, Maine, says he did some singing and a great deal of poetic recitation when he was nineteen. On one occasion he recited the Moore poem:

> O sailor boy! sailor boy! peace to thy shade!
> Around thy white bones the red coral shall grow,
> Of thy fair yellow hair threads of amber be made,
> And every part suit to thy manion below.

He spoke and threw his arms upward. Then he thrust them out in every direction, "as the spirit moved me or the sentiment prompted." It was of utmost importance, Neal says, for every action to seem natural and unforced, as if the whole body were responding to the poet's meaning.[75]

One final consideration involves the elaborate form of acting associated with some songs, described as "singing in character." Such a performance went beyond facial changes and arm gestures and necessitated a singer's acting out the song's text. An appropriate costume was worn; various props were utilized. The effectiveness of such a performance is illustrated by Charlotte Cushman's celebrated portrayal of "Megs Merrilies." The acting "made the blood" of Madame Vestris, a veteran singer, "run cold," despite Miss Cushman's having only a passable and slightly trained voice.[76]

Unfortunately, most contemporary accounts of such acting-singing lack detailed descriptions. For instance, William Clapp says Clara Fisher sang *The White Sergeant* with "a glorious military *abandon* in her voice [and] a martial and bold carriage of her person, which was irresistibly delightful. Never was a song better *acted* than the piece in question and its popularity was therefore unbounded."[77] He supplies no further details. In another description, Joseph Ireland writes of Mrs. Pownall's singing *Needs Must or The Ballad Singers* on crutches to an enthusiastic audience.[78] Again, a description of the scene is omitted.

Slightly more information is given of John Hutchinson's manner of singing Russell's *The Maniac.* This vocalist says he sang it to the accompaniment of his brothers on violin and cello. As Judson and Asa Hutchinson played the prelude, John crouched behind them, out of view. The fingers of both hands raised the hair on his head and brought it disordered over his eyes. Then he rose up "with the expression of vacancy inseparable from mania," and began singing. Critics asserted his performance "froze their blood."[79]

A lengthier account of singing in character comes from the actor-singer Noah M. Ludlow. One day in 1822, while appearing in New Orleans, he says he received a cut-out portion of the New York *Mirror* from his brother. Printed on the sheet were the verses of Woodworth's *The Hunters of Kentucky.* Requiring a new song for his benefit performance, Ludlow asserts that he joined these words to the tune of *Miss Baily.* The evening of the performance saw the theater packed with rough-and-ready river men. To please them, he provided himself with a rifle, and dressed in buckskin (shirt, leggings, moccasins, and an old slouched hat), as a way of depicting the song. His appearance on the stage was greeted with heavy applause, the thunder of stomping feet, and prolonged whoops. As he sang the first stanza, he came to the line: "There stood John Bull, in martial pomp, *but here was old Kentucky.*" On the last five words, he removed his hat, hurled it on the floor, brought his rifle into firing position, and took aim. The singing and acting made a hit with the crowd. The Battle of New Orleans, the song's subject, was still vivid in the minds of the men, many of them having participated in the fight. At the song's conclusion, everyone stood up, excitedly shouting their approval. Ludlow sang *The Hunters of Kentucky* thrice that evening. Later, he toured the West and performed it before enthusiastic audiences everywhere.[80]

This kind of performance was also common in England. It is known that around the year 1810 three London bass singers, Higman, Tinney, and George Smith, were performing William Shield's *The Wolf,* a song about human rapaciousness, in costume and with appropriate actions. Higman sang it while wearing Spanish clothing, boots, a brace of pistols, dagger, and sword. As he sang about the predatory human wolf, Higman stalked up and down the stage. On the last strain, he commenced walking "extravagantly," stamping his feet and wildly looking about. On the words: "Then to rifle, rob, and plunder," he flourished his sword, whipped out a pistol, and charged off the stage.[81]

Songs sung in character did not always require much action. If the piece was connected with a stage character, told a story, or allowed a visual depiction of a situation, occupation, or human condition—a blind boy, a freezing match girl, a storm-buffeted sailor—then singing in character was appropriate, certainly for professionals, and also for amateurs if they were so inclined. In contrast, if a song was devoid of incident, lacked specificity of any kind, then the singer depended more on vocal delivery and interpretation to make the subject come alive. The hosts of laments on recently deceased young ladies longed for by lonely and ever-loving young men belong in this last category.

Singing in character was most prevalent in Period I, still general in Period II, and least practised in Period III, when most songs were not first heard in stage works, as had heretofore been the practice. During all three periods, however, singing in character remained one of several interpretative possibilities for the ballad singer.

Given the audience's yearning to extract every drop of human sentiment from a song, it is no surprise that face, hands, and body were allotted important roles in the portrayal of a composition. If dressing for a part and acting realistically further enhanced emotional communication, then of course they too were employed. Nineteenth-century Americans recognized none of the emotional constraints on outward behaviour that curb the open venting of feelings in twentieth-century society. After all, externalized feelings were extensions of the inner turmoil that so many persons in this romantic age chose to feel so acutely. Without embarrassment, the ballad singer seized on every means calculated to stir the sensibilities of his listeners.

Notes

1. Evelyn Foster Morneweck, *Chronicles of Stephen Fosters' Family*, II, (Pittsburgh, 1944), 437-38.
2. Charles Durang, "The Philadelphia Stage, The Second Series, 1822-1830," XVII, from the Philadelphia *Sunday Dispatch*; clippings without pagination, at Houghton Library, Harvard University. The series began on 29 June 1856. The interpolations described were common affairs both in America and England; see Durang, "Second Series," XXXII; also, "Remarks of D-G," in James Cobb, *The Siege of Belgrade* (London, n.d.), pp. 5-6. *Description of a Play* is a song composed by Henry Bishop.
3. George P. Upton, *Musical Memories* (Chicago, 1908), p. 219.
4. [James Boardman], *America, and the Americans* (London, 1833), pp. 336-37.
5. Oscar G. Sonneck, *Early Concert-Life in America (1731-1800)* (Leipzig, 1907), p. 213.

6. Thomas Goodwin, *Sketches and Impressions*, ed. R. Osgood Mason (New York, 1887), pp. 280-82.

7. *The Memorial History of Boston*, ed. Justin Winsor, IV (Boston, 1881), 421-22.

8. Walt Whitman, *Prose Works, 1892*, ed. Floyd Stovall, Collected Works, III (New York, 1964), 696.

9. Ernst C. Krohn, *Missouri Music*, II (New York, 1971), 12; Bernhard, Duke of Saxe-Weimar Eisenach, *Travels Through North America during the Years 1825 and 1826*, II (Philadelphia, 1828), 39.

10. New York *Musical World*, 15 May 1852, p. 288.

11. New York *Musical Review*, 21 December 1854, p. 440.

12. Ibid, 27 June 1857, p. 193.

13. Boston *Euterpeiad*, 4 November 1820, p. 126; 11 November 1820, p. 130; Edward F. Rimbault in *Grove's* s.v. "Braham, John."

14. Reprinted in *Dwight's Journal of Music*, 18 December 1852, p. 87.

15. Thomas Ryan, *Recollections of an Old Musician* (New York, 1899), p. 18.

16. William W. Clapp, Jr., *A Record of the Boston Stage* (Boston, 1853), pp. 437-38. The song *I Dreamt that I Dwelt in Marble Halls* is reproduced in the Musical Supplement.

17. Durang, "The First Series, 1749-1821," LV. This series began 7 May 1854, in the Philadelphia *Sunday Dispatch*. The song *The Bay of Biscay O!* is reproduced in the Musical Supplement.

18. Louis C. Madeira, *Annals of Music in Philadelphia and History of the Musical Fund Society* (Philadelphia, 1896), p. 159.

19. "The First Series," XLI.

20. Henry Phillips, *Musical and Personal Recollections*, I (London, 1864), 235. The many travel books and studies of American society, written by British travellers to America, that appeared during the years before 1860, were almost unanimous in their hostility to American democratic life, and caused many Americans, in turn, to become hostile to British visitors. Two of these books are Mrs. Basil Hall's *The Aristocratic Journey* (New York, 1831) and Mrs. Frances Trollope's *Domestic Manners of the Americans* (London, 1832).

21. Phillips, II, 110-13.

22. An account of this benefit is given in Joseph N. Ireland, *Records of the New York Stage from 1750 to 1860*, II (New York, 1867), 366-67.

23. Milton Gerald Hehr, "Musical Activities in Salem, Massachusettes: 1783-1823" (Ph.D. diss. Boston University, 1963), p. 173.

24. Bernhard, II, 81.

25. Boardman, p. 204.

26. See, for example, William Hancock, *An Emigrant's Five Years in the Free States of America* (London, 1860), pp. 90-93; Russel Nye, *The Unembarrassed Muse* (New York, 1970), pp. 145-46.

27. H. Earle Johnson, *Musical Interludes in Boston, 1795-1830* (New York, 1943), p. 109.

28. Boston *Euterpeiad*, 9 September 1820, p. 96.

29. *A Handbook of American Music and Musicians*, ed. F. O. Jones (Canaseraga, New York, 1886) s.v. "Hutchinson Family."

30. Hans Nathan, "The Tyrolese Family Rainer, and the Vogue of Singing Mountain-Troupes in Europe and America," *Musical Quarterly*, XXXII (1946), 63-79.

31. *The Autobiography of Mark Twain*, ed. Charles Neider (New York, 1959), p. 61.

32. Carol Brink, *Harps in the Wind* (New York, 1947), pp. 19-20.

33. New York *Musical Review*, 9 January 1858, p. 5.

34. Brink, p. 78.

35. Boston *Musical Gazette*, 2 March 1846, p. 22.
36. New York *Musical Review*, 30 May 1857, p.167.
37. Brink, p. 41.
38. Reprinted from the New York *Evening Mirror*, in *Dwight's Journal of Music*, 28 May 1853, p. 62.
39. Brink, pp. 40, 82; and the Boston *Musical Gazette*, 1 March 1847, p. 22, respectively.
40. Boston *Euterpeiad*, 27 April 1822, pp. 19-20.
41. George Root, *The Story of a Musical Life* (Cincinnati, 1891), p. 18.
42. Reprinted in the New York *Musical World*, 1 August 1852, p. 407.
43. Henry Dickinson Stone, *Personal Recollections of the Drama or Theatrical Reminiscences* (Albany, 1873), p. 10.
44. Frances Courtney Wemyss, *Twenty-Six Years of the Life of an Actor and Manager*, I (New York, 1847), p. 125.
45. Ireland, II, 176.
46. Ireland, I (1886), 546. See above.
47. *Charlotte Cushman: Her Letters and Memories of Her Life*, ed. Emma Stebbins (Boston, 1879), p.87.
48. See Ireland, I, 294; II, 278; Boston *Euterpeiad* 22 December 1821, p. 157.
49. Ireland, I, 330-31.
50. Boston *Euterpeiad,* 31 March 1821, p. 4.
51. New York *Musical World,* 4 September 1852, p. 13.
52. Thomas Hastings, *Dissertation on Musical Taste* (New York, 1853), p. 88. That Hastings is referring to all kinds of secular songs, including the parlor song, is established on pages 17-21.
53. *Dwight's Journal of Music,* 19 May 1855, p. 55.
54. The Mary Nichols collection is in the library at Old Sturbridge Village, Massachusetts, shelf-number 780.82 N51.
55. Boston *Euterpeiad,* 25 May 1822, p. 36; 8 June 1822, p. 44.
56. Root, p. 18.
57. "Advertisement," in Thomas Moore, *National Songs* (London, 1858)
58. Charles E. Pearce, *Sims Reeves* (London, 1924), pp. 37-38.
59. *The Singer's Companion* (New York, 1854), p. 117
60. "Madame Catalini's Concert," Boston *Euterpeiad,* 29 July 1820, p. 71.
61. Hastings, p. 81.
62. Ireland, II, 3.
63. Anna, Comtesse de Bremont, *The World of Music* (New York, 1892), pp. 61-62.
64. *Dwight's Journal of Music,* 15 January 1859, p. 329.
65. *A Selection of Irish Melodies,* III, with symphonies and accompaniments by Sir John Stevenson, and words by Thomas Moore (London, 1813), 28.
66. *I'd Be a Butterfly,* Ballad, music by Thomas Haynes Bayly (New York, ca. 1830).
67. Chapter 8 will give a further account of such directions in each of the three periods. In general, American and British practices were that printed traditional airs and simple composed songs have the least, more musically complex songs the most, dynamic and other expressive indications.
68. "Ballad Singing," from the *Southern Literary Gazette,* reprinted in the New York *Musical Times,* 27 December 1851, p. 118.
69. Boston *Euterpeiad,* 23 June 1821, pp. 50-51.
70. New York *Musical Pioneer,* 1 February 1856, p. 71.
71. "Musical Drama," Boston *Euterpeiad,* 8 December 1821, p. 148. A similar appraisal of the singing may be found in Ireland, I, 330-31.
72. Brink, pp. 41-42.

73. Reprinted in *The Family Minstrel,* 15 August 1835, p. 108.

74. William Cox, "Crayon Sketches," in Clara Fisher Maeder, *Autobiography,* ed. Douglas Taylor (New York, 1897), p. 133.

75. John Neal, *Wandering Recollections* (Boston, 1869), p. 32.

76. *Charlotte Cushman,* p. 78.

77. Clapp, p. 255.

78. Ireland, I, 106.

79. Brink, p. 40.

80. Noah M. Ludlow, *Dramatic Life as I Found It* (1880; reprinted., New York, 1966), pp. 237-38.

81. Phillips, I, 19.

Chapter 5

Minstrel Songs and Parlor Melodies

Many middle-class Americans of the mid-nineteenth century objected to the kind of speech that came from the mouths of black-faced minstrel singers. As their stock-in-trade, these stage entertainers employed jokes, biting satires, grotesque dances, and songs with texts in an imitation-Negro dialect.[1] Since some minstrel works, usually subtitled as "Ethiopian Songs," are known to have been heard in genteel parlors and do occur in the music collections left behind by well-bred Americans, two questions arise: what minstrel-song type was, and what types were not, sung in polite circles alongside the very proper parlor ballad, and what features distinguish the minstrel from the parlor work?

Minstrel pieces should not be confused with the parlor songs on Negro-humanitarian themes which were written in the late-eighteenth century by English composers—songs like William Reeve's *The Desponding Negro* (ca. 1792) and John Ross's *The Dying Negro* (ca. 1799). The issue of slavery weighted the consciences of Americans. Abolitionists sprang up to contend against this hated institution of the South. In Period III, hundreds of anti-slavery compositions similar in subject matter to the earlier British songs were written by American composers in sympathy with the Abolitionist movement, for example Benjamin Hanby's *Darling Nelly Gray* (Boston, 1856), and Jesse Hutchinson's *The Bereaved Slave Mother* (Boston, ca. 1855). What principally distinguishes these works from minstrel songs are three elements: none of them employ dialect, few move faster than *andante,* and most center on sad and sentimental themes.

Unquestionably, such songs belong in the parlor, not the minstrel, category. For members of polite society, their performance demonstrated a broad, indiscriminate awareness of brotherhood without the danger of being considered radical Abolitionists, or having to perform some nasty task attendant on a real commitment to emancipation. For a few, singing these songs was a way of expressing personal feelings of true concern over a despicable aspect of American society. For whatever reasons they were performed, such songs were often purchased and sung by amateur musicians of genteel backgrounds.

The first two stanzas of *The Bereaved Slave Mother,* which are to be sung "Andante con Espressivo," clearly demonstrate the serious, though bathetic, nature of such lyrics:

Oh! deep was the anguish of the Slave Mother's heart,
When call'd from her darling forever to part;
So grieved that lone Mother, that heart-broken Mother,
In sorrow and woe.

The lash of the Master her deep sorrows mock,
While the Child of her bosom is sold on the Block;
Yet loud shrieked that Mother, poor heart-broken Mother,
In sorrow and woe.

The high coefficient of sentimental emotionalism is obvious. The scene is calculated for maximum effect; a listener immediately feels the piercing thrust of pathos. A direct message and vivid representation obviate the freight which the imagination might have been called on to bear. In short, the song is the quintessence of a sentimental parlor composition.

One can find a few mid-nineteenth century parlor compositions on Negro subjects, whose texts contain one or two phrases and symbols derived from minstrel works. For example, the second stanza of L.V.H. Crosby's *The Slave Mother* (Boston, 1853), by a musician who composed both parlor and minstrel songs, includes references to Foster's *Oh! Susanna* and to banjo playing:

But now the chains are on his feet,
The lash is o'er his head,
With grief she cries would it be right,
To wish that he was dead,
She learns her little child to talk,
She teaches it to pray;
And sing "Susanna don't you cry,"
And on the Banjo play.

The song's subject is a slave mother's forced separation from her child. Only one word in dialect occurs in the text; it is the cruel white "Master," not the slave, who utters it. The composer wishes to encourage the listener to feel strongly a mother's suffering. No levity or grotesquerie mars the delineation. The song *Susanna* and the banjo appear as conventional symbols. They enable Crosby to explicate economically the intimate bond that ties mother to child.

The difference between parlor and minstrel song is made easier to understand if one examines a composition that could never be mistaken for a sentimental and genteel work, and that seems to have been very rarely performed by cultivated Americans. If a sheet-music copy of the minstrel song *Long Time Ago!* (1836) is looked at, one sees a cover-lithograph of a raggedly dressed, wild looking Negro, his head wrapped in a bandanna and his hands holding a shot gun, which threatens to go off at any second. The song's text goes as follows:

I was born down old Varginee,
  Long time ago.
O Massa die an make me free,
  Long time ago.
O I ax massa ware he gwoin,
  Long time ago.
He grab a Gun and Dog to show im,
  Long time ago.

He say he gwoin to killa Niggar,
  Long time ago.
He aim he Gun, he pull de trigger,
  Long time ago.
He shoot de Niggar trough de libber,
  Long time ago.
Vich made de Niggar kick an quiver,
  Long time ago.[2]

Evidently the uncouthness of the lithograph figure and the lack of refinement in the text repelled middle-class singers. To them, killing people even in jest was not funny. To sing about shooting someone in the liver, "Vich made de Niggar kick an quiver," would have seemed a demeaning activity and shocking for anyone with pretensions to sensitivity. Well-bred ladies and gentlemen were expected to shun such examples of regressive taste. The song *Long Time Ago!* appears in none of the private collections of music that the author has studied, and nineteenth-century writers never report hearing it in polite circles.

Yet some melodies set to objectionable minstrel texts did strike many members of genteel society as extremely attractive. These music lovers found themselves in the unhappy position of admiring the music but refusing to sing the words. Such was the case with *Long Time Ago!*

Fortunately for them, remedies were at hand. When the English composer Charles E. Horn came to America, he rearranged the melody of *Long Time Ago!* adapting it to a new and far more acceptable text supplied by George P. Morris. In the *Southern Literary Messenger,* November 1839, Horn is quoted as saying that he found the tune so beautiful he enlisted Morris's aid. He was certain that, given a new form, the song could "command" the interest of the "serious listener." The remodeled *Long Time Ago!* did become popular with the middle class and soon found its way into many parlors, under the title *Near the Lake Where Droop'd the Willow:*

> Near the Lake where droop'd the willow,
> Long time ago!
> Where the rock threw back the billow,
> Brighter than snow;
> Dwelt a maid, beloved and cherish'd,
> By high and by low!
> But, with autumn's leaf, she perish'd,
> Long time ago![3]

The subject, the death of a young lady, is a favorite among the parlor-song themes; the somber mood, a contrast to the ludicrous caricature in the minstrel version. This parlor-song contrafactum was now sung in public by the ballad singers of English and American polite society, including Horn's own wife, known as Miss Horton, who popularized it in America, and John Parry, baritone soloist, who sang it in England.[4] Its frequent performance in genteel homes is evidenced by its ubiquitous appearance in the extant music collections from that time. Many copies of the song show evidence of frequent use.

As with *Long Time Ago!* and *Near the Lake,* a large number of tunes employed in both parlor and minstrel pieces were traditional airs and, of course, in the public domain. It is, therefore, hardly surprising to discover that the traditional melody used in *Lubly Fan Will You Cum Out To Night?* published by Keith of Boston, in 1844, as a minstrel song composed by Cool White (John Hodges), also was issued by Reed of Boston in 1843, as the tune of *'Tis Midnight Hour,* a sentimental parlor ballad composed "by an Amateur." Nor is it surprising that another minstrel song published by Keith, in 1843, *The Fine Old Colored Gentleman* by Dan Emmett, shares the same melody with an English parlor song, *The Fine Old English Gentleman* (New York, ca. 1836). The melody of both compositions is an adaptation of an air already old in the eighteenth century.[5]

Significantly, only the parlor-song versions of these tunes seem to have been purchased and performed in any numbers by the middle class. Rarely do their Ethiopian versions occur in the extant music collections from before 1860. Moreover, the minstrel versions are seldom mentioned in contemporary music periodicals like the *New York Musical World* and *Dwight's Journal of Music,* and whatever mention is made is usually derogatory.

Toward the end of the forties and into the fifties, the Ethiopian songs began to share both the subject matter and musical style of the non-dialect sentimental parlor compositions. Only a mild, half-hearted attempt at dialect and an addition of a harmonized choral refrain reveal the slender link to the exuberant, comic minstrel-song type. One contemporary source describes the changes taking place in minstrel pieces as a "bleaching process."[6] Possibly, as the controversy over slavery increased in intensity, fewer people found the themes of comic minstrel songs something to laugh at, and more men and women balked at singing anything in dialect. It may well have caused the purchase of the run-of-the-mill minstrel composition to fall off. In the fifties, one comes across several writers who speak of the drop in the home performance of minstrel works. While some of this reportage was wishful thinking on the part of writers who disliked the minstrel idiom, enough agreement is evident to suggest at least a temporary hiatus in the purchase of these songs, save for the few that managed to achieve high popularity. It follows that composers and publishers would explore new avenues for encouraging an increase in sales.

Interestingly, the same song was occasionally published in both a dialect and non-dialect version, because the publisher hoped by so doing to attract different buyers. One work of this type, *Come Along Wid Me, or The Darkies' Serenade,* by H. Avery (Boston, 1853), has as its text:

> Oh! come along wid me love, come wid me,
> De stars am shining bright,
> While de silver moon am gilding ebry tree,
> Wid her galvanicumizing light,
> All de darkies hab clear'd out some and gone to rest,
> And ebry ting am still;
> Except de pulverations ob dis breast,
> Dats a clippen cloppen like a mill.

The lover's serenade is of frequent occurrence in parlor compositions. But because dialect was employed, some levity was mixed with the sentiment, and words like "galvacumizing" seemed too bizarre, this song may not have appealed to all potential buyers. For reasons that can only be conjectured, Oliver Ditson, the Boston publisher, issued the identical music in 1857, with a new text and title, *Come Along With Me, or The Sparker's Serenade:*

> Oh! come along with me, love, come with me,
> The stars are shining bright,
> While the silver moon is gilding ev'ry tree
> With her pure and ever gentle light;

All our friends have now retired, and gone to rest,
And ev'ry thing is still,
Except the palpitations of this breast,
Which is clicking, clacking like a mill.

Surely the publisher, at least to some extent, had in mind reaching members of polite society who might have been put off by the cruder text.

On occasion, middle-class singers found minstrel works attractive despite the dialect. Foster's *Old Folks at Home* (1851) was one such song; his *Nelly Was a Lady* (1849) another. The strong sentimental cast of both songs explains, in part, why many cultured Americans purchased and sang them:

Down on de Mississippi floating,
Long time I trabble on de way,
All night de cottonwood a toting,
Sing for me true-lub all de day.

(Chorus)
Nelly was a lady—
Last night she died,
Toll de bell for lubly Nell
My dark Virginny bride.[7]

The tone is serious; the subject common to many sentimental parlor ballads; the dialect less obtrusive than in *Long Time Ago!* and *Come Along Wid Me.*

Nevertheless, at times even this more refined type of text seemed undistinguished to some and was exchanged for another. To cite one instance, *The Singer's Companion,* a songbook published in New York in 1854, contains the music of Foster's *Nelly Was a Lady.* But it is printed with a new non-dialect text written by J.A. Turner. Nowhere does the original Foster lyric appear. The song, retitled *Jessie Was a Fair One* begins:

There pinions bright were round us flitting
To bear my Jessie's soul away,
While 'neath the oak we were sitting,
Amid the blooming flow'rs of May

(Chorus)
Jessie was a fair one,
Last May she died;
Shed a tear for Jessie dear,
My bright, my gentle bride.[8]

Underneath the title is a revealing editorial comment: "This is an 'Ethiopian Melody.' The air is touching and beautiful. As we have never seen any other words adapted to it than the common-place ones, 'Nelly was a Lady,' we have endeavored to substitute others that will be more generally acceptable.[8]

In some instances amateur singers did their own textual substitution. Indeed, for those amateurs who loved the melody of a minstrel song and disliked the lyric, a substitution of their own for the printed words was a practical solution to their dilemma. The practice must have been common in the 1840s and 1850s. Sometimes the new, non-dialect verse is found written under the music. Just as often, it is written on a separate sheet of paper, which is then pasted onto the sheet-music. In a few instances, the substitute text is not pasted in but inserted loosely between the pages.

As an example of such substitution, in a bound music collection that once belonged to a Miss Celeste Ingall, now in Houghton Library, is the minstrel work *The Boatman's Dance,* with a written-in non-dialect text that begins: "Oh sweet the spring." That Miss Ingalls was a genteel lady is indicated by an inscription in the volume, written by a G.A. Stewart: "Celeste est une bonne et gentie fille: Tous les monde li sait. Oui. Certainment!" It is difficult to imagine this gentlewoman ever attempting to sing the original comic-dialect words.

In the fifties the gap between the two song-types became so narrow that American composers moved back and forth between them with ease. The differences between minstrel and parlor song are often almost nonexistent in works by Stephen Foster. When Foster first conceived his parlor work *Maggie By My Side* (New York, 1852), he intended it as an Ethiopian song in dialect, *Fanny By My Side,* which began:

Roll on ye breakers
    O'er de troubled tide
Fair wedder all de day
    With Fanny by my side.

He later changed his mind and refashioned it into a parlor piece. In Foster's published version the above stanza became:

Roll ye dark waves
    O'er the troubled tide:
I heed not your anger,
    Maggie's by my side.[9]

Another composer solved the minstrel-parlor song question in

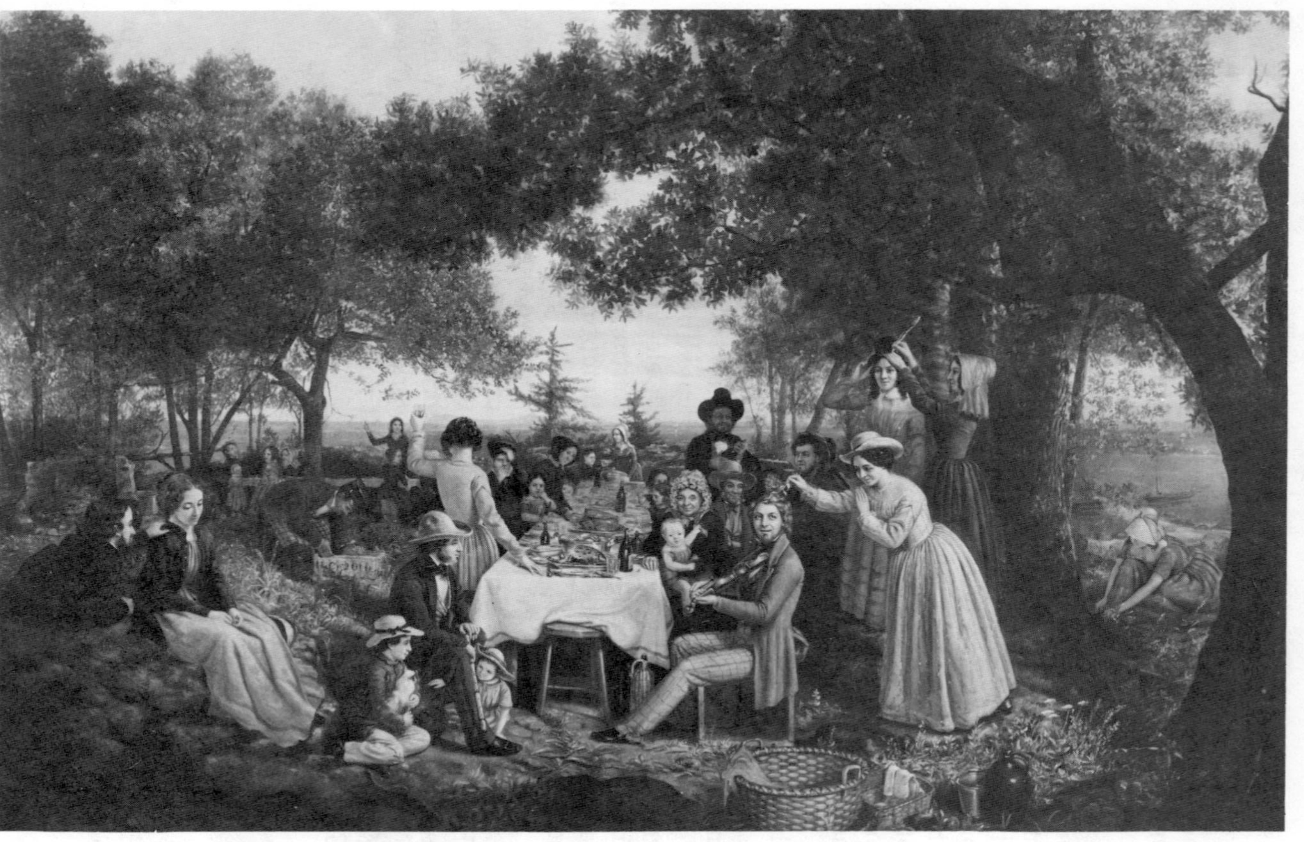

A "Pic-Nick" Camden, Maine. Reprinted with permission from the Museum of Fine Arts, Boston.

an amusing way. The same Avery mentioned earlier as responsible for the two versions of *Come Along With Me* tried to satisfy all tastes with one and the same song, *Come Take a Sail* (Boston, 1853), by describing it as "a new Ethiopian Melody designed for the home circle." True, the music has some of the jauntiness of comic minstrelsy. But there is nothing offensive in the words:

> Oh! Wont you come, my Rosy dear,
> And take a sail with me,
> My boat is laying just out here,
> And only waits for thee.

Avery could just as easily have described the song as a parlor "Ballad."

As minstrel and parlor works approached each other in musical style and theme, and as minstrel shows increasingly introduced sentimental parlor songs into their formats, more and more middle-class ladies and gentlemen attended the public performances of the minstrel men. Most mentions of members of the middle class singing minstrel songs identify men as the performers, not women. Once in a while gentlemen even sang the less nice, comic types of Ethiopian airs. One of the few descriptions of men doing so is given by a foreigner, Frederika Bremer. While on an 1850 visit to America, she was traveling away from Waterville, Wisconsin, in a public coach, just after a musical convention had been held in that town. On board were several "good tempered" gentlemen, one of them a schoolmaster from Mississippi. That evening after they had stopped for the night and had finished dinner, the men "began singing negro songs, and sang 'Oh Susanna,' 'Dandy Jem from Caroline,' and others very well, and in character."[10]

There seems to have been a great deal of uncertainty and contradiction in American middle-class attitudes toward the minstrel songs. This uncertainty surfaces in an 1853 letter sent to *Dwight's Journal of Music* by a Southern lady. While calling Ethiopian works "equivocal proofs of taste," she admits she has heard them sung by whites and blacks in the South with a power and pathos unknown to Northerners. She continues: "When I heard Jenny Lind sing 'Home, Sweet Home' it caused such an emotion as I never before experienced; it might be exquisite *homesickness*. 'Old Folks at Home,' as I heard it shouted from house to house, from the fields and in the valleys, has an effect scarcely inferior. . . ."[11]

Mid-nineteenth-century writers on music conceded Foster's talent as a composer. Some hoped, nonetheless, that he would concentrate on writing music to texts acceptable to refined tastes. Richard Storr Willis, editor of the New York Musical World, for example, voiced the opinion of many in the middle class when he wrote in 1853: "Mr. Foster possesses more than ordinary abilities as a composer; and we hope he will soon realize enough from his Ethiopian melodies to enable him to *afford* to drop them and turn his attention to the production of a higher kind of music. Much of his *music* is now excellent, but being wedded to negro idioms it is, of course, discarded by many who would otherwise gladly welcome it to their pianos."[12]

Further insight into middle-class attitudes toward minstrel songs is provided by the views of one musician and the reactions of two people who read these views in print. A harsh criticism of minstrel music appeared in 1853, written by Augusta Browne, a composer of parlor music only. She wrote that minstrel music had to be considered "melodic trash" that threatens "in a fair way to cast all sentimental music in the shade." The New York Musical World reprinted her criticism as well as two letters from readers commenting on what she had written.

One of the letters, from a writer in Point Coupee, Louisiana, is especially valuable for baring the ambivalence of feeling in some Americans toward Ethiopian songs. Annoyed by the Browne criticism, the anonymous writer states: "I see Miss Augusta Browne sneers at the negro melodies. Let her compose one which, like *Old Folks at Home,* shall be sung, played, and whistled from Maine to California, in four months after it is published, and I will concede her right to ridicule them if she likes. I don't like the negro words myself, and wish you would put Foster to compose the airs, Morris to write the songs, and Maeder to harmonize them."[13]

Polite society's discomfort over minstrel songs seems to have been owing chiefly to the more aggressive and ill-bred comic texts, as seen in *Long Time Ago!* and to the commonplaces of the "negro" dialect. Hardly any writers on music, other than Augusta Browne, describe these compositions as "melodic trash." One who did agree with her was John Sullivan Dwight. In his *Journal* of 19 November 1853, he writes of *Old Folks at Home:*

> We wish to say that such tunes, although whistled and sung by everybody, are erroneously supposed to have taken a deep hold of the popular mind; that the charm is only skin deep; that they are hummed and whistled without musical emotion . . . that they persecute and haunt the morbidly sensitive nerves of deeply musical persons, so that they too hum and whistle them involuntarily, hating them even while they hum them; that such melodies become catching, idle habits, and are not popular in the sense of musically inspiring, but that such and such a melody breaks out every now and then, like a morbid irritation of the skin.

Augusta Browne and John Sullivan Dwight notwithstanding,

unease over Ethiopian songs seems to have centered on the lyrics, not the music. Interestingly, Stephen Foster himself observes, in an 1852 letter to E.P. Christy, the minstrel-troupe manager: "I find by my efforts I have done a great deal to build up a taste for Ethiopian songs among refined people by making the words suitable for their taste, instead of the trashy and really offensive words which belong to some songs of that order. . . ."[14]

In conclusion, one must state that the comic types of minstrel pieces are rarely mentioned as heard in polite circles. A few minstrel songs on more serious subjects, invariably sentimental in tone, are found scattered here and there through the collections that have come down to the present day. Only Foster's sentimental Ethiopian songs, and George P. Knauff's *Wait for the Wagon* (1851), a work designated as a minstrel song but whose text includes not a single word in dialect, seem to have been heard with any frequency amongst the cultivated, and thus appear as exceptions to the rule. For the most part, the more genteel citizens of the United States preferred, if they heard them at all, to listen to these more vulgar manifestations of popular taste in the public concert hall, and only occasionally in the privacy of their homes. Performance in their parlors might have hinted at more than a casual involvement with such music. On the other hand, the anonymity attending public viewing permitted the enjoying of what were generally considered equivocal examples of artistic propriety, without resulting in any obligations on the part of the listeners.

Composers, publishers, and writers on musical matters were certainly aware of the love-hate attitudes of refined Americans regarding minstrel song. They knew that these were the people with the means to purchase songs in quantity. They had to take cognizance of the cloaks of gentility worn by many amateur singers of the 1840s and '50s. Perforce the minstrel song had to change in response to these considerations.

Notes

1. See Hans Nathan, *Dan Emmett and the Rise of Early Negro Minstrelsy* (Norman, Okla., 1962).
2. *Long Time Ago!,* a favorite Comic Song and Chorus, arranged by William Clifton (New York, 1836).
3. *Near the Lake Where Droop'd the Willow,* a Southern Refrain, sung with enthusiastic applause by Miss Horton, the words by G.A. Morris, the symphonies composed, adapted, and arranged by Charles E. Horn (New York, 1837).
4. *Long Time Ago or Near the Lake Where Droop'd the Willow,* Ballad, sung by Mr. John Parry, the symphonies and accompaniments composed by Charles E. Horn (London, n.d.).
5. William Chappell, *Popular Music of the Olden Time,* I (London, 1859), 299-300.

6. "Obituary, Not Eulogistic," *New York Musical Review,* 7 December 1854, p. 418.

7. *Nelly Was a Lady,* Foster's Ethiopian Melodies No. 1, as sung by the Christy Minstrels, written and composed by S.C. Foster (New York, 1849).

8. *The Singer's Companion* (New York, 1854), p. 238.

9. John Tasker Howard, *Stephen Foster, America's Troubadour* (New York, 1953), p. 211.

10. Fredrika Bremer, *The Homes of the New World,* trans, Mary Howitt, I (New York, 1853), 649.

11. "Letter from a teacher at the South," *Dwight's Journal of Music,* 26 February 1853, p. 164.

12. *New York Musical World,* 29 January 1853, p. 75.

13. *New York Musical World,* 8 September 1853, p. 28. George Morris was a writer of lyrics for parlor songs, editor of the *New York Mirror,* and a friend of Richard Storrs Willis. James Gaspard Maeder was an English vocalist, music teacher, and composer of parlor songs; he lived and worked in Boston.

14. Howard, p. 196.

Chapter 6

The Economics Of The Parlor Song

The sheet-music publisher catered to a more specialized and elusive market than did the general publisher. Accordingly, the risks were greater. His customers were those relatively few Americans who found nothing morally wrong in performing secular songs, had some musical training and leisure, and commanded the purchase price of the music. The publisher himself had to be musician and businessman enough to evaluate a song in relation to its selling potential. One or two errors could prove financially disasterous to those who were undercapitalized.

Marketing and profiting from the production of songs involved at least five different factors, all interdependent and essential. Music had to be printed and copyrighted, if possible; competition met; the songs retailed; the music advertised; the stock of works replenished. The publisher tried to sell at least enough copies of an issue to cover the expenses of engraving, printing, and advertising. The initial number of copies printed in a first edition might number a hundred or less, rarely more than a thousand.[1] If the song became popular, the publisher had to rush out additional copies to exploit the increased demand, especially since rival publishers might be tempted to put out pirated copies and thus dilute profits.

Some songs were in demand only for a few years. For example, Oliver Shaw's *Mary's Tears* seems to have remained popular from 1817 to about 1825. On the other hand, a few pieces remained popular for decades. Henry Bishop's *Home! Sweet Home!,* first issued in America around 1823, continued popular throughout the century. Further, a successful composer like Isaac B. Woodbury might write several songs which sold well enough to require several reprintings. Woodbury's *Be Kind to the Loved Ones at Home* (1847) went into at least twelve editions; *Take Me Home to Die* (1850) into fifteen; *He Doeth All Things Well* into sixteen.[2] Regrettably, of how many copies an "edition" consisted is uncertain. And some publishers may have engaged in some puffery to encourage further purchase.

No composer or publisher could predict what would sell. George

Root states that, after composing *There's Music in the Air,* he threw the song into a drawer "as not being of much account." When required to supply the New York *Musical Review* with a composition, some months later, he "sent this for want of something better." The work swiftly caught on. Its popularity, Root asserts, "illustrates" a composer's "not knowing when we do that which will touch the popular heart."[3] Unfortunately, several failures accompanied every success. These diminished profits.[4] Poor selections, bad timing, over-pricing, the reluctance of professional musicians to perform one's publications, and limited access to marketing channels could easily result in severe losses.

The United States in 1800 had about eighteen known publishers of sheet music, none of them native Americans, with establishments in Philadelphia, New York, Boston, and Baltimore. The most important of these were Benjamin Carr and George Willig of Philadelphia, George Gilfert, James Hewitt, and John Paff of New York, and Peter Albrecht von Hagen of Boston.[5] In this early period, the engraving and printing of music was often done for the publishers by outside firms. In some cases the work was sent to England. The United States was then almost entirely rural; the population small and concentrated along the Atlantic seaboard. Perforce the number of new issues per year was low. To publish four or five titles a month was considered a highly ambitious undertaking for one firm. As an example of the activities of a publishing firm from these early days, on 1 January 1794 Benjamin Carr advertised in Dunlap and Claypoole's *Amerian Daily Advertiser:* "B. Carr and Co. inform the public that having settled a correspondence with the principal publishers of music in Britain, etc. from whom they are constantly receiving supplies of the newest music—together with several originals in their possession from which they wish to present amateurs with a selection of the most esteemed, they will, for the future, *publish a new song, or piece of music, every Monday,* and by the continuance hope to make their publications a register of fashionable music."[6]

American cities grew swiftly. Hundreds of new towns sprang up where twenty years before only wilderness existed. A flourishing middle class found itself with enough leisure to think of taking up music. Inevitably the demand for sheet-music grew, as did the number and size of music publishing firms. By 1860 the number of publishers had increased to about ninety, now scattered all over the United States, from the Atlantic to the Mississippi. The giants, like Oliver Ditson of Boston, and Firth, Pond and Co. and William Hall and Son of New York, had large, almost completely integrated operations. One writer stated in 1856 that Ditson's "list of sheet-music and music books is said to be the largest in the world; and while he publishes largely for the million, furnishing the country with music that all can sing and appreciate, he does not neglect the more advanced musician." And of the Hall firm: "This house have [sic] sent Wallace's, Gottschalk's, Root's (Wurzel,) Converse's, and other similar publications from Maine to Oregon, the Sandwich Islands, and Australia."[7]

Through hundreds of retail outlets and thousands of mail orders, these publishers purveyed their sheet-music to people in every settled corner of America. Clearly, the dominant firms of the 1850s no longer resembled the modest and undercapitalized enterprises of fifty years before.

Song-Publishing Activities

The sheet-music songs published in America before 1860 were normally printed from pewter, sometimes copper, plates. On these plates, staff lines were incised, then notes and lettering punched in with steel die stamps; and finally, slurs and other non-standardized markings drawn in with a graver.[8]

One of the earliest advertisements of a sheet-music issue occurred in the Boston *Chronicle,* 17 October 1768: "The New and Favorite LIBERTY SONG, IN FREEDOM we're Born, &c. Neatly engraved on COPPER PLATE, the size of half a sheet of Paper. Set to MUSIC for the VOICE, and to which is also added, A Set of Notes adapted to the GERMAN FLUTE and VIOLIN, Is just published and to be SOLD at the *LONDON Book-Store, King-Street, Boston.*"[9] Richard Wolfe, an expert on these matters, says that the first music engraved by means of punching tools was Alexander Reinagle's *A Selection of the Most Favorite Scots Tunes* (Philadelphia, 1787), the engraver being John Aitken.[10]

Music sheets grew in size, from those of 1790 to those of 1860. During the first two decades (1790-1810) of the era under study, they averaged 32.5 centimeters long by 25 centimeters wide. From 1810 to 1840, the dimensions increased to about 34 centimeters long by 25.5 centimeters wide. From 1840 to 1860, they grew to an average of 35 centimeters long by 26.5 centimeters wide. The change in size is not owing to an increase in the size of the engraved plate from which the music was printed. The plates remained about 28 centimeters long by 20 centimeters wide throughout the seventy years. Rather, the change can be attributed to the increasing size of the paper upon which the music was printed. As the years passed, the music was provided with progressively wider margins.

During the 1790s, engraver, printer, and publisher were usually different people. Publishers chose between at least twenty-five different engravers in Philadelphia, Boston, and New York.[11] The plates completed, the publisher could then have copies printed until the plates wore out. Reinagle had much of the music he published in Philadelphia, around 1787-89, printed for him by Thomas Dobson, also of Philadelphia.[12] Publishers sold the music in their own retail stores. They also mailed bulk consignments of music at discounted prices to independent retailers in other cities and towns, for local resale. In the second decade of the nineteenth century, the Franklin Music Warehouse of Boston became one of the largest music dealers in America, carrying and offering for local and mail-order sale what the firm claimed was all the sheet-music published in America, as well as a large selection of music published in Europe.[13] Sheet-music publishers normally concentrated on secular vocal pieces and light piano works, leaving the issuance of sacred music, much of it printed by means of moveable type, to general publishers or to those specializing in sacred music. Music stores tended to carry mostly sheet-music; general book stores, sacred music. The country store of many a small town included a few secular and sacred works among its paper goods and stationary.[14]

From 1800 to 1820, performances in the growing number of theaters and concert halls increasingly brought songs to the public's attention. Astute publishers took account of what was sung in public. If a song pleased a sizeable group, the alert entrepreneur hastened to make it available for general purchase. This practice is commented on by a writer in the New York *Euterpeiad:* " 'Away, away, etc. to the Mountain's Brow' was first sung by Miss Hughes at the Park Theatre, N.Y. on Friday, and in five days three [sic] several publishers presented their respective copies to the inspection of the purchasers. One publisher, Mr. Hewitt, came out with his copy in about *three days and a half* after the first night of its performance."[15]

As sales increased, so also did the number of publishing houses. Competition became intense. Each firm tried to make the appearance of its songs attractive in order to attract customers. Therefore, a decorative title-page began to preface the music itself. Prior to 1820, a few songs had been published with a small engraved illustration on the upper part of the first page. Beginning with the 1820s, the title-page of many songs was given over to a lithographed vignette, usually the portrait of a favorite singer or the depiction of the song's main subject matter or sentiment. The vignette, the publisher hoped, would help sell the music.

While Catherine Hayes was touring America, several songs she was singing, among them Moore's *The Harp that Once Thro' Tara's Halls* and Hook's *Within a Mile of Edinburg Town,* were published by Ditson and by Reed, both of Boston. On each title-page is the singer's portrait, and her signature reproduced below. Presumably, she received some recompense for her endorsement, a practice already well-established in England. In this regard W.T. Parke states of the English musical scene of around 1828: "Ballads [are] continually sung... by our most popular singers, some of whom will sing any production... provided the composer or publisher will pay them down a sum of money more or less exorbitant. This expensive system which originated in the backwardness of the lovers of music to buy songs, however good, that had not been sung in public, has at length been partially superseded by the new mode of heading them with a cheap lithographic engraving, which causes them to be purchased with avidity!"[16] Although certainly surmisable, no evidence of similar payments by American publishers exists.

As an added inducement to the ladies, some firms printed songs on tinted paper, in shades of blue, pink, and yellow mostly. Scores of such songs, the majority of them issued in the late twenties and early thirties, occur in the still-extant private music collections of women of that time, an indication the publishers had succeeded to some extent. Around 1830, a New-York publisher, George Bourne, is reported to have published *She Never Blamed Him Never* not only on lilac-tinted paper but with the pages "scented by some aromatic essence."[17]

Sales increased; so also did the amount of music published. Three or four hundred titles altogether are known to have been published in the eighteenth century. As demand expanded in the first quarter of the nineteenth century, almost ten thousand titles appeared.[18] Gradually, activities once shared by several small firms (engraving, printing, distribution, and retail sales) came under one direction. The Ditson Company of Boston started modestly in 1834 as an offshoot of the store belonging to Samuel Parker, who was a book, stationary, and piano retailer, and a publisher of a limited amount of music. By the fifties, Ditson had become a leviathan among music publishers. For example, within a two-week period comprising the last week of February and the first of March, 1856, the company issued thirteen vocal and eleven piano compositions, and one book of voice exercises. In the next two weeks, at least thirty-one items came out. The songs by American composers were priced at 25¢ each.[19]

In the 1857 New York *Musical Review,* a writer describes, possibly with some exaggeration, Ditson's new quarters at 277 Washington Street as having an enormous basement floor devoted to wholesale sheet-music sales; a ground floor for the display and retail sale of American and foreign publications; an upper floor which housed the engravers and stampers, and a huge supply of paper for sheets and books; and another floor where from 25 to 30 men operated twelve printing presses, printing sheet-music from engraved plates. The firm was said to have an inventory of 9,000,000 sheets of music and 50,000 engraved plates, and to use about 1000 reams (about 50,000,000 sheets) of paper yearly in the sheet-music operation alone.[20] On the last page of John Ordway's *Parlor Glees,* which Ditson issued in 1859, the firm claims its sheet-music publications "comprise upward of 20,000 pieces" of vocal and piano compositions, and offers to send its catalogue free of charge to any address.

The Ditson Company of the fifties was both a secular and a sacred music publisher, printing music in sheet and book format. As the century unfolded the company bought up many of its competitors, established new, company-controlled outlets in important centers like New York City, Philadelphia, Chicago and Cincinnati, and achieved an impressive volume of production and sales.[21]

Whether a giant like Ditson or a smaller, struggling company, the publisher, when not reprinting European works, depended on the creative efforts of composers in America to keep his presses rolling, however ill-equipped some of these writers might have been in musical theory. Since great technical skill was unnecessary to compose a typical song, most published American compositions came from amateurs and half-trained professionals. A song's title-page sometimes identifies the composer as "an amateur," as in *It is Not that I Love You Less* (Philadelphia, ca. 1820); or "a Gentleman," as in *Know Ye The Land* (Baltimore, ca. 1824); or "a Lady," as in *Thou Hast Wounded the Spirit that Loved Thee* (Baltimore, 1846). Probably to compliment and retain the goodwill of their students, small publishers who were also music teachers (a common combination) might issue music composed by persons studying under them. This helps explain why some songs displayed in Gottlied Graupner's small music store in Boston were the creations of his pupils, all of them amateurs.[22]

There were an extraordinarily large number of errors in chord construction, modulation and voice leading in the published works of amateurs. Yet they are not alone. Professional composers were equally prone to error. One writer in the Boston *Euterpeiad,* while praising the melodies of the well-liked song composer Thomas Wiesenthal, also points out the "defects in the scientific construction of his harmonies."[23] Even the extremely popular composer Henry Russell was criticized for the many mistakes in his compositions. An 1854 reviewer of Russell's song *Cheer, Boys, Cheer* writes: "Good words by Charles Mackay, and the music is more chaste and less pretentious and incorrect than most of this author's [Russell's] songs."[24]

A song's success had nothing to do with its musical correctness. A writer in the 1857 New York *Tribune* admits that no one knows the rules for constructing a popular song: "From shrinking men and from unlettered men come the melodies which fasten themselves upon the life of the world." He says the famous *Marseillaise* was an accidental creation; *Home! Sweet Home!* a hack job written for a manager greedy for novelties; and *Hail, Columbia* a spur-of-the-moment sort of piece. He concludes by pointing out that the masses take up the singing of popular songs without worrying over who wrote them or why—though all feel gratitude "towards those who have cheered our loneliness, elevated our hopes or assuaged our grief." With popularity, a song ceased to belong to the composer or publisher but became "especially the property of the people."[25]

Yet who could tell the publisher what would become popular? He examined hundreds of manuscripts, gambled on a few, and rejected the majority as unlikely to impress his customers. Most rejections were the work of amateurs. On a number of occasions the publisher seems to have decided he could not take the risk of general publication since the market would be too limited. One reason for the limited market was that many pieces by amateurs were slipshod imitations of currently popular compositions. Also commanding a negligible market were music teachers' compositions intended for sale to students. In instances where sales might not cover costs, several publishers printed the music only when the composer paid for all expenses and allowed the publisher a profit for the services rendered. For example, a spokesman for the Ditson firm, in 1859, after discussing the problems involved in the publication of songs by amateurs and music teachers, agrees his firm would be willing to put out such songs if the composer guaranteed the costs.[26]

Some establishments even advertised that they would print sheet-music for anyone who paid the expenses. Billings, Taylor and Aikman of New York was active in this business. The company offered in 1852 to print by the stereotype process 50 copies of one page of music for $4., 100 copies for $5., with additional copies at $2. per 100.[26] The stereotype process, a 1771 discovery of Alois Senefelder, was based on the lithographic transfer principle. This involved writing on a specially conditioned stone with some greasy matter, then printing ink copies from it. Later a metal surface was substituted for the stone.[28] The New York firm's charge of $13. for 500 copies comes to 2.6¢ a page. Thus a two-page song cost 5.2¢ and a four-page song 10.4¢. Presumably Billings, Taylor and Aikman also realized a profit.

Seven years later, in a "Reply to Inquiries Related to Publication of Music," the directors of the Oliver Ditson Company complained that most song manuscripts they received were not worth publishing. Moreover one in ten of the songs they did publish realized only enough to cover costs, and one in fifty proved successful. The firm, therefore, had either to decline the offer of music they could not justify publishing on their own account or require the composer to buy a certain number of copies to help defray the expenses. They had decided on the latter course. Their charges, to cover costs, would be $2. per page for engraving, $1.50 per 100 sheets for paper, and 75¢ per 100 sheets for printing. A full title-page would cost from $5. to $10.; a half-title, $2. to $3. These charges also covered reading and correcting the proofs.[29]

The composer's cost was $4.25 for producing 100 copies of one page by the engraved-plate process; for 500 copies, $13.25, making it slightly more expensive than the stereotype process. A four-page song without title-page cost 10.6¢. Assuming a conservative 1:22.5 ratio as the value relationship of pre-1860 dollars to 1977 dollars ($1 equals $22.50 in 1977), [30] a four-page song without title-page cost $2.37 in 1977 dollars. These figures are important because they help clarify the relationship of costs to retail price in the sheet-music publishing business. Since the publisher's usual retail selling price for a four-page song, 25¢-30¢ (or about $5.63 to $6.75 in 1977 dollars), was comfortably higher than his costs, which undoubtedly were well below 10¢, he was allowing himself a good measure of profit, even allowing for failures and discounting. Cost figures for the years before mid-century have not been discovered.

Copyright and Competition

Good profit margins notwithstanding, a publisher needed protection from competing firms, who were ever ready to pounce at the scent of success and kill sales by offering their own reprints of a "hit." He, therefore, tried to enlist the aid of governmental authority. From the first days of the United States a clamor arose for some sort of copyright law.

Today the Copyright Office defines copyright as, "That body of exclusive rights granted by statute to authors for protection of their writings. It includes the exclusive right to make and publish copies...to make other versions...and to perform the work in public."[31] In the seventy years under study here, the definition of musical copyright was by no means so explicit. And even when the law articulated a specific right of the copyright-holder, taking action against a violator was not always worth one's trouble.

The first passage of copyright laws came soon after American independence. By 1783 four states—Connecticut, Massachusetts, Maryland and New Jersey—had passed copyright laws of some kind.[32] These laws, nonetheless, proved unsatisfactory since they gave protection only within a state's borders. Pirating across state lines went on at will.[33] The need for national regulation became obvious. Therefore, in 1790 the first Federal Copyright Act was passed. It protected the works of citizens and all other residents in the United States for fourteen years, and included provisions for renewal for another fourteen. Regrettably, protection was denied works first published in other countries. Nor was music specified as coming under the copyright act, possibly because, as Robert Burton speculates, it was still a "comparatively unimportant potential source of revenue for composers."[34] Nevertheless from the beginning, composers and publishers acted as if the law applied to music.

Under the law, a copy of a work's title-page was to be deposited before publication, and a copy of the work itself deposited within six months of publication.[35] The act was amended in 1802 to require all such publications to carry a notice of copyright.[36] Music was not named specifically as entitled to protection until 1831. At that time the period of protection was changed to twenty-eight years, the renewal period remaining fourteen years as before.[37] In 1856 the act was again amended to include the performance of all dramatic works.[38] Composers waited another thirty-five years for the first international copyright law.[39]

In the years before the 1802 law requiring a work to bear a copyright notice, such an indication is rarely found printed on songs published in America. Occasionally the information "Entered according to law," is printed on the first page. For instance, Benjamin Carr's *Ellen Arise* (Philadelphia, ca. 1798) is so described. However, most sheet-music songs published by Benjamin Carr, Peter A. von Hagen, Alexander Reinagle, and other composer-publishers bear no copyright information whatsoever.

From 1802 to about 1823 the legend "Copyright secured," or "Entered according to law," neither given with a date, is normally found on the first page. Thus, most Carr and Hewitt songs issued after 1802 include the words "Copyright secured" on the first page.

James J. Fuld, in *The Book of World-Famous Music,* rev. ed., (New York, 1971), p. 16, states that the copyright law effective from 1 January 1803 on required the year of copyright to be shown on the printed works. Yet, of the hundreds of songs in the Boston Public Library and the Houghton Library of Harvard University, a vast majority of those published before 1823 show no copyright date. The same is true of the songs published before 1823 that are listed in the

Sonneck and Wolfe bibliographies of early American music. Both Sonneck and Wolfe have relied on publisher's addresses, advertisements and other public notices for the dating of the music they list. When, for instance, a publisher's address is printed on the music, the year he conducted business from that address, discovered in the annual directories of an urban area, can give an approximate date for a composition's publication.

Three cautions must be observed, however. Plates sometimes were engraved, then stored away for months before they were used.[41] Or old plates may have been used at a later date, with the original address obliterated and a new one engraved. To cite one instance, Ditson printed for years from plates bearing his 135 Washington Street address, the firm's location from 1838 to 1844. The company moved to 115 Washington Street in 1844; to 277 Washington Street in 1857. On several songs printed at the 277 Washington Street location, the music's first page gives the 135 Washington Street address; the title-page or a Ditson catalogue appended after the music gives the new 277 Washington Street address.[42] At times the title-page describes the song as a favorite of a singer popular in the early twenties, while the title-page of another copy of the same song, printed from the same plates, claims it a favorite of a singer popular a decade or more later. For a few songs, concealing the date of publication or refurbishing the title-page was a publisher's strategem to reinvigorate sales.[43]

Beginning about 1823 (one can cite some earlier instances) the full date of copyright began to appear on the first page of most works, except of course reprints of foreign publications. A typical issue of this time is Arthur Clifton's *The Apparition of a Dandy*. On the bottom of the title-page appears: "Entered according to Act of Congress the first day of October, 1823, by the Author." This style of dating appears on other compositions of the twenties, including works composed by Arthur Clifton, John Cole, James Drake, George Jackson, Charles Gilfert and Thomas Wiesenthal.

With the enactment of the 1831 law, the day and month were dropped from the notice. Now the typical legend is like that appearing on John Hewitt's *The Mountain Bugle:* "Entered according to act of Congress in the year 1833 by G. Willig, Jr. of Baltimore." Willig was the publisher.

Undated and non-copyrighted songs, after 1823, were normally either the works of amateurs that publishers felt were not worth copyrighting or reprints of foreign publications. Since no international copyright existed prior to 1891, American publishers reprinted at will anything from Europe without requesting permission or paying royalties.[44] As early as 1793 Carr was offering "all the newest music reprinted from European publications" for sale.[45] Gilfert made the same claim in 1795.[46] Twenty-two years later, the Franklin Music Warehouse advertised it was constantly receiving new music from England, "which is daily reprinting by the Proprietors."[47] Similarly, Blake, on the page of Moore's *Irish Melodies*, which he issued without the permission of the London holder of copyright, states: "G.E. Blake has just received by the Edward and Charles, from London, a supply of Musical Instruments and some new Music, which he will republish with all imaginable expedition."

That such a practice was taken for granted and scarcely called for special comment is evident in a report on the reprinting of music composed by a Providence, Rhode Island, musician, Oliver Shaw, by a London publisher. In the Boston *Euterpeiad*, John Rowe Parker observes only that the republication is a credit to "our fellow countryman," especially since it was issued in the form of "an elegant volume."[48] Parker does not bother to mention that Shaw would gain nothing from the sales in England.

Therefore the gesture made by William Pond, the New York publisher, after the death of the British composer Michael Balfe, was exceptional. Pond voluntarily sent £300 to Balfe's widow in England for the right to reprint *Il Talismano*. Balfe's biographer, William Barrett, found the action so astonishing that he writes at length of the incident: "This was the only financial recognition of Balfe's merit received from the great country, where his operas and songs were well known and as welcome as they were in several European cities. Balfe never complained of this, never alluded to the want of understanding between the two nations. He was perfectly well acquainted with the state of things nearer home. International copyright, as it existed, was practically a dead letter."[49]

Because they had only the cost of production, American publishers easily competed with foreign ones. The latter also had the purchase of copyright, the original risk in publishing a work and trans-oceanic shipping costs to add to their expenses. As a consequence the domestic copy was priced below the foreign original, in most cases driving the import off the American market.[50] Hence, except for the years around 1800, when domestic publication was limited, most music purchased in America was American published.

At the same time that they were reprinting European works, American publishers increased their publication of music composed in America. For example, the 1854 *Dwight's Journal of Music* quotes the remarks of an unidentified reporter who claims the Copyright Bureau of the Department of State had 300 volumes of such music dating back to 1819. Each volume averaged 250 pages. It took only one volume to hold the songs filed from 1819 to 1834. A second volume contained songs from 1834 to 1838, during which time the publication of music by native composers increased rapidly. Two volumes covered the years 1840-41; three volumes, 1843; five volumes, 1847; six for 1850; eight for 1854. By 1854 an average of 2,000 sheets of new music (about 650 new songs) were being registered annually.[51]

Without question the copyright of a fast-selling song was a valuable "commodity." This is stressed in an 1858 article, entitled "Applications for the Use of Tunes," by the editors of the New York *Musical Review*.[52] They write that, in common with other publishers, they were constantly asked for "gratuitous" permission to reprint copyrighted tunes.[53] Their response was to refuse permission since valuable property would be given away. With tunes just introduced and having as yet no "established pecuniary value," the editors were willing to make exceptions, provided they approved the circumstances of republication and the number of copies printed. With favorite songs, however, rights would not be waived so easily. A businessman neither could afford nor would have the disposition to give these rights away. Fortunately for the copyright owner infringement brought heavy penalties, justified because copyrights cost a great deal. Of the many thousands of tunes published, only a few proved of commercial value. These few had to compensate for the many losses a publisher incurred. The editors close by stating their view that copyright laws protect from duplication by others, original melodies and the arrangements of old tunes, which often require more effort and skill than original compositions. [54]

The laws, nonetheless, were not as strictly enforced as the editors of the *Musical Review* would have liked their readers to believe. Suing copyright infringers was a never-ending and time-consuming activity, so George Root claimed. He spoke from his experience as a composer and publisher. Root writes that after passage of the 1856 law controlling performances of a composer's work, he found it "more trouble than it was worth to enforce it, and I soon gave up the effort." People, he adds, were accustomed to helping themselves to each other's compositions and could not be stopped.[55]

Pirated editions of favorite songs appeared constantly. In an attempt to discourage their purchase, copyright holders sometimes printed a notice on the legitimate edition of a song, asking the public not to purchase illegal reprints, which were purported to be laden with errors. For this reason John Sinclair's *Come Sit Thee Down,* published in 1842 by Parker and Ditson of Boston, includes the statement on its title-page: "Only correct copy. A Pirated and incorrect copy having been published at Baltimore the Public is respectfully cautioned against purchasing the same. J.S."

Another dodge used by a competitor was to affix the title of a well-liked song to different music, hoping thereby to take in the gullible. Unhappy about this practice, Daniel Johnson includes a warning in the twelfth edition of his popular *The Carrier Dove* (New York, 1841): "The Popularity of this Song has induced persons in Philadelphia, Baltimore, and New York to publish music with the title of the 'Carrier Dove.' The publisher of this Song would respectfully remind purchasers: that the Genuine Copy has the Imprint of New York, Published at 201 Broadway, by Atwill." Since a song's title was unprotected under the law, such deception was freely practiced during the 19th century.[56]

Retailing the Music

The publisher could little afford to wait for customers to come to him. Survival necessitated aggressive merchandising. If he conducted his business shrewdly, he prospered and won over increasing numbers of Americans to the circle of song lovers. Assuredly, the thousands of works sold were directly attributable to the winning-over of hordes of new customers, who otherwise might have felt disinclined to purchase music. To strengthen sales, every publisher and every wholesale and retail outlet dealing in music from different publishers tried a variety of strategies. Because music lovers in small towns could obtain at best only a limited selection of songs locally, city dealers offered to mail the newest music to anyone, anywhere mail was deliverable.[57] If a customer wished currently fashionable music, the dealer offered to make a selection for him, guaranteed to please or money back. In 1856, William Hall claimed his firm had mailed music even to Australia.[58] That same year, Cook and Brothers, New York music dealers, advertised: "Great inducements offered to Music-Teachers and Dealers [presumably the small independent retailers]. Being practical musicians, we examine all the new music as received from every quarter of the Union, and select the best to fill orders. Music selected by us may, if not liked, be exchanged within six months for any other pieces. Music mailed free of postage.[59]

Advertising outside the urban centers was a problem that Russell and Richardson of Boston tried to solve in singular fashion. In the 1858 New York *Musical Review* they inserted at the bottom of an advertisement of recently published music: "N.B.--EDITORS: Russell and Richardson will send you two dollars' worth of their latest musical publications (postage free) if you will give the above advertisement (including this offer) one insertion in your paper."[60] Some publishers sold their songs in the theaters and concert halls where the music was being sung.[61] Most advertised their songs as identical to those performed by prominent vocalists presently appearing in town.[62]

If a song sold well, its "Answer" was sure to follow, more often than not composed by a different person, a practice evident in America from the beginning. In 1799, for example, Peter Albrecht von Hagen of Boston and George Gilfert of New York were selling *I Have a Silent Sorrow* and also offering "the answer to this song." An amusing comedy of Answers began in 1850. F.D. Benteen of Baltimore issued *I Would Not Die in Spring Time* by "Milton Moore," a pen-name Stephen Foster assumed occasionally. Almost a year later Benteen brought out *An Answer to the New and Beautiful Song, I Would Not Die in Spring Time, or I Would Not Die in Summer Time,* now with Foster named as composer. Later in 1851, Lee and Walker of Philadelphia published *I Would Not Die in Winter* by "J.H. Milton," another Foster pen-name. Finally in January 1852 appeared John Hewitt's parody answer *I Would Not Die at All.*[63]

Song composers and publishers tried to exploit subjects of current interest. For this reason when *Uncle Tom's Cabin* became a stage hit: "every music publisher...[had to] have his 'Little Eva' song...and all the minor composers were...as busy on this theme, as if it were the one point of contact for the time being with the popular sympathies. Verily 'Uncle Tom's Cabin' has much to answer for, in calling forth such a crop of musical weeds. For these things seek the sun, not by virtue of their music, but by virtue of their titles, and so make music play a slavish part."[64]

Little detailed information on the sale of songs prior to the late forties is extant. During the fifties, a five-thousand-copy sell-out was "considered a great sale." The nation-wide hit *Old Folks at Home,* issued in 1851, had sold 40,000 copies by September 1852 and was well on its way to breaking all sales records. Firth, Pond, and Company claimed two, and sometimes three, presses had to run constantly in order to satisfy the demand for this one song.[65] Of all the American publishers, Firth, Pond was the most willing to divulge the number of copies of individual songs, particularly those of Foster, sold. Only successes, never failures, are mentioned. Toward the end of 1854 an advertisement in the New York *Musical World* states that *Old Folks at Home* has sold over 130,000 copies; *My Old Kentucky Home,* 90,000; *Massa's in De Cold Ground,* 74,000; and *Old Dog Tray,* 48,000 copies in six months. A few weeks later this same firm advertised Francis Brown's *Will You Come to My Mountain Home?* as achieving a sale of nearly 90,000 copies since it was published a dozen years earlier.[66] These figures should be treated with caution. The publisher may well have inflated them, employing a come-and-get-them-while-they-last trick in order to encourage sales.

Around 1800 the typical song was one to two pages long and sold for around 25¢ a copy, which was high for those times. The 25¢ of that year was about the same as $5.63 in 1976. After fifty years the typical song was four to five pages long but still sold for about 25¢-30¢ a copy, owing to increased competition, lower paper costs and more efficient printing and distribution. For a few songs by British musicians resident in the U.S, therefore copyrightable, like those of the admired Dempster and Wallace, the price per copy could range as high as 50¢ to $1.00. Why the British compositions commanded a higher price than their American counterparts is unexplained by contemporary writers. Perhaps these British composers demanded and got a larger sum for the rights to their songs, or a British name was more prestigious than an American one. Whatever the reason, works by British composers residing in the U.S. were never lower but frequently were higher than American compositions.

The printed figures on title-pages, nonetheless, were not always the true retail prices. Discounts were often available. For example, a reporter writes in the New York *Euterpeiad,* on 15 July 1830 that dealers were selling music at 30-40 percent off listed prices that year.[67] When sales dropped markedly, as they did in depression years, music dealers quickly reduced prices. For instance, the severe summer slump of 1857 forced Horace Waters of New York to offer his entire stock of music and instruments for greatly reduced prices.[68]

Further information on pricing policies is revealed in the *Musical Review.* On January 1855 William Hall and Son, of New York City, halved the prices on non-copyrighted music; stating not the "fictional" but the "reduced"price would henceforth appear on each copy.[69] The object of the reduction was to compete successfully with non-copyrighted music. The reporter mused on the subject: "It would seem to the uninitiated that the course taken by them was calculated to produce a result just the contrary. It is, however, assumed that the larger portion of music bought by the public is purchased of, or on the recommendation of music-teachers. The pupil pays the retail price but the teacher gets from the dealer a commission. It is argued that if non-copyright music be reduced, as proposed, no commission, or at best a very small one, can be allowed to teachers, while on the copy-right music, at the old price, the same liberal prerequisites will be enjoyed by them as before."[70]

Hall and Son was immediately boycotted by all the other publishers, who ceased supplying its retail outlets with their music. Competition became intense. Despite Hall and Son's claim that its action would increase the sale of music by native composers, the price reduction may have encouraged the increased sale of non-copyright songs to customers buying without a teacher's advice.

Other publishers had to reduce prices. Within a few days of the Hall announcement, Schuberth and Company, a New York house dealing mainly in imported music, said it too would compete by cutting prices by one-half. The firm anticipated a considerable loss, since its original editions were corrected by and purchased from the composer and cost a great deal more to get ready, publish and ship across the Atlantic.[71] Because the price-war began to hurt all publishers they induced William Hall to settle with the rest of the trade. Four months after the start of discounting, they all agreed on a new price schedule aimed at realistically reflecting the current market. Republished foreign music would be priced thusly: one page, 5¢; two, 8¢; three, 10¢; four, 15¢; one and a half sheets, 20¢; two sheets, 25¢; and a lithograph title-page, 5¢.[72] The next month they agreed that one house would desist from printing a non-copyright piece already issued by another. This last agreement was meant to place American works on the same footing as foreign ones, each having one publisher.[73]

Yet prices remained unstable. During economically depressed times, they dropped drastically. In 1858, for example, a financially-troubled year, dealers sold music at 1¢ a page, sometimes for even less.[74]

The Composer's Earnings

A composer of highly popular songs rarely profited to any extent from sheet-music sales. He rarely received royalties, but usually sold all his rights for a relatively small sum. On a large majority of title-pages, the publisher states he is the copyright holder.

The most prominent musicians failed to garner more than a pittance for their hits. One of the most popular composers in America was Henry Russell. The publishers who held the American copyrights to his songs made fortunes. Yet the composer stated that he profited from them only through the original sale to the publisher and through his own performances, travelling and singing his works throughout the United States. In his autobiography he complains: "I have composed and published in my life over eight hundred songs, but it was by singing these songs and not by the sale of the copyrights that I made money. There was no such thing as a royalty in those days [the late thirties and forties], and when a song was sold it was sold outright. My songs brought me an average price of ten shillings each, that is to say, my eight hundred songs have represented about four hundred pounds to me, though they have made the fortune of several publishers."[75]

At the beginning of his career a composer was fortunate to get published at all. If published, he usually signed away all his rights for little or no recompense. The young and inexperienced Stephen Foster, pleased to be published though unknown, gave two songs—*Old Uncle Ned* and *Oh, Susannah*—gratis to W.C. Peters, the Cincinnati publisher. Shortly, Peters realized a profit of $10,000 from the two songs. Foster never received a cent.[76]

Another young composer, more astute than Foster, did manage to win more from a publisher. George Root persisted in demanding and eventually won $1200 from Russell and Richardson for the copyright of *Rosalie, the Prairie Flower.*[77] Root explained that he first offered this and five other songs to Nathan Richardson for $600 but was laughed at for his temerity. Root refused to lower the price, and Richardson then agreed to pay the composer a royalty instead. Only after Root had made $3000 on *Rosalie* did the publisher buy him out.[78]

In contrast, Foster, constantly in need of money and a terrible businessman, sold all his interests in thirty-seven of his songs to Firth, Pond in 1857. He received $1872.28, "approximately two-thirds of the composer's asking price." Among the works sold at this price were *Old Folks at Home, My Old Kentucky Home, Old Dog Tray, Massa's in De Cold Ground,* and *Nelly Bly,* all of them still enjoying brisk sales.[79]

Royalty agreements were almost unheard of, at least until around 1850. Morrison Foster, brother of Stephen, gives information on one such agreement, that between his brother and Firth, Pond, in 1849. The composer was to be paid three cents for every copy of every song sold. Later a similar agreement was concluded with F.O. Benteen of Baltimore.[80] John Tasker Howard, the Foster biographer, claims the royalty was two cents a copy after expenses had been met; he adds that Firth, Pond, in 1853, boosted the royalty payment to ten percent of the retail price. Because ten percent of the usual price of a Foster song was about three cents, it would appear that Morrison Foster was thinking about the 1853 agreement.[81] Most Foster songs were priced at 25¢ to 38¢ a copy.[83]

Russell, Foster, John Hewitt, and other composers all expressed unhappiness over the way publishers took the lion's share of the profits. Some tried to fight the system by having the songs published "For the Author." A few, like Reinagle, Shaw, Horn,

Ordway, Root and Winner, set up their own publishing enterprises at one time or another.[83] At the same time they augmented their incomes by teaching, performing music, and maintaining music stores.[84]

The only non-complainers were amateurs. They wrote perhaps one or two songs and had no expectation of any payment. Publishers usually did not copyright their compositions. In one instance failure to copyright the song lost the publisher a large sum of money. John Hewitt wrote *The Minstrel's Return from the War* in 1825. His brother, a publisher, issued the song reluctantly, describing it as "Written and Composed by J.H.H." Because he felt the song would have no sale, he neglected to copyright it. When the song became a success and was "sung all over the world," the publisher missed making, according to John Hewitt, "at least $10,000."[85]

One of the rare composers to make a living from the sale of his works was Foster. Although his publishers made enormous profits, he himself did earn a modest but comfortable living from royalties for about a decade. Between November 1849 and January 1857, Firth, Pond paid him about $1350 annually.[86] Other composers were less fortunate. Scarcely anything they wrote ever matched the sale of a Foster song. If something did make money, the lack of a royalty agreement insured all profits went to the publisher, who felt this was only just since he alone had the expense and the risk of issuing and marketing a new song.

It is a wonder that so many composers continued to write songs. Of course, the amateurs would have done so anyway, without regard for recompense. One should add that a good number of professionals wrote music in order to provide themselves with suitable vehicles for performance. Music, also, was commissioned by concert singers, publishers and theater managers. For whatever reasons, songs were written and published by the thousands. Most failed or sold only enough to return expenses. A smaller number proved profitable.

The economics of the song market was affected by a complex of relationships—between publisher, composer, lyricist, performer, teacher and amateur; also between publishing firm, music dealership, theater and concert hall, school, private music studio and parlor. The successful song originated anywhere. No one knew the secret for success, then as now. No patron of the arts sponsored its composition. Any composer, highly trained or not trained at all, might write one. The newly introduced song had to attract an audience in order to continue to exist, no matter who wrote it. If it failed, it was quickly forgotten. If it succeeded, the song was swiftly taken up by throngs in all parts of the nation. The hope that one of their songs would win wide acceptance motivated the composer and publisher in the nineteenth century.

Notes

1. These estimates are derived from Richard J. Wolfe, "Early American Music Engraving and Printing" (Unpublished work), pp. 270-273.

2. Robert Marshall Copeland, "The Life and Works of Isaac Baker Woodbury, 1819-1858" (Ph.D. diss., Univ. of Cincinnati, 1974), p. 136.

3. George Root, *The Story of a Musical Life* (Cincinnati, 1891), p. 98.

4. See the New York *Musical Review,* 23 Jan. 1858, p. 17

5. Oscar G. Sonneck, *A Bibliography of Early Secular American Music,* rev. William Treat Upton (New York, 1964), pp. 575-89.

6. Sonneck, pp. 65, 219.

7. New York *Musical Review,* 12 Jan. 1856, p. 2.

8. Christine Merrick Ayers, *Contributions to the Art of Music in America by the Music Industries of Boston, 1640-1936* (New York, 1937), pp. 87-88. A detailed study of how music is engraved and printed can be found in William Gamble, *Music Engraving and Printing* (London, 1923). Other processes for printing music include the use of music type (used mainly for books), and lithography (used from the mid-twenties on for the reproduction of the ornaments on title-pages, but not used for the music itself to any extent until after 1860, at least not for first editions).

9. Henry M. Brooks, *Olden-Time Music* (Boston, 1888), p. 86.

10. Wolfe, "Early American," pp. 55-56.

11. Sonneck, pp. 577-89; Wolfe, *Secular Music in America, 1801-1825,* III (New York, 1964), 1133-78.

12. Sonneck, p. 68. See also William Arms Fisher, *One Hundred and Fifty Years of Music Publishing in the United States* (Boston, 1933), p. 24.

13. H. Earle Johnson, *Musical Interludes in Boston, 1795-1830* (New York, 1943), p. 259; Brooks, p. 173.

14. Johnson, p. 238. Almost all extant copies of sheet-music comprise secular songs, dances, marches and variations on popular tunes.

15. New York *Euterpeiad,* 15 Oct. 1831, p. 138. See also the statement on Gottlieb Graupner of Boston, in Johnson, p. 39.

16. W.T. Parke, *Musical Memoirs,* II (London, 1830), 256.

17. New York *Euterpeiad,* 2 August 1830, p. 59.

18. See Sonneck for 18th century titles, the Wolfe *Bibliography* for early 19th century titles.

19. New York *Musical Review,* 8 March 1856, p. 71; 22 March 1856, p. 85.

20. *Review,* 22 August 1857, pp. 262-63.

21. *A Handbook of American Music and Musicians,* ed. F.O. Jones (Canseraga,N.Y., 1886) s.v. "Ditson, Oliver"; also *The American Supplement,* ed. Weldon Selden Pratt, Grove's Dictionary, 2nd ed., VI (Phila., 1926) s.v. "Ditson, Oliver"; Thomas Ryan, *Recollections of an Old Musician* (New York, 1899), pp. 116-18. For a study of the Ditson firm's expansion into Chicago, see Eva M. Knock, "Music Merchandising Moves into a House of Many Mansions," *Notes* of the Music Library Association, Second Series, I (1944), 16-24.

22. Jones s.v. "Graupner, Gottlieb."

23. Boston *Euterpeiad,* 10 March 1821, p. 199.

24. New York *Musical Review,* 30 March 1854, p. 109; also the comments on

Foster's musical training, in John Tasker Howard, *Stephen Foster, America's Troubadour* (New York, 1953), pp. 107-8, 116.

25. Reprinted under the title "Popular Songs," in *Dwight's Journal of Music,* 27 June 1857, pp. 99-100.

26. Ibid., 1 January 1859, p. 319.

27. New York *Musical World,* 20 Nov. 1852, p. 192.

28. See A. Hyatt King, *Four Hundred Years of Music Printing* (London, 1968), pp. 25-7.

29. *Dwight's Journal of Music,* 1 Jan. 1859, p. 319.

30. The ratio is based on a study of 19th century wages and prices made by Stanley Lebergott, of the U.S. Bureau of the Budget. He found average annual wages for non-farm labor in 1800 were $250 to $300. By 1830, wages had dropped 25%; by 1869 they had returned to the level of sixty years earlier. When wages and prices are compared, real wages went down 10 to 20% from 1800 to 1820, and returned to the 1800 level by the 1850s; Stanley Lebergott, "Wage Trends, 1800-1900," *Trend in the American Economy in the Nineteenth Century,* Studies in Income and Wealth, XX1V (Princeton, 1960), 462-82.

31. Sidney Shemel and M. William Krasilovsky, *This Business of Music,* rev. ed., ed. Paul Ackerman (New York, 1971), p. 109.

32. *How the Public Gets Its New Music* (New York, 1933), pp. 11-13; published for the American Society of Composers, Authors, and Publishers.

33. Margaret Nicholson, *A Manual of Copyright Practice* (New York, 1956), p. 5. For an example of the difficulties involved in invoking the laws, see Irving Lowens, "Andrew Law and the Pirates," *Music and Musicians in Early America* (New York, 1964), pp. 58-88.

34. *How the Public,* p. 13; Robert J. Burton, "Copyright and the Creative Arts," *One Hundred Years of Music in America,* ed.Paul Henry Lang (New York, 1961), pp. 284-5.

35. Nicholson, p. 5.

36. Ibid., pp. 5-6.

37. Ibid., p. 6; *How the Public,* p. 13. Further information on musical copyright is in Burton, p. 285; David Friedman in *The International Cyclopedia of Music* s.v. "Copyright, Musical"; and T. Solberg, *Copyright in Congress: 1789-1904* (Wash., D.C., 1905), pp. 29-33.

38. Helmut Lehman-Haupt, *The Book in America,* 2nd ed. (New York, 1951), p. 107; Herman Finkelstein, *Public Performance Rights in Music and Performance Right Societies* rev. ed. (New York, 1961), p. 2; Burton, p. 285.

39. Don Lacy, "The Quagmire," *The Saturday Review,* 27 Nov. 1971, p. 24.

40. Johnson, pp. 239-40.

41. Harry Dichter and Elliott Shapiro, *Early American Sheet Music... 1768-1889* (New York, 1941), pp. 166-248, contains many instances of publishers selling or permitting others to use their plates.

42. See Dichter and Shapiro, p. 185, for Ditson's different addresses; Wolfe, *Bibliography,* I, xxii, for a statement concerning reissues from James Hewitt's plates by Geib of New York.

43. *Dwight's Journal,* 26 June 1852, p. 94; also Carleton Sprague Smith, "Introduction" to Wolfe, *Bibliography,* I, ix.

44. James J. Fuld, *The Book of World-Famous Music,* rev. ed. (New York, 1971), p. 24.

45. Printed on a copy of Dibdin's *Jack at the Windlass* (Phila., ca. 1793).

46. Printed on a copy of Hook's *I Never Lov'd Any Dear Mary But You* (New York, ca. 1795).

47. Brooks, p. 173.

48. Boston *Euterpeiad,* 9 July 1821, p. 45.
49. William Alexander Barrett, *Balfe: His Life and Work* (London, 1882), p. 244.
50. Ayers, pp. 1-10; Fisher, pp. 21-31; N.Y.*Musical Review,* 8 Aug. 1857, p. 250; Ruth F. Finley, *The Lady of Gody's, Sarah Josepha Hale* (Phila., 1931), p. 45.
51. Reprinted from the Washington *Globe,* 3 Nov. 1854, in *Dwight's Journal,* 11 Nov. 1854, p. 43.
52. The editors were Lowell Mason Junior and Daniel Gregory Mason.
53. The editors refer to melodies for voice; note, later in the paragraph, the reference to "favorite songs."
54. New York *Musical Review,* 23 Jan. 1858, p. 17.
55. Root, p. 118.
56. For a statement on the non-applicability of copyright to titles of songs, see Shemel and Krasilovsky, p. 119.
57. "Notes of a Short Tour Westward," *Dwight's Journal* 19 June 1852, p. 84.
58. New York *Musical Review,* 12 Jan. 1852, p. 84.
59. Advertisment in the N.Y. *Musical Review,* 12 Jan. 1856, p. 10.
60. *Review,* 20 Feb. 1858, p. 63; 6 March 1858, p. 79.
61. See, for example, Sonneck, *Bibliography,* under "May Day in Town."
62. In the Boston *Euterpeiad,* 22 Dec. 1821, p. 129, the Franklin Music Warehouse advertises the availability of exact versions of songs performed by Mr. Philipps and Mrs. Holman. The singers were in Boston.
63. Evelyn Foster Morneweck, *Chronicles of Stephen Foster's Family,* II (Pittsburgh, 1944), 389; Howard, pp. 183-5.
64. "Musical Review," *Dwight's Journal,* 31 July 1852, p. 135.
65. New York *Musical Review,* 11 Sept. 1852, p. 202.
66. Ibid., 13 Jan. 1855, p. 24.
67. "Music and a Reduction," possibly written by Charles Dingly, the editor, New York *Euterpeiad,* 15 July 1830, p. 51.
68. New York *Musical Review,* 8 Aug. 1857, p. 250.
69. Ibid., 4 Jan. 1855, p. 7. The publisher's announcement states: "Since the study of Music has become an essential branch of education, a reduction in the price of Sheet-Music has been demanded by the public."
70. Ibid., 18 Jan. 1855, p. 28.
71. Ibid., 18 Jan. 1855, p. 17
72. Ibid., 19 May 1855, p. 161.
73. Ibid., 16 June 1855, p. 107.
74. New York *Musical Gazette,* 29 May 1858, p. 165.
75. Henry Russell, *Cheer! Boys, Cheer!* (London, 1895), p. 198. This English singer-composer lived in America from 1833 to 1841, during which time he composed, sang publicly, and sold to American publishers many of his most popular songs. He then returned to England, where he continued his musical career.
76. Morrison Foster, *My Brother Stephen* (Indianapolis, 1932), p. 35.
77. New York *Musical Review,* 6 Feb. 1858, p. 34.
78. Root, p. 111.
79. Howard, pp. 265-70.
80. Morrison Foster, pp. 41-42.
81. Howard, pp. 152, 237.
82. Howard, pp. 245-6; N.Y. *Musical Review,* 19 Jan. 1854, p. 31; 2 March, p. 78; 8 June, p. 207; 28 Sept., p. 330.
83. Dichter and Shapiro, pp. 166-248.
84. See the many references to these composers and others, in John Tasker Howard, *Our American Music,* 4th ed. (New York, 1965), and Gilbert Chase, *America's Music,* 2nd ed. (New York, 1966); also in more specialized studies, like

Oscar G. Sonneck's *Early Concert-Life in America* (Leipzig, 1907) and *Early Opera in America* (New York, 1915); Joyce Ellen Mangler, *Rhode Island Music and Musicians, 1733-1850* (Detroit, 1965); as well as the references to contemporary and earlier composers in periodicals of the period; and the biographical entries in Sonneck's *Bibliography,* pp. 497-531, and Wolfe's *Bibliography* (where they are arranged alphabetically by name).

85. Quoted in Howard, *Our American Music,* p. 166, from the composer's own memorandum, written on the original song manuscript, now in the Library of Congress.

86. Howard, *Foster,* p.266, based on papers once possessed by the successors to Firth, Pond, now in the Library of Congress. Howard, p.272, estimates Foster's total average yearly income during these years to have been $1425.84, basing his figure on information obtained from Stephen Foster's "Account Book."

Chapter 7

The Subject Matter Of Parlor Songs

In their own way the Americans of that time were sensitive to the world around and within them. The human condition received an intimate articulation in novels, paintings, poetry and song. These art forms set forth a limited number of recurring themes, which encompassed ideas and feelings that society thought of paramount importance. Again and again they were called upon to express the permanencies and vagaries of life.

The subjects receiving the greatest attention in the parlor ballads were those of affection and love, mortality and time, lamentation over death, estrangement, religious feeling, social criticism, praise of nature and didacticism.[1] Although no one of these themes is unique to the nineteenth century, their manner of presentation and the less frequent incidence of other possible subjects do point to a consistent outlook that unifies the era.

The Ambience of the Song of Affection

By far the most popular theme in the parlor ballads is affection, either love that is usually tender and sometimes passionate for the person of the opposite sex,[2] or devotion to parents, siblings, children and friends, or attachment to an inanimate object associated with one or more loved persons.

The Maid of Athens, words by Lord Byron, music by Isaac Nathan (New York, ca. 1817),[3] is more impassioned than most songs and a type only occasionally found in the private music collections of amateurs. Its first and third stanzas are:

Maid of Athens, ere we part,
    Give, oh give me back my heart:
Or, since that has left my breast,
    Keep it now, and take the rest.
Hear my vow before I go,
    My life, my life, I love you

By that lip I long to taste;
    By that zone-encircled waist;

By all the token-flowers that tell
What words can never speak so well;
By love's alternate joy and woe,
My life, my life, I love you.

In contrast, British and American musicians composed a greater number of works, especially during Period I, that treat love in a light vein. The gentle raillery of *Cousin John,* music by Alexander Reinagle (Philadelphia, ca. 1805), is by no means rare:

Tell me, tell me truly, gentle cousin John,
He is blind but you can see,
Where is little Cupid flown, gentle cousin John.
Let him fly, but not to me
When that wicked brat is gone,
Then good morrow, then good morrow, cousin,
Cousin John.

Love has bows & arrows, gentle cousin John,
Should he aim a shaft at you,
Arrows mortal every one, gentle cousin John.
That same shaft may wound me, too.
When that cruel deed is done,
Then good ev'ning, then good ev'ning, cousin,
Cousin John.

Love has chains and fetters, gentle cousin John.
Hymen is a cruel knave,
For he puts those fetters on, gentle cousin John;
Makes his best of friends a slave.
Farewell love when that is done;
Then good night ah, then good night, dear cousin,
Cousin John.

After 1810 people may smile now and then in their songs; but they also suffer more. The mention of Cupid grows scarce. Love turns serious. Its sadder aspects dominate. Grave themes predominate: a girl is forced by her parents to foresake her lover and marry another, or she is deserted by a lover after he has seduced her; a man suffers with unrequited love, or because of a prolonged absence in a land distant from his beloved; and lovers are constantly parting or parted, never to meet again. Several of the era's song cliches about the spurned lover appear in *Thou Hast Learned to Love Another, or Farewell, Farewell, Forever,* music by Charles Slade (Boston, 1845). It begins:

Thou has learned to love another,
Thou hast broken ev'ry vow;

We have parted from each other,
And my heart is lonely now;
I have taught my looks to shun thee,
When coldly we have met,
For another's smile hath won thee,
And thy voice I must forget.
Oh, it well to sever
This heart from thine forever,
Can I forget thee? Never!
Farewell, farewell, forever.

Although the first line of the above song gives the reason for the separation, it is more usual not to explain. The poet instead concentrates on the emotions evoked. Thus the listener can become absorbed by the central sentiment without being distracted by questions of why or how the parting came about. If he wishes, the listener is free to adduce any number of explanations. Possibly with this consideration in mind, the unnamed author of *At Eve I Miss Thee When Alone,* music by L.V. Crosby (Boston, 1847), says nothing about why the lovers have parted. The references to evening, loneliness, weeping, flown hopes, fleeting time, prayer, "thy gentle form," "tresses dark," "thy snowy bosom," and "fairy bark" are common in parlor-songs written after 1810:

At eve I miss thee when alone,
Beneath the darkling bough I stray
To muse on hopes that all have flown
Upon time's fleeting wing away.
We met, we loved, we parted ere
A cloud had o'er our pathway swept,
And when I saw the dewy tear...
Upon thy cheek...I turned and wept.
At eve I miss thee when alone,
Beneath the darkling bough I stray
To muse on hopes that all have flown
Upon time's fleeting wing away.
A gentle sky with sunbeams warm,
Will carry soon above us smile,
And I shall clasp thy gentle form,
Fair as the sylphs of Scio's isle.
And when I smooth thy tresses dark
That o'er thy snowy bosom steal,
I'll pray kind heaven our fairy bark
Shall ne'er life's rugged tempest feel.
At eve I miss thee when alone, [etc.]

The themes of the love song reflected the attitudes held by most nineteenth-century Americans toward the role of affection in the relationship between man and woman. These Americans thought of love as the bond which created enduring personal, family and societal relationships. With it came the emotional security and feeling of permanency they craved, and which they thought were often denied them in the hurly-burly of the outside world. The respected contemporary observer Alexis de Tocqueville comments that these Americans considered it important to practice restraint and observe order in private lives, the home and the intimacies of marriage. He also said the American woman was considered the protector of morals. By loving her and winning her as his bride, a man hoped to insure a happy and tranquil life for himself. "There is certainly no country in the world," Tocqueville concluded, "where the tie of marriage is more respected than in America or where conjugal happiness is more highly or worthily appreciated.

In short, one's ambitions might be defeated, acquaintances prove treacherous and worldly matters unsettling; but love, once given, had to be steady and honorable, untainted by the indelicate or vulgar. It therefore follows that the songs enjoyed by those Americans, as Thomas Hastings, wrote, "should be such as to inspire us with sentiments of refinement, and of virtuous sensibility. In this way, [music]...blends innocent amusement with useful thoughts and contemplations."[5]

Most love songs employ lyrics that exemplify the values of American society while at the same time affording "innocent amusement." This is seen in R.G. Shrival's *Oh! Share My Cottage, Gentle Maid* (Baltimore, 1843). The song depicts a lover whose object is an honorable marriage. His plea to his beloved is genteel. No hint of anything indelicate intrudes:

Oh! share my cottage, gentle maid,
It only waits for thee
To give a sweetness to its shade,
And happiness to me.
Here from the splendid gay parade,
Of noise and folly free,
No sorrows can my peace invade
If only bless'd with thee.

The melody heard in conjunction with these words breathes innocence and is attractive to sing. All in all, it was a winning composition in the forties.

In the years before 1840 love songs had appeared, though at no time were they numerous, which exhibited some vulgarity and touched on the physical aspects of love. These compositions appeared in America during the transitional years between the era of eighteenth-century frankness and Victorian reticence about such matters. An American lady from Period III would have felt embarrassed by the repartee between lovers in Alexander Reinagle's *Says I to Dear Laura* (Philadelphia, ca. 1803). After a young man has proposed marriage the following exchange takes place:

> Says she if we've children, pray what shall we do,
> The merrier the more, says I with a leer.

Such frankness occurs in scarcely any of the love songs published after 1840.

Another song, Charles Gilfert's *Return, O My Love* (New York, 1827), is exceptional because it mentions physical contact between lovers, and because a woman describes and even endorses the contact:

> Return, O my Love and we'll never part.
> While the moon her soft light shall shed,
> I'll hold thee fast to my throbbing heart,
> And my bosom shall pillow thy head
>
> ....
>
> The breath of the woodbine is on my lip
> Empearl'd in the dew of May;
> And none but thou of its sweetness shall sip,
> Or steal its honey away.

In contrast to this Gilfert composition, songs published after 1840 hardly ever describe lovers touching each other.

One song from Period II, Alexander Ball's *Thou Can'st Not Forget Me,* the lyric by "Amelia of Louisville, Ky." (Baltimore, 1838), is unique for its portrayal of the effects of passion. And it is told from a woman's point of view. Moreover, it evokes an atmosphere of sensuality extraordinary in the song literature of the time:

> Thou canst not forget me, too long thou hast flung,
> Thy spirit's soft pinion o'er mine.
> Too deep was the promise, that round my lips clung,
> As they softly responded to thine.
> In the hush of the twilight, beneath the blue skies,
> My presence will mantle thy soul,
> And a feeling of softness will rush in thine eyes,
> Too deep for thy manhood's control.

Though songs like this were in the minority in the earlier years of the century, they are nearly nonexistent after 1840. Indelicate allusions are almost completely banished. Extreme circumspection surrounds mention of physical contact between lovers. It is sometimes proper to contain a line such as "I kiss'd her lip and left her side,"[6] or "I shall clasp thy gentle form."[7] In most compositions, however, the lovers neither kiss nor clasp each other.

Indeed, the evidence is strong that during most of the first sixty years of the nineteenth-century, and especially in Period III, those few songs which treat love as a physical passion were quite unpopular. Contemporary writers on music seldom mention them as being in public performance; musical amateurs scarcely ever purchased them.[8]

An important reason for the unpopularity was that to mid-century Americans physical passion, like the serpent in the Garden, had the power to destroy the soul, to dominate reason, and to make a shambles of duty and moral obligations.[9] They seem to have felt of love songs as Edgar Allan Poe did of poetry, that passion should be excluded, and if introduced, treated as having "the general effect as do discords in music."[10]

Without question the most admired compositions from all three periods rarely allude to strong desire. The highly discreet tone of songs like George Root's *The Hazel Dell* (New York, 1853) contributed to their widespread popularity in Period III:

> In the Hazel Dell my Nelly's sleeping,
> Nelly loved so long;
> Any my lonely, lonely watch I'm keeping,
> Nelly lost and gone.
> Here in moonlight often we have wandered
> Thro' the silent shade,
> Now where leafy branches drooping downward
> Little Nelly's laid.

Root writes that in 1853: "*The Hazel Dell* began the run which was not to end until the boys whistled it and the hand organs played it from Maine to Georgia, and no ambition for a songwriter could go higher than that."[11]

A majority of the love songs share several important characteristics. In most the "I," usually a male, speaks and reveals his inmost feelings. The lovers are commonplace persons drawn from the middle or the non-urban lower class. Rarely do they represent the rich or well-born.[12] They normally dwell in "cots" or "cottages," on mountains, in valleys or by the sea. If a wealthy or noble suitor woos a maid with promises of mansions and riches, as he does in *Mary of the Glen,* words by Charles Eastman, music by George Root (New York, 1952), the maid is expected to spurn him for someone more humble. In the Eastman-Root song, Mary replies that her heart is given to honest "Willie, who labors with the men" and who "has neither land nor leases."

Also characteristically, the love songs portray the idealized woman as a native American who is pious, gentle, pure, sweet and graceful. Her hair, eyes and skin are light; her figure is slender. During her youth she is carefree and smiles easily. But regrettably her health is often poor. She may die young, leaving a loyal lover to lament nostalgically over her passing. If she is widowed, or the man who loves her dies before he marries her, or he casts her aside for another, she must either endure severe and lasting agony or lose her life.[13]

This idealized woman is found in most of the songs from Period II and III. Typical representations occur in Stephen Foster's *Sweetly She Sleeps, My Alice Fair* (Baltimore, 1851) and *Gentle Lena Claire* (New York, 1862), and in J.R. Thomas' *Blue-Eyed Jeannie* (Boston, 1856) and *Annie Law* (New York, 1857). The first three songs have lyrics by the composers; the last, one by W.W. Fosdick.

In contrast to the idealized woman, now and then a foreign lady is mentioned. She has darker eyes and hair and swarthier skin. She hypnotizes men with her innate seductiveness. Yet, this dark lady seldom marries anyone.[14] In *Oh! Must We Part to Meet No More?*, words and music by Laura A. Hewitt (Baltimore, 1851), a foreign lady is introduced, at least in the imagination of a woman who is bidding farewell to the man she loves. The American woman is desolate. She knows they will "meet no more... cruel fate decreed it so." She first tells him she is a "drooping plant whose feeble tendrels cling to thee." Then in the last stanza she cries out:

> Yes, thou wilt roam through foreign climes
> And smiling seek the dazzling throng,
> List fondly to some dark-eyed maid,
> The while she breathes her syren-song.

A further characteristic of the love song is the stereotyped manipulation of natural phenomena to project the dominant emotional tone of the lyric. When the beloved is described, the setting is often one of cheerful sunlight, singing birds, glittering brooks, verdant meadows, and blooming flowers. The weather turns mild; the season is spring or summer. Melodious sounds and gay activities prevail.

Such is the setting for Foster's dream of the past contained in the first stanza of *Jeanie with the Light Brown Hair* (New York, 1854):

I dream of Jeanie with the light brown hair,
    Borne like a vapor on the summer air;
I see her tripping where the bright streams play,
    Happy as the daisies that dance on her way.
Many were the wild notes her merry voice would pour,
    Many were the blithe birds that warbled them o'er.
Oh! I dream of Jeanie with the light brown hair,
    Floating like a vapor on the soft summer air.

Nature is also invoked to contrast past happiness with present sorrow brought on by love thwarted and lovers parted. As compared with the summery past, the present is autumnal or wintry in this kind of song. Now the reference may be to the chill of night, rain or snow falling on a bleak countryside, and natural sounds suggestive of grief. In the second and third stanzas of the Foster song, named above, the speaker puts aside his dream of past happiness and grows aware of his yearning for the departed Jeanie. He hears her melodies "sighing like the night wind and sobbing like the rain," and observes, "Now the nodding wild flowers may wither on the shore."

If the song portrays the nocturnal tryst of young lovers, then nature turns benign, as in John Ordway's *Witching Love by Moonlight* (Boston, 1857):

Lovely flowers by moonlight,
    Sleep when daylight's gone,
Placid shades of twilight,
    Beckon love to come.
Come to rural happy bowers,
    Queenly moon invites;
She will strew thy path with flowers,
    Tipt with golden light.

Witching love by moonlight
    Ever bright and fair;
Shining with the starlight,
    Cupids watching there.

The sight and sounds of nature create a mood of disquiet when lovers remain eternally separated by distance or death. In H.S. Thompson's *Marion Lee* (Boston, 1858), the woman awaiting the return of her loved one is unaware that he has drowned at sea. Nevertheless, nature signals the hopelessness of her wait and the defeat of her expectations:

Come to me love for here I am waiting,
    Sadly and lone by the dark rolling sea;

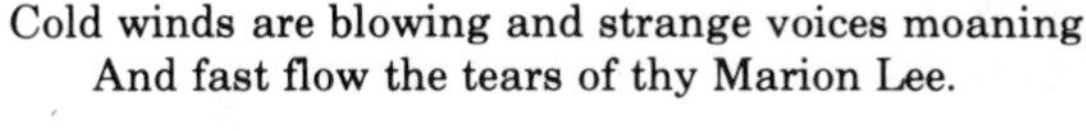

Cold winds are blowing and strange voices moaning
    And fast flow the tears of thy Marion Lee.

. . . .

Long have I watched thro' the night's gloomy shadows,
    Gazing far out o'er the dark troubled sea;
Striving in vain, thro' mists that are hov'ring,
    To catch but one glance of thy proud bark and thee.

The Subjects of Affection

The lyrics to the American love songs from Period III differ from those of earlier songs and from contemporary British compositions. These American songs show their dissimilarity in the smaller variety of motifs used, the more conventionalized presentation of these motifs, and the high incidence of a very limited number of subjects peculiarly mid-century American in their emotionally charged delineation of lovers' situations. Among these subjects about nine are prominent.

The first is one of leave-taking, of lovers saying farewell, possibly forever. This theme was an entirely appropriate one for people living in the decades of long and dangerous sea voyages, constant western movement, and young men striking off to seek their fortunes. Years could pass before a man and woman met again. Death frequently intervened and made reunion impossible, at least in this life. Saying good-bye to home and dear one was already an often heard theme in pre-1840 American songs, examples being George Jackson's *One Kind Kiss* (Boston, ca. 1809), and the production of a "Young Lady of Georgia," *No More* (Philadelphia, 1836). After 1840, however, the song of farewell is made to bear a heavier emotional burden, as in *Come Love and Sit Awhile by Me,* by H.S. Wheaton (Boston, 1847). Here, a man is about to depart, apparently never to return and with no explanation given for his leaving. Nor is it revealed where he is going. The song begins:

Come, love, and sit awhile by me,
    That, once more, ere we say farewell,
My soul may give itself to thee
    And all its grief and sadness tell.

The first stanza ends with a warning to his beloved that their "cherished hopes. . . now must die." In the second stanza he senses her torment:

Thy gentle heart throbs wearily
    Beneath the grief that's brooding there.

Thy soul's deep joys, pressed heavily,
Shrink crushed in all thy love's despair.

and suggests, although without much conviction, that "passing time shall soothe thy pain." The song concludes typically with his prophecy of eternal and hopeless love and constant sorrow for himself:

I still shall see thee—but in dreams—
I still shall love thee—but in vain—
No hope from out the future gleams!
No joy shall thrill my soul again!

The parting in Mrs. C.E. Habicht's *The Sun Is In the West* (Boston, 1848) is depicted in slightly dissimilar fashion. Now the speaker concentrates on his own, to the exclusion of his beloved's, feelings. He vows to love her always. In a world that will remain joyless, her memory will be "A lamp within a tomb/To burn tho' all unseen/. . .To light—tho' but a gloom."

Now and then a song of this type shows the narrator simulating gaiety while suffering inwardly. This is the message of John C. Andrew's *Come, I've Something Sweet to Sing You* (New York, 1848):

Come, I've something sweet to sing you
And a parting word to say,
Nay gaze not thus upon me
That tonight I seem so gay,
For though my lips look mirthful
And my cheek is glowing too,
Ah, my heart is very joyless
For its thoughts are all on you.

Some songs of affection describe a person, usually a young woman, as still waiting and expecting the return of a loved one after a long separation.[15] In most such songs, the woman watches at the seashore for one who is a sailor or traveler to distant lands.[16] Like the subject of leave-taking, that of the waiting woman is old, an instance from Period I being Francis Hopkinson's *My Love Is Gone to Sea.*[17] After 1840 most waiting women appear lonely, distressed and perched upon a promontory overlooking the water. The scene painted in Charlie Converse's *The Rock Beside the Sea* (Philadelphia, 1857) reveals the recurring conventions of this type of song:

The wild waves' thunder on the shore,

The curlew's restless cries,
Unto my watching heart are more
Than all earth's melodies.
Come back; my ocean rover, come!
There's but one place for me,
Till I can greet thy swift sail home,
My lone rock by the sea!

One variation shows the watcher unaware that the awaited one is dead. In Foster's *Willie, My Brave* (New York, 1851), no one has the courage to "tell her of the fragile bark that sank beneath the ocean." At the song's end, she abandons hope and dies.[18]

In the third type of love song, lovers remain separated with no expectation of ever meeting again. Although eternal separation and attendant miseries was dealt with in works from Period I and II, [19] it became one of the most ubiquitous of all mid-century subjects. The viewpoint is almost always a male's.[20] As in other song types, the emotions are all; the why, where and what of the situation hardly receive mention. Running through all is the sentiment in *Jenny Grey,* words by Benjamin Jones, music by George Poulton (Boston, 1855), that the beloved's "image clingeth to memory yet/And this bosom still beats for thee, sweet Jenny Grey." The speaker promises forever to "remember [her] in sorrow, in joy and in pain/One heart shall be faithful unchangeable still."

Foster wrote several songs of this type. Invariably he has a male speaker describe an idealized woman, then repeatedly ask where she has gone. The speaker provides no answers and never really expects a reunion. Two such Foster works are *Laura Lee* (Baltimore, 1851) and *Where Has Lula Gone?* (New York, 1858).

An occasional minstrel song pictures the permanent separation of slaves who are lovers. Unlike non-dialect compositions, the minstrel ones state the reason for separation. Either one of the two slaves has been sold and sent to a new owner, as in James Carter's *Cynthia Sue* (Boston, 1844), or the man has thrown over his enslavement and escaped to the North, as in *Young Clem Brown,* words by Marshall S. Pike, music by L.V.H. Crosby (Boston, 1846).

The fourth type is an elegy on the beloved, uttered by a disconsolate lover, and usually over a young woman's grave. For years poetry and song had favored this subject, many British examples appearing throughout the eighteenth century.[21] As early as the 1790s, American music publishers were reprinting songs of this kind, like James Hook's *Lucy Gray of Allendale* (Philadelphia, ca. 1794) and Charles Dignum's *Fair Rosale* (New York, ca. 1797). On the whole, the lyrics of these pieces seem highly artificial.They are written mostly in the third person and concern themselves with unreal people, like the classically inspired shepherds and shepherdesses who inhabited a world distant from the concerns of everyday men and women. Moreover, gracefulness takes precedence over feeling.[22]

The New York publication of Morris and Horn's *Near the Lake Where Droop'd the Willow*, in 1837, initiated a tremendous rise in the popularity of the elegiac song of affection. This composition attracted a vast following almost overnight. In it one finds most of the conventions that reappear with regularity in the Periods II and III songs of this type: a beautiful and idealized "maid, belov'd and cherished" by high and low is buried "near the lake where droop'd the willow"; and a bereaved lover, who can never forget her, watches and weeps over her grave.

Most often a weeping willow, sometimes a yew or cypress, overhangs the grave. In a special study on the symbolic use of the willow, John W. Draper states that the tree was at one time the symbol of distressed lovers. Not until after the weeping variety of the tree had arrived from China a little before the middle of the eighteenth century and had begun to supplant the yew and cypress in cemeteries did it become the symbol of death.[23]

The willow still symbolizes distressed lovers in Francis Hopkinson's song of 1788, *Beneath a Weeping Willow's Shade.*[24] Nevertheless, according to Draper, by the end of the eighteenth century the weeping willow had become widely accepted in America as a death symbol. It was planted in burial grounds and appeared with some frequency on gravestones.[25] During the 1820s, American songs pictured the tree as drooping over graves situated near a body of water:

> By the side of yon streamlet,
> There grows a green willow,
> Which bends to its surface,
> And kisses each wave;
> Under whose dark shades,
> With the sod for his pillow,
> In peace rests the spirit,
> Of William the Brave.[26]

Then, with the 1840s a young woman almost invariably lies buried beneath the tree.[27]

The composers of the elegiac songs seem to have been in agreement with Edgar Allan Poe in his explanation of a poet's approach to writing, as set forth in his essay on "The Philosophy of Composition." Poe asks himself what is the most melancholy of topics. "Death" is the answer. How does a poet make death a proper

For Eunice Anney 1813. Reprinted with permission from the Museum of Fine Arts, Boston.

subject for poetry? By uniting it to beauty. Furthermore, the death "of a beautiful woman is unquestionably the most poetic topic in the world and equally is it beyond doubt that the lips best suited for such a topic are those of a bereaved lover."[28]

Two elegiac songs conforming to the Poe dictum have already been cited, Emerson's *Cora Bell* and Root's *The Hazel Dell.* Among the many examples of this type that Foster wrote,[29] *Eulalie* (New York, 1851) may possibly have been the one most directly influenced by Poe's poetry. The change of the death symbol from a willow to a yew was made, at least in part, for the sake of the assonance "yew-tree, Eulalie." The last stanza reads as follows:

Streamlet chanting at her feet
  Mournful music sad and sweet,
Wake her not, she dreams of me
  'Neath the yew-tree, Eulalie!
Eulalie, but yesternight,
  Came a spirit veiled in white,
I knew it could be none but thee,
  Bride of Death, lost Eulalie.

The fifth type of song involving affection explores the feelings of a rejected lover, a subject with a long history in poetry and song. Two early parlor works on this theme are James Hewitt's *How Happy Was My Humble Lot* (New York, ca. 1800) and *When First Maria Won My Heart* (New York, ca. 1807). During the 1830s the song lyrics centering on a lover's rejection assumed the characteristics associated with mid-century works. One begins to see the change in *The Broken Heart,* words by R.H.H., music by Edwin Merriott (New York, ca. 1830), and *There Was a Time,* "Words from the Lady's Book," music by Tau Delta (Philadelphia, 1833). The author of the last lyric is still somewhat reticent in his depiction of feeling. His speaker appears saddened but does not sound terribly disordered by his rejection, as the song shows at the beginning:

There was a bright and sunny time
  When ev'ry hope was gay
But the vision's gone, and each fairy dream
  Has floated far away!
There was a time when I believed,
  She whom I lov'd was true:
I twin'd her roses, flowers she gave,
  But ah! her flowers were rue.

After 1840 the personal emotion becomes more naked. Note the suffering laid bare in the ending of *Hopeless Love,* words and music by J.T.S. Sullivan (Philadelphia, 1849):

Tho' in this world I ne'er may possess thee,
    Tho' those charms I may never embrace,
Tho' these lips, love, may never caress thee,
    I still worship thy beauty and grace;
Oh would that I never had met thee,
    Thou bright vision of all that is fair,
Or that power were mine to forget thee,
    I had vanquished this aching despair.

Why must the speaker never again possess the one he loves? Why must he succumb to despair? The usual reason given is the one loved has married another. The turning away is owing to fickleness or the insistence of parents. Since the marriage state was as immutable as death itself, neither a divorce nor a liaison being conceivable, all that the speaker has left is the never-ending ache of unsatisfied love. As the "Lady" writes in the last stanza of her song *Thou Has Wounded the Spirit that Loved Thee* (Baltimore, 1846): "Thus we're taught in this cold world to smother/Each feeling that once was so dear."

Another "Lady" ends her song of rejection—*My Hopes Have Departed Forever* (New York, 1851)—with a reference to willows and death. The speaker here is a woman:

He came, but another had rifled
    His heart of the love once my own,
I grieved, but my anguish was stifled,
    And shrank from his cold formal tone.
The sun is now sinking in billows,
    That roll in the far distant west,
But morning will shine through the willows,
    And find me forever at rest.

Fortunately for the mental health of mid-century singers, happier compositions also existed. One form the happier pieces took was the idyllic composition in praise of a still-living and presumably approachable beloved, as in J.R. Thomas' *Annie Law,* words by W.W. Fosdick (New York, 1857), and Foster's *Fairy-Belle* (New York, 1859). Some happy songs the musical public enjoyed have a suitor beg his beloved to come with him, away from the grimness and sorrow of the world that surrounds her. Through marriage they can both escape to a joyful existence elsewhere. The elsewhere may be an isolated mountain side, as in Francis H. Brown's *Will You Come to My Mountain Home?* or an island paradise, as in Henry Williams' *Bermuda's Fairy Isle,* words by T.M.Y. (Boston, 1854), or a faraway exotic land, as in John Baker's *The Burman Lover* (Boston, 1849).

Still another variety was the serenade. The titles of two popular serenades from Period II, *The Lone Starry Hours,* words by

Marshall S. Pike, music by James Power, and *Twinkling Stars are Laughing, Love,* words and music by John Ordway (Boston, 1855), give an indication of the contents. No surprises are tucked away in any of the verses. The suitor in the former song twice sings a conventional refrain:

When no winds through the low woods sweep, love,
    And I gaze on some bright rising star,
When the world is in dream and sleep, love,
    Oh! wake while I touch my guitar.

In some serenades the speaker does not sing to his beloved but simply thinks of her while she sleeps. He wishes the dreamer all the joys and none of the unhappiness in life, as in *Oh, Were I a Bird,* words and music by J.T.S. Sullivan (Philadelphia, 1846), and *Sweetly She Sleeps, My Alice Fair,* words and music by Stephen Foster (New York, 1851).

The last variety of love song to be described is good-humored and often makes sport of the sentimentality pervading the other types. The amusing *Joe Hardy* of James Pierpont (Boston, 1853) pokes fun at the solemn commonplaces infesting the love songs, and restores the emotional equilibrium of singer and listener, as evidenced in these first two stanzas:

Yes, I know that you were my lover,
    But that sort of thing has an end,
Tho' love and its transports are over
    You know you can still be my friend:
Don't kneel at my feet I implore you,
    Don't write on the drawings you bring,
Don't ask me to say I adore you,
    For indeed it is *now* no such thing.

I confess when at Bangor we parted,
    I swore that I worshipped you then,
That I was a maid broken hearted,
    And you the most charming of men;
I confess when I read your first letter,
    I blotted your name with a tear,
I was young then, but now I know better,
    Could I tell that I'd meet Hardy here?

More biting are the following verses by Nathaniel Parker Willis, a versifier who also wrote his own fair share of sentimental lyrics:[30]

Your love in a cottage is hungry,
    Your vine is a nest of flies—

Your milkmaid shocks the Graces,
    And simplicity talks of pies!
You lie down to your shady slumber
    And wake with a bug in your ear,
And your damsel that walks in the morning
    Is shod like a mountaineer.

True love is at home on a carpet,
    And nightly likes his ease—
And true love has an eye for a dinner,
    And starves beneath shady trees.
His wing is the fan of a lady,
    His foot's an invisible thing
And his arrow is tipped with a jewel,
    And shot from a silver string.[31]

In contrast to the ever-present love songs, parlor works that stress devotion to family and friends are relatively scarce before 1820, begin to increase in number from 1820 to 1840, and become prominent after 1840. Especially popular were the paeans to Mother, exemplified in *Welcome, Mother!*, words and music by John Hewitt (Baltimore, 1834). The absolute devotion of the son, as expressed here, pervades all such songs. The wonder is that sufficient love remained to direct toward others. The first two stanzas read:

Welcome, Mother! now I greet thee,
    Can I all my feelings tell?
How this heart has long'd to meet thee,
    Since my lips breath'd out "farewell"!
Welcome, Mother! while I press thee
    Fondly to my youthful heart
Every word I speak will bless thee,
    While I know how dear thou art.

Welcome, Mother! I have often
    Traced thine image in my dreams;
Memory's touch the spell would soften,
    Dressing like in golden beams.
Love, foresaken—'midst the smiling,
    Longing for some absent one,
I have stood—one though beguiling,
    'Twas the thought of thee alone.

As songs of devotion to family and friends rose in popularity, so did songs on objects associated with those loved. A counterpart to the Hewitt song is *The Old Arm Chair,* words by Eliza Cook, music by Henry Russell (Boston, 1840), in which an armchair becomes a surrogate mother. This exaggerated affection for a piece of furniture seems to have given no pause to the singers of the time. Instead of feeling embarrassment, they sang the following lines with apparent sincerity:

I love it, I love it; and who shall dare
To chide me for loving that old arm chair.
I've treasured it long as a holy prize,
I've bedew'd it with tears, and embalmed it with sighs;
'Tis bound by a thousand bands to my heart;
Not a tie will break, not a link will start,
Would ye learn the spell a mother sat there,
And a sacred thing is that old armchair.

Unabashed amateur singers in the thousands purchased the composition.

Though affection was likely to be bestowed on anything old and associated with a person's past, the most frequent recipients of affection were a family's or mother's Bible, a church, schoolhouse, tree, flower or home. Home songs grew in number with the popularity of *Home! Sweet Home!*, words by John Howard Payne, music by Henry Bishop, and issued in New York and Philadelphia within a few months of its first London airing in 1823. Soon, several similar songs composed by Americans achieved success: William Wetmore's *The Cot Beneath the Hill* (1841), L. Heath's *The Cot Where I Was Born* (1844), Judson Hutchinson's *The Cottage of My Mother* (1848), E.A. Hosmer's *O Give Me a Home by the Sea* (1851), John Ordway's *Going Home* (1855), and Stephen Foster's *My Old Kentucky Home* (1853). Home as rustic dwelling representative of childhood's innocence and a mother's love, the commonplaces of the type of parlor song, is the subject of J.R. Thomas' *The Cottage by the Sea* (New York, 1856):

Childhood's days now pass before me,
Forms and scenes of long ago;
Like a dream they hover o'er me,
Calm and bright as ev'ning's glow.
Days that knew no shade of sorrow,
When my young heart pure and free,
Joyful hailed each coming morrow
In the cottage by the sea.

Fancy sees the rosetrees twining
'Round the old and rustic door,
And, below, the white beach shining,
Where I gathered shells of yore.
Hear my mother's gentle warning,
As she took me on her knee;
And I feel again life's morning,
In the cottage by the sea.

What though years have rolled above me,
    Though 'mid fairer scenes I roam
Yet I ne'er shall cease to love thee,
    Childhood's dear and happy home!
And when life's long day is closing
    Oh! how pleasant would it be;
On some faithful breast reposing,
    In the cottage by the sea.

The wish to regress into a state akin to infancy even when death approaches, as revealed in the last four lines, is a reflection of the womb-tomb, birth-death syndrome that underlies a good number of the parlor-song lyrics.

The Other Subjects of Sentimental Song

Like affection, mortality and time is the theme of songs from all three periods. In such works, beauty, youth and happiness are described as ephemeral; all living things are subject to aging and decay; and relentless time is ruler over life. *Carpe diem* is the main sentiment of *Come Chace that Starting Tear Away,* words by Thomas Moore, music arranged by Henry Bishop (New York, ca. 1822):

Come chace that starting tear away,
    Ere mine to meet it springs;
To night, at least, to night be gay,
    What e'er tomorrow brings!;
Like sunset gleams, that linger late,
    When all is darking fast,
Are hours like these we snatch from fate,
    The brightest and the last.
Then chase [sic] that starting tear away,
    Ere mine to meet it springs,
To night at least, to night be gay
    What e'er to morrow brings.

Man receives warning of his mortality in the pessimistic *Love Not!* words by Mrs. Norton, music by John Blockley (New York, ca. 1833). The first two stanzas read:

Love not! Love not! Ye hapless sons of clay,
    Hope's gayest wreaths are made of earthly flowers;
Things that are made to fade and fade away,
    Ere they have blossom'd for a few short hours.
Love not!

Love not! Love not! The thing you love may die,
    May perish from the gay and gladsome earth,

The silent stars, the blue and smiling sky,
  Beams on its grave, as once upon its birth.
Love not!

The song's sentiments addressed the feelings of inner conflict that were deeply felt yet at the same time fashionable in this romantic age. Men and women, wearied by life and seeing the inevitable deterioration that crumbled the beauty about them, endorsed its message. *Love Not!* was incredibly popular during the thirties.

From this subject it is a short step to the next, lamentation and death, expressed either as an elegy on the idea of death in general, or as mourning for a particular person. Infrequent in Period I, laments increase in Period II and are numerous in Period III. One special lament, that of a young man over the grave of his beautiful beloved, has already been discussed.

A rather macabre example of the general commentary on death is *The Old Sexton,* words by Park Benjamin, music by Henry Russell (Boston, 1841):

Nigh to a grave that was newly made
  Leaned a Sexton on his earth worn spade.
His work was done and he paused to wait
  The fun'ral train through the open gate.
A relic of bygone days was he,
  And his locks were white as the foamy sea—
And these words came from his lips so thin,
  I gather them in! I gather them in!

I gather them in! for man and boy
  Year after year of grief and joy
I've builded the houses that lie around
  In ev'ry nook of the burial ground.
Mother and daughter, father and son
  Come to my solitude, one by one.
But come they strangers, or come they kin,
  I gather them in! I gather them in!

Many are with me, but still I'm alone
  I'm king of the dead and I make my throne
On a monument slab of marble cold
  And my sceptre of rule is the spade I hold,
Come they from cottage or come they from hall,
  Mankind are my subjects—all, all, all.
Let them loiter in pleasure, or toilfully spin—
  I gather them in! I gather them in!

In many laments, the death of a famous person is the subject, as in *The Burial of Allston,*[32] words by Miss H.F. Gould, music by John

Braham (Boston, 1846). The lyric describes "Allston's noble shrine of clay/He from dust hath passed away."

The fourth category of subject estrangement, deals with alienation of feeling or physical separation from loved ones. Although found in Period I, compositions involving estangement did not achieve their highest popularity until after 1820. The romantic anguish and self-pity of the lonely wanderer, a frequent theme, are vented in the first stanza of *Alone, Alone,* words by S.S. Steele, music by Thomas Comer (Boston, 1847):

> Like a doomed shade I wander,
> To dark despair a prey,
> As streams thro' vales meander,
> Where sun ne'er sheds a ray;
> Each tree around seems bending
> To the breeze that bears my moan,
> While pining echo mocks my sigh,
> And cries, "Alone, alone."

Another recurring theme is on a prisoner suffering and without hope for release, as in *The Gallery Slave,* words by James Perciaval, music by Elam Ives, Jr. (Philadelphia, ca. 1835). The song recalls the unfortunate American sailors imprisoned by the Barbary corsairs. Most of the captives had expired in torment, owing to the heavy labors exacted by their ruthless masters. The third and fourth stanzas develop as follows:

> And oft as around him the billows were roaring,
> He struggled to sweep his broad oar through the wave,
> I've marked him in tears his lost freedom deploring,
> I've marked the poor heart-broken slave.
>
> "Ah! ne'er shall I meet my lost friends," he was crying,
> "Oh! ne'er shall my woes and my sorrows be o'er!"
> Then faintly his voice on his pallid lips dying,
> He sigh'd as he tugg'd at the oar.

Occasionally a song centered on an innocent young bride exhanging her home for an unknown future. The first stanza of *The Bride's Farewell,* words by Miss M.L. Beevor, music by Thomas Williams (Boston, ca. 1830), sets forth a typical scene:

> Farewell, Mother! tears are streaming,
> Down thy pale and tender cheek,
> I in gems and roses beaming,
> Scare this sad Farewell may speak;
> Farewell, Mother! now I leave thee,

(Hopes and fears my bosom swell)
One to trust who may deceive me,
Farewell, Mother! Fare thee well.

This composition contrasts with the usual popular song of a hundred years later, in which marriage opens the door to paradise and the heart to rapturous delight.

The remaining types of subject matter, while by no means rare were less common.

Sacred song, though characteristic of the output of one or two early composers (Oliver Shaw, for example), becomes common only in the years after the great success of *Rocked in the Cradle of the Deep,* words by Mrs. Willard, music by J.P. Knight (New York, 1840). Some sacred works are in the form of a prayer and therefore difficult to distinguish from contemporary hymns. The difficulty is compounded because hymns like Lowell Mason's *Watchman Tell Us of the Night* (Boston, 1830) were also published for solo voice with piano accompaniment. Hymn settings in this format were purchased by the same Americans who enjoyed sacred and other parlor songs. Unlike parlor songs, however, hymns are subtitled as such and never as ballads. They are considered vocal compositions in praise of God and suitable for congregational and individual worship.

Nevertheless, the line dividing sacred song and hymn is impossible to draw since both are stylistically so similar. Hymns were freely sung by soloists in concert and at home; sacred parlor songs were included in church services. The prayer-like texts of some parlor works are exemplified in the opening lines of *Rocked in the Cradle of the Deep;*:

Rocked in the cradle of the deep,
I lay me down in peace to sleep;
Secure I rest upon the wave
For Thou, O Lord, has pow'r to save.
I know Thou wilt not slight my call,
For Thou doest mark the sparrow's fall!
And calm and peaceful is my sleep,
Rocked in the cradle of the deep.

On the other hand, many sacred songs do not resemble prayers. Instead, they make reference to a Biblical incident, as with Oliver Shaw's *Mary's Tears,* words by Thomas Moore (Providence, ca. 1817), which begins:

Were not the sinful Mary's tears
An off'ring worthy Heav'n,

When o'er the faults of former years
She wept and was forgiv'n?

Other compositions have only a tenuous claim to sacredness. Thus, the subject of Isaac B. Woodbury's *He Doeth All Things Well* (Boston, 1844) is really the death of a sister:

I remember well my sorrow, as I stood beside her bed,
And my deep and heartfelt anguish, when they told me *she was dead;*
And oh! that cup of bitterness—*let not my heart rebel,*
God gave—He took—He will restore—"*He doeth all things well!*"

Much less encountered than sacred songs are compositions critical of contemporary society. When they do appear, they bewail society's insensitivity to suffering, indifference to vice, and acceptance of slavery and oppression. During late Period II and into Period III, Henry Russell and members of the Hutchinson Family composed and sang many such pieces—in support of the American Indians and of women's rights, and against slavery, gambling and drunkenness. A few of these pieces are Russell's *The Indian Hunter* (Boston, ca. 1840), *The Gambler's Wife* (New York, 1841) and *The Dream of the Reveller* (New York, 1843), and Jesse Hutchinson's *Get Off the Track* (Boston, 1844). The last piece advocates the abolition of slavery.

During the forties the Irish migrated in great numbers to America in an attempt to escape the potato famine of their homeland. A number of songs, among them F.N. Crouch's *Kathleen Mavourneen* (New York, ca. 1840) and William Dempster's *The Lament of the Irish Emigrant* (Boston, 1840) describe the poignancy of parting from home and loved ones. *Give Me Three Grains of Corn,* words by Mrs. A.M. Edmond, music by O.R. Gross (Boston, 1848) tells of the starvation that caused the exodus and the indifference of the rich and powerful in England to the suffering of those who remained. The first and sixth stanzas of this song are:

Give me three grains of corn, mother,
Only three grains of corn;
It will keep the little life I have
Till the coming of the morn.
I am dying of hunger and cold, mother,
I am dying of hunger and cold,
And half the agony of such a death
My lips have never told.

. . . .

There is many a brave heart here, mother,
  Dying of want and cold,
While only across the channel, mother,
  Are many that roll in gold.
There are rich and proud men there, mother,
  With wondrous wealth to view,
And the bread they fling to the dogs to-night
  Would give me life and you.

One wonders how many of the singers were titillated by the verses and at the same time indifferent to the real hardships and new prejudices the Irish immigrants endured after their arrival in America.

Praise of nature, the seventh type of subject, usually depicts a generalized rural scene, less often a seascape or a particular place that is geographically identifiable. Songs of this kind, found mostly during Period I and rarely after 1830, are well exemplified in the first stanza of *May Morning,* author unknown, music by P.A. von Hagen (Boston, ca. 1802):

The mellow lustre of the Morn
  Was mingling with the Golden Beam,
That gilt the tear upon the Thorn,
  And danc'd upon the dimpling Stream.
The grove and landscape hill and green,
  Whose charms drew Splendor from the ray,
Had dress's with Smiles their Gayest mien,
  To welcome in the morn of May.

Perhaps because insufficient personal feeling is involved and too much of the outer, too little of the inner, world is explored, relatively few such songs became popular in Period III. Without a strong personal emotion emanating from each line, the praise of nature in itself must have seemed an empty gesture, consequential only when given a human dimension.

The last type of subject—the teaching of a moral lesson—is illustrated by the obvious message in John Barnett's *The Butterfly, the Moth, and the Bee* (Boston, ca. 1827). Here the poet contrasts the "Butterfly and Moth so fair, silly idle thoughtless pair," with the industrious bee. The song ends:

See, ah see, yon cruel boy
  The gaudy Butterfly destroy,
And, victim to delusive joy
  The Moth expires in flame.
The Bee, still cheerful, busy, gay,
  Renews its toil from day to day,
'Tis Industry that points the way

To Virtue and to Fame.

This song, a favorite in its day, exemplifies the kind of instruction coated with music that the young were made to down on a daily basis. Public schools and private seminaries doted on lessons set to pretty tunes.

In the majority of parlor songs, the "I" and the "you" or "thou" predominate. The versifiers try to express (to use Wordsworth's phrase) "the spontaneous overflow of powerful feeling."[33] In simple and emphatic terms, they set forth events, conditions and feelings common to all humanity. Above all, they desire that "elementary feelings...be more accurately contemplated and more forcibly communicated."[34] According to Alba Warren, a scholar and writer on nineteenth-century poetic theory, these writers of verse held their object was poetic truth, with beauty "the outward manifestation of truth."[35]

The characteristics of poetic beauty aimed at by the authors of parlor-song lyrics, as far as could be ascertained, are consistent with the conclusions reached by Francis Jeffrey[36] in his highly influential "Essay on Beauty" (1811), in which he describes beauty as purely subjective, "nothing more than the reflection of our own inward emotions, and is made up entirely of certain little portions of love, pity, or other affections, which have been connected with these objects." The poet, Jeffrey says, employs "objects" that are "the inseparable concomitants of emotions, of which the greater part of mankind are susceptible; and his taste will then deserve to be called bad and false if he obtrude upon the public, as beautiful, objects that are not likely to be associated in common minds with any interesting impressions."[37]

What Jeffrey neglects to add is that the beauty he delineates is often suffused with self-pity, suffering, loneliness and yearning,[38] experienced by stock figures placed in stock situations: freezing match girls, abandoned orphans (frequently blind or maimed), minstrels serenading their ladies, knights returning to their anxious damsels, lonely wanderers, sailors on foundering ships, soldiers wounded on battlefields, prisoners without hope of release, innocents dying, brigands and their captive maidens, and nubile and desirable young women pictured variously as Scottish or Irish lasses, Moorish maids, American Indian girls and Arabian or Grecian beauties.

The favorite stance of these stock figures is summed up in Henry Bishop's *I'm Saddest When I Sing,* the lyric by Thomas Haynes Bayly (Philadelphia, ca. 1840):

You think I have a merry heart

Because my songs are gay,
But oh they all were taught to me
By friends now far away:
The Bird retains his silver note
Though bondage chains his wing,
His song is not a happy one—
I'm saddest when I sing.

I heard them first in that sweet home
I never more shall see,
And now each song of joy has got
A plaintive turn for me.
Alas! 'tis vain in winter time
To mock the songs of spring;
Each note recalls some wither'd leaf,
I'm saddest when I sing.

Of all the friends I us'd to love,
My harp remains alone,
Its faithful voice still seems to be
An echo of my own:
My tears when I bend over it
Will fall upon its string,
Yet, those who hear me little think
I'm saddest when I sing!

The central figure in texts like this indulges in an exaggerated protestation of sorrow described in the popular commonplaces of the time. In some lyrics, the reason for the protestation is unrevealed. In others, a pathetic but stereotyped situation is invented, seemingly to elicit the proper emotional response. For example, to insure the emotions proper to tragedy, what better than an anguished mother and child perishing by slow degrees in *The Snowstorm*?[39]

The poetic texts favored for musical setting were careful to portray the more delicate and refined emotions. The extremes of joy, grief, rage and despair were usually avoided or muted. Feeling was confined within the bounds of propriety and moderation. Simplicity in language and situation helped evoke the "pathetic" and "sublime."[40] In this regard, the descriptive scenes in Henry Russell's *The Maniac* (1840) and *The Gambler's Wife* (1841) were exceptions whose popularity had few counterparts in parlor-song literature.

Monk Lewis' lyric for *The Gambler's Wife* describes the death of a mother and child after waiting in vain for the husband's return:

Nestle more closely, dear one, to my heart!
Thou art cold! thou art freezing! but we will not part!
Husband! I die! Father! it is not he!

Oh, God! protect my child! hush,—the clock strikes three.

They're gone! the glimmering spark hath fled!
The wife and child are number'd with the dead.
On the cold earth outstretch'd in solemn rest
The babe lay frozen on its mother's breast.

The gambler came at last—but all was o'er,
Dread silence reign'd around—the clock struck four.

Russell's songs were popular. But lyrics like the above, each stanza filled with exclamation marks, failed to win approval when set by others.[41] In contrast, the typical songs that became favorites with the American public require less intense emotional responses, as can be seen in Robert Burns' *Auld Lang Syne,* Thomas Moore's *My Heart and Lute,* Thomas Haynes Bayly's *Long, Long Ago* and Stephen Foster's *Old Folks at Home.* They are all on serious subjects. Indeed, the incidence of comic and lightly playful songs amongst the popular favorites is low after Period I. *Mamma, Mamma,* words by Thomas Haynes Bayly, music by Jonathan Blewitt, a prolific composer and singer of comic songs, published in New York around 1833, is typical of the inconsequentiality of this type:

Why don't the men propose, mamma?
Why don't the men propose?
Each seems just coming to the point,
And then away he goes!
It is no fault of yours, mamma,
That every body knows;
You fete the finest men in town,
Yet oh they won't propose!

Only exceptionally and mostly in Period I were songs with narrative rather than lyrical texts among the favorites. These Period-I narratives usually involve national or patriotic themes. The music is sometimes original with the composer, but more often an adaptation of a traditional melody. One popular narrative song, *The Arethusa,*[42] words by Prince Hoare, music attributed to William Shield,[43] describes the battle between the Arethusa, an English ship, and the Belle Poule, a French ship, in the English Channel, June 1798. It begins:

Come along ye jolly sailors bold
Whose hearts are cast in honor's mould,
While England's glory I unfold,

The Hollingsworth Family, George Hollingsworth. Courtesy, Museum of Fine Arts, Boston.

Huzza for the Arethusa.
She is a frigate, tight and brave,
As ever stemm'd the dashing wave;
Her men are staunch to their fav'rite launch,
And when the foe shall meet our fire,
Sooner than strike we'll all expire,
On board the Arethusa.

After Period I, narrative songs (at least the few popular ones) exhibit the same sentimental cliches found in other popular songs, as can be seen in *The Tempest,* words by James T. Fields, music by Nathan Barker (Boston, 1849):

We were crowded in the cabin,
Not a soul would dare to sleep,—
It was midnight on the waters,
And a storm was on the deep.
'Tis a fearful thing in winter
To be shattered by the blast,
And to hear the rattling trumpet thunder,
"Cut away the mast!"

So we shuddered there in silence,—
For the stoutest held his breath,
While the angry sea was roaring,
And the breakers talked with death.
And as thus we sat in darkness,
Each one busy in his prayers,—
"We are lost! " the captain shouted,
As he staggered down the stairs.

But his little daughter whispered,
As she took his icy hand,
"Isn't God upon the ocean,
Just the same as on the land?"
Then he kissed the little maiden,
As he spoke in better cheer,
And we anchored safe in harbor,
When the moon was shining clear.

While the authors may base their texts on real or imagined incidents, which are sometimes described in a paragraph printed on the first page of a published work, their verses try to capture only the emotional essence of the situation and forego narration. This distinction between possibly factual incident and its sentimental retelling is made in the song *Let Me Kiss Him for His Mother,* words and music by John Ordway. A paragraph on the title page states the "Ballad" was prompted by the death of a young man from Maine. He died in New Orleans, among strangers, from yellow fever. At the funeral service, as the coffin lid was about to be closed, an elderly woman stopped the lid's movement and said: "Let me kiss him for his mother."[44] Typically this incident does not lead to a musical narration by Ordway. Instead, his lyric becomes an exercise in bathos:

Let me kiss him for his mother,
    What though left a lone stranger here;
She has loved him as none other
    I feel her blessing near.
Though cold that form lies sleeping,
    Sweet angels watch around;
Dear friends are near thee weeping,
    O lay him gently down.

(Chorus)
Sleep dearest, sleep,
    I love you as a brother,
Kind friends around you weep,
    I've kissed you for your Mother.[45]

It is difficult today, in an age with such different aesthetic values, to evaluate fairly a poem like Ordway's.[46] To twentieth-century tastes, his excessive emotionality shrinks to nothing the aesthetic distance between author and subject, his studied simplicity exploits one strong though stereotyped experience to the exclusion of depth, variety and subtlety—a criticism which is levied on most parlor-song texts.

On the other hand, these lyrics were not meant for reading but for singing strophically, thus encouraging an overall unity of expression to accommodate the repetition of melody. At the same time, the music, unassuming as much of it is, remains in the brighter major, rather than the minor, mode. In this fashion the composer relieves the sentimentality of the text and contributes an extra dimension to the whole that is difficult to define. When one lives day after day with these parlor compositions and hears them as songs (that is, at all times as a unity of words and music), a good number of them seem to shed their excessive sentimentality and emerge as fundamental and moving statements on the human condition. Furthermore, the real beauty of several of their melodies, though incapable of being readily analyzable, has merits comparable to that of the better art and folk songs.

Both the creators of these songs and the society for whom they were written felt their music should engage the listener's emotions first and stimulate his intellect second, if at all—certainly a conclusion safe to draw after an examination of the hundreds of sheet-music examples still extant. Moreover, the most successful songs [47] were found to involve the most unambiguous themes set to the plainest melodies. The titles of a majority of the songs telegraph the central theme: *Absence, The Captive Knight, Home! Sweet Home!, Do They Miss Me at Home?* and *Old Folks at Home.* To the extent that such songs flourished, they were valid for their time and society.

We must keep in mind that the nineteenth-century Americans who enjoyed the sentimental parlor song, and wept or smiled at its message, were quite aware of the problems troubling their society.[48] They certainly had first-hand knowledge of friends and family members who had left loved ones behind and traveled great distances, sometimes never to return. The American West and the oceans had swallowed up many of these travelers. In addition, a tragic number of the women they knew did die young, especially during or just after childbirth.[49] Love under these circumstances took a buffeting and was so depicted in song.

In the restless, constantly changing nineteenth-century social environment, where mobility and competition allowed little room for the development of warmth and intimacy between individuals, the relationship of suitor to beloved, husband to wife, and children to parents became of great consequence.[50] The importance of love and the other "pure" emotions in cementing personal relationships, therefore, was stressed.

It is clear that these Americans lived constantly with life's harsh truths.[51] It is just as clear that when they turned to song for entertainment, they preferred that these truths be softened with sentimentality. To relive the actualities of the American experience in song that held nothing back would have seemed incomprehensible to them. Instead, they wished some relief from the stark reality of their existence.[52] For sentimental songs to take on a recreative and therapeutic function, realistic details were suppressed, situations generalized and the violent emotions muted.

As for the composers and versifiers of the songs, their attitude is well expressed by George Root when he states that in his time few people knew, required or understood artistic songs such as those of Schubert. His choice was to write in artistic isolation or attempt to meet the needs of the American people. He chose the latter and was "thankful" when he "could write something that all the people would sing."[53] What he wrote had to be simple and sentimental, since it was this kind of musical composition alone that would "be received and live in the hearts of the people."[54]

Given the democratic temper of the time and the felt need to articulate what was a "people's music,"[55] the creators of the

American parlor song behaved like representatives of the people and did give shape to a musical genre with meaning for their own age. For this, at least, they should receive credit, and their compositions respect.

Notes

1. For an extensive discussion of poetic subjects, see Elizabeth Drew, *Poetry* (New York, 1959), pp. 101-252; see also Robert Hillyer, *In Pursuit of Poetry* (New York, 1960), pp. 116-17; Walter E. Houghton and G. Robert Strange, *Victorian Poetry and Poetics* (Boston, 1959), p. 4; James William Johnson in *The Princeton Encyclopedia of Poetry and Poetics* s.v. "Lyric." William Wordsworth, in the Preface to the 1815 edition of his poetry, classifies poetry as narrative (with the poet as narrator), dramatic (in dialogue form, the poet not appearing in his own person), lyrical ("containing the Hymn, the Ode, the Elegy, the Song, and the Ballad"), the Idyllium ("descriptive of external nature"), didactic, and satirical; William Wordsworth, *Poetical Works,* ed. Thomas Hutchinson, rev. ed. Ernest De Selincourt (London, 1936), p. 752. While parlor songs are found that fit all of Wordsworth's categories, the narrative, dramatic, and satirical types are not often seen.

2. Michael R. Turner, in the Introduction to *The Parlour Song Book* (New York, 1973), p. 17, states that in nineteenth-century parlor songs, "affection between male and female was seen to be of an inferior quality to the noble devotion of man for his maker, of a mother for her baby, or one comrade for another in adversity." He states further that "many girls, nurtured on drawing-room ballads, apparently went to the altar expecting in married life no more alarming contact with their husbands than the tickle of a manly whisker. It is surprising therefore, that so many middle-class marriages were happy as well as fecund."

An examination of hundreds of parlor-song texts, dating from 1790 to 1860, proves the first statement to be false. A reading of nineteenth-century observations on American life, by authors as diverse in outlook as Alexis de Tocqueville, Francis J. Grund, Mrs. Trollope, George Root, John Hewitt, and Samuel Clemens, proves the second statement of Turner to be inapplicable to most American girls, who knew quite well where babies came from.

3. Also set to music by William Horsley (Philadelphia, ca. 1814), and George Kiallmark (Philadelphia, ca. 1821).

4. Alexis de Tocqueville, *Democracy in America,* trans. Henry Reeve, ed. Francis Bowen, I (New York, 1945), 315-16. Much the same thing has been written by recent historians, such as Carl Bode; see his *American Life in the 1840s* (New York, 1967), pp. xiii-xiv, 55.

5. *The Musical World and New York Musical Times,* 11 December 1852, p. 227.

6. *Agnes May,* words by Anson C. Chester, music by Henry Tucker (New York, 1853).

7. *At Eve I Miss Thee when Alone,* music by V.H. Crosby (Boston, 1847).

8. The author of this study has examined several hundred song collections that once belonged to Americans who lived in the last decade of the 18th century and the first sixty years of the 19th century. Among the thousands of compositions seen, only a small handful make any reference to physical passion.

9. William Charvat, *The Origins of American Critical Thought, 1810-1835* (New York, 1968), pp. 13-16.

10. Edgar Allan Poe, "The Philosophy of Composition," *The Complete Poems and Stories of Edgar Allan Poe,* ed. Arthur Hobson Quinn and Edward H. O'Neill, II (New York, 1970), 981.

11. George F Root, *The Story of a Musical Life* (Cincinnati, 1891), p. 89.

12. Some pre-1840 songs had knights and their ladies as subjects; for example, John Hewitt's *The Minstrel's Return from the War* (New York, 1827) and *The Knight of the Raven-Black Plume* (New York, ca. 1833). Hewitt, however, reflected the views of the American South, which was considerably taken with the ideas of chivalry. After 1840, as the settlements in the Mid-West, populated mainly by ordinary people from New England, grew, the music publishers increasingly issued songs that centered on every day people and their experiences, in order to accommodate the tastes of the populous Northeast and Northwest. At the same time, they felt it less and less necessary to cultivate the preferences of the largely rural South, with its limited market, and hardly any songs were issued on chivalric themes; see Charvat, pp. 300-301; and John Bayley, *The Characters of Love* (New York, 1960), pp. 282-3.

13. This picture of the idealized woman is found not only in the love songs, but in most of the American literature of the period; see Charvat, p. 22; Leslie A. Fiedler, *Love and Death in the American Novel,* rev. ed. (New York, 1932), p. 228; Ralph Boas, "The Romantic Lady," in *Romanticism in America,* ed. George Boas (New York, 1961), p. 63.

14. This type of woman also appears in contemporary American literature; see Fiedler, p. 296; Charvat, p. 23.

15. One composition, the minstrel song *The Yellow Rose of Texas,* by J.K. (New York, 1858) is unusual in that a man speaks and says he is returning to the woman he loves after a prolonged separation from her. Another song, told from the viewpoint of the absent man is Foster's *Gentle Lena Clare* (New York, 1862).

16. In one or two songs the watcher is a rustic maiden living in a "dell" or "glen," as in *The Absent Soldier,* words by William Lewers, music by S.O. Dyer (New York, 1847).

17. *Seven Songs for the Harpsichord or Forte Piano* (Philadelphia, 1788), p. 2.

18. For another example of this song type, see the lyric to Thompson's *Marion Lee* quoted earlier in this chapter. The same subject, from a man's viewpoint is found in Charlie C. Converse's *Aileen Aroon* (Boston, 1853).

19. See the British song, *The Beautiful Maid,* words by Thomas Dibdin, music by John Braham (New York, ca. 1802); also *The Link is not Broken,* words by a "Gentleman of Boston," music by E.T. Coolidge (Boston, 1835).

20. One of the few songs with a woman's point of view is *Come Back,* words by Letty Linwood (Brooklyn, 1856).

21. See Sickels, p. 186.

22. Sickels, p. 188, states that the artificialness was true also of 18th century poetry.

23. John W. Draper, "Notes on the Symbolic Use of the Willow," *The Funeral Elegy* (New York, 1929), pp. 335-37.

24. *Seven Songs,* pp. 3-4. The willow continues to be used in some British songs as the symbol of distressed lovers, into the first decade of the 19th century, for example, in Sir John Stevenson's *The Willow,* first issued in Philadelphia by Benjamin Carr, around 1801, and in John Braham's *The Willow Tree,* words by Thomas Dibdin, also first issued by Carr, around 1808.

25. Draper, p. 337.

26. *William the Brave,* words by a "Young Lady of Kentucky," music by Charles Gilfert (New York, 1823). The well-known psychiatrist C.G. Jung, in *Analytical Psychology* (New York, 1968), pp. 130-32, 138, 177, speaks of water as an archetypal symbol of death, especially when connected with a tomb.

27. Some examples of elegiac songs of affection employing the willow as the symbol of a beautiful woman's death are *Bessie Gray,* words by W.R. Lawrence, music by George Poulton (Boston, 1854); *Alice Clair,* words by J.M. Fletcher, music by

Lyman Heath (New York, 1853); and *Annie Lisle,* words and music by H.S. Thompson (Boston, 1860). Examples of minstrel songs, in dialect, that are of this type are *Nelly Was a Lady,* words and music by Stephen Foster (New York, 1849), and *Jenny Lane,* words and music by R. Bishop Buckley (Boston, 1850).

28. *The Complete Poems,* II, 982. Two of Poe's poems that illustrate his ideas and employ similar conventions as those in the elegiac parlor songs are *Ulalume* and *Annabel Lee.* Since many songs portray the lover as watching over the grave, it is of interest that Norman Brown, a Freudian, states in *Life Against Death* (Middletown, Conn., 1959) p. 100, that man, unlike all other animals, instinctively guards his dead.

29. See *Lila Ray* (New York, 1850), *Gentle Annie* (New York, 1856) and *Virginia Belle* (New York, 1860).

30. Examples of Willlis' poetry may be found in Rufus W. Griswald, *The Poets and Poetry of America* (Philadelphia, 1842), pp. 278-86.

31. James L. Onderdonk, *History of American Verse (1610-1897)* (Chicago, 1901), pp. 145-46.

32. Washington Allston (1779-1843) was an American painter, whose work was highly regarded in England and America during his lifetime.

33. From the Preface to the Second Edition of William Wordsworth's poems; see *Poetical Works,* p. 740.

34. Ibid., pp. 734-35.

35. Alba H. Warren, Jr., *English Poetic Theory, 1825-1865* (New York, 1966), p. 7.

36. English critic, and founder and editor of the *Edinburgh Review.*

37. Rene Wellek, *The Romantic Age, A History of Modern Criticism: 1750-1950* II (New Haven, 1955), 114.

38. See Arnold Hauser, *The Social History of Art,* trans. Stanley Godman (New York, 1951), III, 65.

39. *The Snowstorm,* words by Seba Smith, music by Lyman Heath (Boston, 1843).

40. Thomas Hastings, *Dissertation on Musical Taste* (New York, 1853), pp. 108, 115. The term "natural," as used by several contemporary writers on the parlor song, seems to refer to what they called the "instinctive" and "real" emotions, having no hint of affectation, and common to all mankind.

41. While the singing of such songs might have required more than ordinary ability, it is worth noting that the comparatively difficult Russell works are frequently met with in private collections from before 1860. For performance, they were probably simplified by the less proficient performers; see Root, p. 18.

42. *The Arethusa,* "Sung by Mr. Story at the Federal Street Theatre in the Lock and Key with the greatest applause" (Boston, ca. 1800).

43. Donald O'Sullivan, in *Carolan,* II (London, 1958), 52-53, attributes the tune to Carolan, the early eighteenth-century Irish harper-composer, and cites as the earliest extant source, Walsh's *Compleat Country Dancing Master* (ca. 1730). The tune may also be found in Edward Bunting, *A Collection of the Ancient Music of Ireland* (Dublin, 1840), p. 35.

44. *Let Me Kiss Him for His Mother,* song and chorus, words and music by John P. Ordway (Boston, 1859). Note that this "song and chorus," a designation often appearing on the title-pages of American songs of the fifties, is called a "Ballad" in the description of the incident. The incident may have actually occurred, or may have been invented, in whole or in part, by Ordway to help popularize the song.

45. Ibid., stanza 2 and the "chorus" refrain.

46. Concerning the several theories and problems of poetic criticism, see Laurence D. Lerner and Brewster Rogerson in *The Princeton Encyclopedia* s.v. "Criticism."

47. See the Musical Supplement for a representative collection of the most

popular parlor songs.

48. For an examination of these problems, see Fred Lewis Pattee, *The Feminine Fifties* (Port Washington, 1966), pp. 4-16; also Charvat, pp. 49-50.

49. Pattee, p. 308; Wilma Clark, "Four Popular Poets," *New Dimensions in Popular Culture,* ed. Russell B. Nye (Bowling Green, 1972), p. 193; and Ann Douglas Wood, "Mrs. Sigourney and the Sensibility of Inner Space," *New England Quarterly,* XLV (1972), 177.

50. This kind of relationship is discussed in Robin M. Williams, Jr., *American Society,* rev. ed. (New York, 1960), p. 81.

51. See Tocqueville, II, 208; Onderdonk, pp. 157-58.

52. A conclusion also reached by Pattee, pp. 53-54, and Tocqueville, II, 210-211.

53. Root, p. 83. For a report on the failure of German songs to gain a following in America, see the New York *Musical Review,* 17 April 1858, p. 117.

54. Root, p. 97.

55. Root, pp. 19-20, 95-96; also, the New York *Musical Review,* 16 February 1854, pp. 57-58.

Chapter 8

Musical Characteristics of Parlor Songs

The parlor compositions enjoyed by Americans in the seventy years between 1790 and 1860 occupy a vast middle ground of solo song, from the utterly naive to the highly sophisticated. While none reflect the vulgarity of many minstrel pieces, neither do they attempt the kind of artistry present in the *Lieder* of composers like Schubert and Schumann. Any subtle probing of an individualized experience is absent. The impression that music for singer and pianist constitute an inseparable partnership, with each a vital contributor to the understanding of the whole, is lacking.

One must admit that the qualities that distinguish the art song were considered neither important nor desirable in the parlor songs. But care must be taken not to criticize parlor music for not becoming what it was never intended to be. As with the subject matter of the lyric, the music exhibits recurring and widely accepted procedures which, though they dilute originality, do contribute to ready understanding. And the swift comprehension of message and music was a great desideratum behind the creation of parlor songs.

As steps to understanding, the commonplaces in parlor melodies are examined first; then the elements of melody, harmony, and rhythm, and the approach to the setting of the lyrics in both simple and complex works; finally, the characteristics shared by most parlor songs.

The Melodic Commonplaces

After George Root had achieved stature as a composer of parlor songs, well-meaning friends advised him to direct his high creative abilities toward producing a better sort of music, advice that Stephen Foster had also received. Root replied that few Americans wished to have "songs of a higher grade," and those that did could easily find them among the works of foreign composers. He himself refused to become the composer for an American minority. Instead, he ardently desired to touch the feelings of the "tens of thousands of people whose wants would not be supplied at all if there were in the world only such music as they (the critics) would have."

Furthermore, for him to write a fine "People's song" was more difficult than a more artistic one, "where the resources are greater; where I did not have to stop and say, 'That interval is too difficult,' or 'That chord won't do'."

Granted, to write down a simple song correctly is easy, Root continues, "but so to use the materials of which such a song must be made" in a manner to have a wide appeal "is quite another matter."[1] Root's conviction was that in the entire world, composers like Beethoven, who can "invent. . .new forms and harmonies *that live*" are rare. Most composers recognized as great—Mendelssohn, for one—employ "existing materials in such new and wonderful ways that their music. . .is regarded in an important sense as original."[2] The best American song composers belong in this second category, he concludes.

Root also tried to define originality in the world of popular song. An article in the New York *Musical Review* contains his claim that popular composers store their minds with a large variety of musical forms, tonal combinations, and effects that seem beautiful or striking. Often they do so involuntarily and unconsciously, the source forgotten. The stored information is the composer's "reservoir," from which he may draw at any time. When setting a text, the composer attempts to arrive at the musical shape most suitable for the emotion to be expressed. The form may impress the listener as new, Root writes, but it probably derives from another source. Nevertheless, derived ideas can be given a treatment that seems original. According to Root, one must keep in mind that in evaluating popular works, originality frequently means the sources for melodies are undiscovered.[3]

Root's explanation of the popular composer's "reservoir" helps clarify what puzzled the author of an article on "Musical Drama," printed in the Boston *Euterpeiad*. The writer describes the songs of Henry Bishop as "very singular," because they seem so familiar to the listener. He fails, however, to explain this familiarity when he studies the music. This "impression," the writer says, means Bishop's combination of notes is expressive, for he employs only "the most impressive parts of musical phrases, while, at the same time, it shows his power to multiply, and essentially diversify melody by the conjunction of short, yet striking combinations."[4]

This explanation of the familiarity is unsatisfactory. One turns to the music for clarification.

The melodies do sound as if related. Similar melodic phrases appear in diverse tunes. It took an inspired anthologist consciously or unconsciously to select and then recombine common melodic elements into a new unity called a parlor song, adding enough of a personal touch to convince song lovers of the work's uniqueness. Whether the result was truly new, that is to say something novel presented for the first time, concerned neither the creator nor the listener. Such a consideration had little significance for either.

In the following discussion of the prevailing commonplaces of popular-song melody from all three periods, the opening phrase receives the greatest attention because it dominates the melody and appears at least three times in most songs, closing normally on 2 of the scale in its first, and on 1 of the scale in each later, appearance. Phrases different melodically from the first are heard only once, possibly twice. Typical melodic-phrase forms are A A^1 B A^1 (**Flow Gently, Sweet Afton*) and A A^1 A A^1 B A^1 (*Old Folks at Home).* In most instances the A^1 indicates a slight variation in the phrase's ending in order to permit the passage to close on a perfect, where previously it had closed on a half, cadence.

Half the melodic phrases of the most popular parlor pieces assume one of six shapes. These six common patterns should be understood to indicate general correspondences in the structure of stressed notes, rather than a particularly close relationship between melodies.

By far the greatest number of melodies begin on a stressed 5 of the scale, sometimes preceded by an upbeat on 1 or 3-4. The phrase then rises to a stressed 8 and returns to 5, as in S.M. Grannis' *Do They Miss Me at Home?* (Boston, 1852), which begins as in Example 1. A similar pattern appears in John Fletcher's *When I Saw Sweet Nellie Home* (New York, 1859):

Rhythm:

Scale notes: 3 4 5 5 4 5 6 5 5 8 8 8 8 7 6 8 5

In both songs the phrase closes on 5.

A variation on this pattern occurs in Foster's *Massa's in de Cold Ground* (New York, 1852), where the stressed tone pattern is 5-8-6-5-3-2 (Example 2). In the Grannis and Foster examples the most important tone in the first measure is 5; in the second, 8. Then Grannis' phrase skips down to 5 and moves to 6, where Foster's skips down to 6 and moves to 5. Both procedures are equally favored in phrase patterns of this type. The high incidence of similar melodic phrases may be owing to the ease with which the amateur singer can anticipate the curve of the structure and its sequence of sounds.

The second common phrase pattern also begins on a stressed 5. It then rises to 3 and returns to close on 5, as in E.A. Hosmer's *O Give Me a Home By the Sea* (Boston, 1853) and George N. Allen's *The Ocean Burial* (Boston, 1854). After stressing 5, the phrase at times may close on 2 or 1. This close is found in J.P. Knight's *Rocked in the Cradle of the Deep* (New York, 1840) and G.F. Cole's *O'er the Far Blue Mountain* (Baltimore, 1833). A quotation from the latter is given in Example 3. One curious coincidence should be noticed. In the first three examples of the second phrase pattern, the sea or ocean is referred to in the text. Possibly the wider curve, from 5 up to a sixth to 3, then back again, suggested an ocean swell or, in the case of the Cole song, the upward thrust of a mountain.

The third pattern, illustrated in Foster's *The Voice of By Gone Days* (New York, 1850), begins on 3, rises to 5, then descends to 2 or 1 (Example 4). The melodic curve is gentler, less dynamic though more lyrical, than in the previous patterns. The opening on 3 seems softer and tonally more ambiguous than on 5. Other instances of this pattern are found in Isaac B. Woodbury's *He Doeth All Things Well* (Boston, 1844), Thomas Comer's *Alone, Alone* (Boston, 1847) and Sidney Nelson's *The Bride* (Philadelphia, ca. 1830).

The fourth pattern also begins on 3. But it then rises to 4, returns to 3, and eventually closes on 2 or 1, as in Henry Russell's *The Old Arm Chair* (Boston, 1840), which begins as in Example 5. John Ordway's *Let Me Kiss Him for His Mother* (Boston, 1859) and N.P.B. Curtis' *The Gold Digger's Grave* (Boston, 1850) also share this pattern. Certainly this least dynamic and potentially most monotonous of all the six patterns is well suited to the depiction of death or the aftermath of death, the theme in all three songs.

The fifth pattern, seen in William Dempster's *The Blind Boy* (Boston, 1842), is another that starts on 3. For the first time in any of the patterns, however, rather than rising, the melody descends to 1 before moving to 5 (Example 6). In some other songs of this type, after touching on 1 the phrase descends to the 5 below, as it does in L.V.H. Crosby's *Kitty Clyde* (New York, 1853). Still other songs, after they have reached 1 and moved to 5 make their close on 1 or 2. The melodies in Sidney Nelson's *The Rose of Allendale* (New York, ca. 1830) and William Wetmore's *The Cot Beneath the Hill* (New York, 1841) proceed in this fashion.

The sixth type commences on an upbeat, stresses 1, rises to 3, then either descends or ascends to a 5, often touching on 6 before or after the 5. This pattern is exemplified in William Wallace's *The Bell Ringer* (Boston, 1859). The melodic phrase winding around the tonic note, seen in Example 7, is typical of the pattern. For other instances, see Stephen Glover's *A Home that I Love* (New York, ca. 1845), and *Annie O' the Banks O' Dee* (Boston, ca. 1845), as well as *The Green Cymar* (Boston, ca. 1822), by an unidentified amateur.

To be noticed in most of the examples is a tone that is repeated several times in succession at or soon after the opening of the phrase. Next, most show a rise to 8 or 5, then a return to the starting note. Five out of seven feature a wide upward skip. On the other hand, downward movement tends to be stepwise or through skips of a third. These shared characteristics do make parlor songs sound "familiar." Yet the auditor may find himself unable to account for the familiarity by tracing it "through any succession of notes," as the *Euterpeiad* writer observes.

If one of the melodic phrases already quoted, say that of *Massa's in de Cold Ground* (Example 2), is taken as a starting point, then further melodic commonplaces are easily found. These are not necessarily similarities limited to sounds from one phrase pattern. As might be expected, several Foster compositions reveal a melodic kinship to Example 2. For instance, though *Old Folks at Home* commences on 3 of the scale, it also descends to 1, leaps upward to 8, touches on 6, then descends through the tonic triad 5-3-1 and swings back to close on 2 (Example 8). Two other Foster pieces featuring the striking octave leap, 1-8, and the descent through 6 to 5 are *Farewell, My Lilly Dear* (New York, 1851) and *The Village Maiden* (New York, 1855), whose openings are reproduced in Examples 9 and 10 respectively.

These Foster tunes also resemble the melody of Lady John Scott's *Annie Lawrie* (Boston, n.d.), a composition which first appeared in the late thirties. Prominent in *Annie Lawrie* is the same jump, 1-8 (Example 11). It would be a mistake to assume that Foster necessarily imitated the Scott tune. The sudden ascent to 8 and descent 7-6 of Examples 10 and 11 are characteristic of several parlor-song melodies. *No More,* music "by a young Lady of Georgia" and published in Philadelphia in 1836, a little before *Annie Lawrie's* first appearance in England, also has the skip up to 8, followed by the 7-6 return (Example 12). The same procedure occurs in Samuel Lover's *My Mother Dear* (Boston, 1845), whose opening (Example 13) closely resembles that of *Annie Lawrie.*[5]

One safely concludes that the composers who wrote songs with so many melodic correspondences shared a familiarity with a large body of traditional airs of British origin: English, Welsh, Scottish and Irish. After all, such tunes were the cultural heritage of both British and American composers. On both sides of the Atlantic, these melodies could be heard as part of an aural tradition. They also were readily available to anyone able to afford the purchase price of one of the many published collections of national songs. Even more affordable were the ubiquitous sheet-music issues of national airs and the many cheap songbooks that borrowed liberally from traditional sources.

The question arises whether any of the melodic commonplaces are ascribable to any one of the national musics from the British Isles. After long study and consideration, one must state that so many of the tunes traveled freely from one area to another and became inextricably mingled with each other that it would be hazardous indeed to speak of specifically Irish or Scottish traits, say, in the songs. Moreover, what seems Irish may also appear in the melodies of some Italian songs—an observation made by a few contemporary writers on music.

To elaborate, it is true that Scottish and Irish airs are sometimes structured on gapped scales, the fourth and seventh missing usually. A fondness for skipping from 1 to 6 below and back is a feature of many airs. Some Irish songs exhibit a lowered seventh tone above the tonic and a raised seventh below it. Irish melodies also may start and end on a high note, while Scottish airs may leap about incessantly. Swift ascents and slower downward movements are frequent. On the other hand, English melody is more disciplined and influenced by cultivated musical practices. All seven tones of the scale are present in the melody. The melodic skeleton, however, may outline a pentatonic scale.

As for American tunes, they may exhibit any of the characteristics just enumerated. Furthermore, with Period III and its "music for the millions" concept, deliberate simplification produced an increase in gapped scales and melodic shapes that resembled the traditional airs of the British Isles, rather than the current practices of most English composers. Whether the resemblance of American song to specifically Irish or Scottish musical styles is owing to the simplification process guided by the unconscious influence of a common cultural heritage, or to a conscious modeling of tunes after Irish or Scottish originals is a question hazardous to answer.

Undoubtedly the felt need for uncomplicated music coupled with a cultural memory impressed with the sound of traditional melody must be signalled out. In addition, many American composers did envy the popularity of Burns' Scottish airs and Moore's Irish melodies. They might have followed the melodic procedures of favorite songs like *Auld Lang Syne* and *'Tis the Last Rose of Summer*. Composers, of course, also knew well the previous productions of other parlor-song fabricators and the works from continental Europe that had caught the public fancy. The music of

Pleyel, Rossini, Auber, Donizetti and Bellini was often adapted to fit English texts and also became part of the popular musical literature of America. These French and Italian melodies in their adapted forms were additional models followed by American composers (and British composers, as well). Therefore, one must conclude that traditional airs, older composed songs, and all other music from whatever source that was popular with the masses formed a large part of the "reservoir" into which all the composers dipped. Because of their shared musical background and common approach to writing music, the parlor-song composers would inevitably have composed pieces demonstrating some sort of relationship to one another. If one takes as a starting point the opening of Foster's *Voice of By Gone Days* (Example 4), the kinship to a host of other songs is easily demonstrated. Isaac B. Woodbury's *He Doeth All Things Well* (Boston, 1844), for instance, also includes the repeated 3s. It then skips up to 6, turns back on 5, and descends to 1 of the second measure, before finally closing on 2 (Example 14).Another composition, Charles Horn's *The American Indian Girl* (New York, 1835), starts on a 5 to 3 skip and, like Foster's melody, moves 3-6-5 after the barline, then 5-4-3 before closing on 2. Unlike Foster's tune, here the 1 is touched upon in the first measure, 8 in the third, and 1 at the close as a raised auxiliary note moving to 2 (Example 15). A third song, J.P. Carter's *I See Her at The Window* (New York, 1848), like Foster's tune goes from 3 to 5 to 1 and closes on 2; but like Horn's tune, after 5 and before descending to 1, it rises to 8 (Example 16). A final citation, Peter A. von Hagen's *Anna* (Boston, ca. 1802), has a melody similar to Horn's. It moves from 3 down to 1 after the upbeat, then rises to a stressed 5; it next closes on 2 by way of 4-3 (Example 17).[6]

When the melody used for comparison comes from a composition once extremely popular, then most similar melodies are found to be from later creations and composed by musicians who must have felt its influence. Two such popular and influential songs were Oliver Shaw's **Mary's Tears,*[7], first published in 1817, and Henry Bishop's *Home! Sweet Home!,*[8] first issued in America in the early twenties.

Other significant points of similarity between parlor songs are the shared melodic motives of three to nine notes occurring anywhere in a phrase. A common motive, the sound sequence of 5-10-9-8-7-6-5, or its variant 5-10-9-8-7-6-8-5, can usually be encountered in the forms illustrated by Examples 18 a-f. All quotations are given in the key of C to facilitate comparison. Some tunes reproduce only a part of this sequence—as in Examples 19 a-c, where only the beginning, 5-10-9-8, appears.

Although correspondences between melodic phrases and between motives are readily discovered, similarities encompassing more than one phrase are another matter. One occasionally discovers two songs with so much in common that one suspects the later work was modeled on the earlier. For example, the favorite Scottish air **Auld Lang Syne,* first published by George Thomson in *A Select Collection of Original Scotish Airs* (London, 1798), was reprinted in the United States just at the turn of the century. Its tune, an anonymous one, had appeared in several publications prior to Thomson's.[9] About 1805 James Hewitt wrote and published his *Advice to Ladies,* in New York. The Hewitt tune closely resembles that of *Auld Lang Syne.* Example 20 reproduces the two melodies, with the latter transposed from the key of F to A, for the sake of comparison. The tunes differ in meter and have no correspondences in measures three to five, seven and fifteen. *Advice* has a heptatonic, *Auld* a pentatonic, tune. Nevertheless, both employ the same melodic curves, pause in identical places, and display quite similar melodies. Additional similarities appear when the harmonies of the two songs are compared:

Advice:	I	II V	I	I	I	II V	I^6 IV	I	I	V
Auld:	I		I	IV	I^6 V^{09} of V	V^7	IV	I	I	V^7

Advice:	I	IV	I^6	II V	I^6 IV	I
Auld:	I	IV	I^6 IV^6	V^7	IV	I

Most measures contain identical harmonies, or at least one harmony in common.

Though two tunes may sound similar, an explanation for the resemblance often is difficult to give. Such is the case with John Barton's *The Irish Mother's Lament* (New York, ca. 1840) and "J.K.'s" *The Yellow Rose of Texas* (New York, 1858), as can be seen in Examples 21 a-b. Admittedly, their harmonic schemes are unalike:

Irish:	I	IV I	I V^7 of IV IV	V^7 I	IV V^4_3 of V	V	I
Yellow:	I	I I V^7	V^7 I	I	V^2 I II^6	I^6_4 V	I

Yet, their rhythmic structures are somewhat the same:

After the first two measures, several melodic correspondences are found (Example 22). Unfortunately, the question of whether "J.K." knew the Barton piece can probably never be answered. Besides, from the standpoint of the popular-song world, it is irrelevant.

In conclusion, one cannot say any two tunes are exactly alike. Nevertheless many share similar melodic curves, tone progressions and rhythmic patterns. If Foster's *Willie, We Have Missed You* resembles *Jock O'Hazledean;* the same composer's *Old Black Joe,* John Barnett's *The Spot Where I Was Born;* George Root's *There's Music in the Air,* Henry Bishop's *I'm Saddest When I Sing;* and John Hewitt's *The Minstrel's Return,* John Braham's *The Death of Nelson*—none are necessarily a conscious copy of the other. To be kept in mind is Root's statement that derived ideas can receive a seemingly original treatment, and that the composer draws his melody from a common reservoir of tunes.

The creators of the parlor songs enjoyed by cultured Americans did not venture into unknown musical territories. Both the tunes and words of their songs, however beautiful the sound and moving the text, were composed of shared elements. A poem that reasserted and confirmed communal values was united to a tune that sounded familiar and was easily assimilable. The result was a "people's song" that all could enjoy.

The Simple Type of Parlor Song

Unpretentious strophic songs having attractive melodies and making modest technical demands of the amateur predominate among the parlor compositions. The following songs of the plainest construction, reproduced in the Musical Supplement in their entirety, are listed here by period and title. The simplest among them are indicated by three asterisks after the title.

Period I.

British: *Auld Lang Syne*
Auld Robin Gray
*The Bay of Biscay O!****

American: none

Period II.

British: *Long, Long Ago!****
American: *Flow Gently, Sweet Afton****

Period III.

British: none
American: *The Blue Juniata****
*The Hazel Dell****
*Rosalie, the Prairie Flower****

No American compositions from Period I are given since few were written and none gained a following of any importance. In Period III, the more popular British songs in America were not usually of the simple variety. On the other hand, numerous American composers tried writing pieces that made modest demands on performers.

One striking characteristic of the songs in the Musical Supplement, particularly the simplest ones, is the paucity, if not downright absence, of dynamic and other marks of expression. **How Happy Was My Humble Lot* (New York, ca. 1799), by James Hewitt, a British composer who emigrated to America in 1792, has only one dynamic mark, a single *mp* at the beginning of the keyboard prelude. **Long, Long Ago!,* by the British poet and song composer Thomas Haynes Bayly (first published in London about 1835, then in New York about 1839), has a *"dolce"* in the prelude, a *p* in the keyboard part at the vocalist's entry, and an *mf* in the postlude. Two American compositions, Marion Dix Sullivan's **The Blue Juniata* (Boston, 1844) and George Root's **The Hazel Dell* (New York, 1853),[10] contain no dynamics at all.

In contrast, other forms of music, including many published before the turn of the century, contained much wider use of dynamics. In eighteenth-century London, terraced and graded dynamics were already in use in compositions by Johann Christian Bach.[11] James Hewitt, Benjamin Carr and other composers active in the United States during Period I who use no dynamics in a great many of their simple parlor pieces do include them in other works.[12]

One possible explanation for the minimal employment of dynamics and other expressive indications is the composer's and publisher's decision that the text was sufficient guide for the singer. The singer freely added his own expression so long as it was consistent with a song's sentiment.[13] The vocalist is expected to study every sentence of the text to determine the appropriate interpretation, even if this means altering the published directions, if any.[14] Concurring in this opinion were two well-known singing teachers, Joseph and Horace Bird. They published an instruction book in 1852 that contains many parlor songs with all expression marks omitted; their explanation: "We think the words are in most cases the best guides to expression."[15]

While the singer is expected to rely on the text for appropriate expression, the pianist, having no text to guide him, is presumed to require the aid of printed expression marks.[16] This is a probable explanation for the practices with regard to expressive symbols seen in the sheet music sent to the Boston *Euterpiad*'s subscribers from 1820 to 1823. The subscribers received parlor songs usually with no printed signs, solo piano compositions with many signs.[17] In quite a few songs, among them Hewitt's **How Happy Was My Humble Lot* and Thompson's *Lilly Dale* (Boston, 1852), dynamics occur in the keyboard preludes and postludes, not in sections where the vocalist sings.

One must also conjecture that composers, arrangers, and publishers thought a large number of amateurs neither needed nor used expression marks. In the several hundred private music collections this author has examined, pencilled-in solfeggio symbols, piano fingerings, breath marks, etc., are frequent, but rarely an *f* or *p*. Dynamics are also missing from most songbooks meant for amateurs. For example, the *Boston Musical Miscellany* leaves out all dynamic and tempo indications in both the 1811 edition and the greatly expanded 1815 edition. Likewise, the sheet-music versions of most compositions quoted in the songbook lack dynamics. Nevertheless, several songbooks omitting all expressive indications do contain works whose sheet-music versions have expression marks. To give one instance, *The Gem of Song* (Boston, 1846), pp. 50-51, reproduces J.P. Knight's *She Wore a Wreath of Roses* with no symbols of expression. But the original sheet-music issue does have those signs, several of them assigned to the vocal part. The superfluousness of such markings for America's non-professional singers was certainly a persuasive argument for dispensing with the signs in music intended solely for amateurs.

A knowledge of dynamics was widespread among Period III

singing masters. Yet, knowledgeable musicians like Benjamin F. Baker and George Root neglected printing these signs in their publications. Baker's *The American School Music Book* (Boston, 1845) contains mostly parlor pieces. Baker briefly describes the meaning and use of *f, p, crescendo,* etc. (pp. 37-38); he excludes these signs from the musical selections, sacred and secular.

A great many such publications are teachers' manuals and not intended for students. The teacher copied the music from these manuals onto a blackboard; the students, from the blackboard into their music notebooks.[18] Whether the teacher had his class copy down and learn his recommendations on expression is unclear. Since so many students rarely learned to read music at all, instead learning the music to songs by rote, signs of expression are unnecessary.[19]

Chromatically altered notes are also scarce in simple parlor songs. In so many pieces, one senses the composer's attempt to link his music with those traditional airs, already familiar to Americans, which eschew even a passing accidental in the melody. "Music for the millions" meant, too, the avoidance of the confusions produced in the inexperienced singer by the introduction of sharps, flats and naturals. Half-trained composers like Thomas Haynes Bayly and Marion Dix Sullivan might unconsciously have neglected to utilize chromatics; but assuredly the musically sophisticated George Root deliberately chose to avoid them. In any case, favorite compositions are often entirely diatonic. Examples are **Long, Long Ago, *The Blue Juniata* and **The Hazel Dell.* Hewitt's **How Happy Was My Humble Lot* modulates into the key of the dominant for four measures; the raised fourth tone occurs twice in the melody, at measures 14-15. Otherwise, this work is diatonic. Like the Hewitt song, uncomplicated pieces introducing chromatic alterations in the melody do so only once or twice, and normally as a raised fourth degree over a V of V harmony.

One or two simple compositions inexplicably introduce complications for a few measures, as in William Leeve's **Auld Robin Gray* (New York, ca. 1798). Measures 13-16 replace the major mode with the tonic minor, and the tune features the lowered third degree of the scale. Also out of the ordinary is the chromatic progress from the second to the fifth scale degree in measure 15. In other respects, the song contains nothing difficult to sing.

Already noted was the chromatic alteration that normally takes the shape of the raised fourth rising to the fifth, as in measure 31 of **Flow Gently Sweet Afton.* On occasion a melody may descend chromatically 5-4+-4-3, as in measure 15 of Blockley's **Love Not!* The harmonic progression under the 4+-4 is V^7 of V to V^7.

Approximately one fifth of the parlor songs are completely or almost completely diatonic. One-half have no chromatic changes in the vocal melody, even while they are introduced into the keyboard part below. This is Woodbury's practice in **Be Kind to the Loved Ones at Home*.

Customarily the composer confines most chromatic alterations to the keyboard prelude and postlude. Thus, Lady Scott's *Annie Lawrie* has a V of V harmony in measure 3 and a V° of V in measure 6 of the prelude. The postlude's bass contains two chromatically raised neighboring tones. The rest of the song is bare of chromatics. To give an illustration from the Musical Supplement, in measure 6 of the keyboard prelude to **Near the Lake Where Droop'd the Willow,* Horn writes the harmonies V° of VI-V° of II-II^6—an unusual passage for a simple song. The same harmonies return in the postlude at measure 30. The rest of the song employs only tonic, dominant and subdominant harmonies, the only exception being one V° of V with chromatic alteration confined to the piano part.[20]

To sum up, most simple songs that contain chromatic alterations employ the raised fourth degree as part of V of V. Less often there is the raised fifth of V of VI and the lowered seventh of V^7 of IV. Rarer is the introduction of a chromatically altered nonharmonic tone in the melody.

As might be expected, the prevailing diatonicism is joined to a firm tonal design. Clarity in melody goes hand-in-hand with clarity in key. The amateur never flounders in a sea of tonal ambiguity and perplexing harmonies. The usual harmonic passage begins on I and closes on V or I. As a result, the performer finds few measures whose harmonic progressions he cannot foresee. The musical design is easily recognized; the chordal structure, clearly articulated. Tonic, dominant, and subdominant harmonies predominate. Sometimes heard is the dominant of a closely related key (V of V, V of IV). An analysis of the occurrence of harmonies found in four of the simple songs provides the following information:

A. Hewitt, **How Happy Was My Humble Lot*
I: 45% V: 25% IV: 15% II: 10% V of V: 5%

B. Bayly, **Long, Long Ago!*
I: 70% V: 30%

C. Sullivan, **The Blue Juniata*
I: 75% V: 20% IV: 5%

D. Root, **The Hazel Dell*
I: 55% V: 20% IV: 25%

A summary of the harmonies employed in the simple songs that were examined shows the following—I: 55%, V: 25%, IV: 15%, II: 3%, other: 2%.

One consideration is vital to the understanding of the composer's intent: the drastic limitation in harmonic variety, the adherence to a tonality's primary chords, and the utilization of familiar melodic patterns were not the result of incapability or paucity of creative invention. Rather, these were ways of setting forth musical ideas to achieve maximum recognition and immediate understanding. In the parlor-song composer's mind took place a refining process which in traditional music might require an aural transmission through several generations of performers. The end result, after all superfluities were removed, was a song of plainest construction. Such a composition also might exhibit the same virtues that make folk song attractive.

Most musical phrases are four measures, some two measures, long. While potentially boring to the sophisticated listener, the phrase structure's regularity was an additional aid to the inexperienced listener's understanding. All phrases in **The Blue Juniata* and **The Hazel Dell* are four measures long. **Long, Long Ago* is mostly in four-measure divisions; measures 13-16 have two two-measure phrases. In **How Happy Was My Humble Lot,* phrases subdivide into distinct two-measure half phrases.

Each phrase ends on a cadence on the dominant or tonic triad usually, on the subdominant occasionally. Chiefly the Scottish-type ballads, such as *Within a Mile of Edinburg* and **Auld Lang Syne* favor the endings on the subdominant. These ballads can be denominated as pseudo-folk songs written for publication and intended to please a genteel class.[21] The words of the latter song, for instance, are "amplifications" by Robert Burns of an old Scottish text; the melody is an adaptation of a traditional Scottish air, "The Miller's Wedding." The new words and melody were fitted together and the music harmonized for publication in *A Select Collection of Original Scotish Airs* (London, ca. 1798).[22] In measures 12 and 20, **Auld Lang Syne*'s melody makes a half close on the sixth degree; in measures 15-16 and 23-24, it makes a full close by moving from the first down to the sixth, to the fifth, and then up to the first degree. In these measures, as in many other Scottish-type airs featuring it, the tone on the sixth degree acts like a functional dominant.[23]

Throughout the eighteenth century, harmonizing melodies that made the sixth degree prominent in this fashion was a problem for arrangers and publishers. In **Auld Lang Syne,* the tone is harmonized with the subdominant triad, a solution already arrived at in William Thomson's *Orpheus Caledonius,* 2nd edition (London,

1733).[24]

Normally, phrases are treated in pairs, as antecedent and consequent in an eight-measure strain. The strain almost invariably closes on the tonic, with the melody lighting on the scale's first degree. Over half the simple compositions are in two, the remainder in three, strains. Songs hardly ever extend longer than three strains, possibly out of consideration for the amateur's and listener's limited span of attention and inability to cope with music of any great length in one composition.

These uncomplicated melodies almost sing themselves. Difficult skips (augmented fourths, major sevenths and the like) are seldom encountered. Tunes proceed mostly by conjunct motion, less by skips of a third (usually through the first, third and fifth degree) or by note repetition, and least by leaps wider than a sixth.[25] Some tunes move mostly by conjunct motion, as in **Long, Long Ago!;* others by a combination of conjunct motion and repetition, as in Russell's *The Old Arm Chair* (Boston, 1840); and still others by small skips, as in **The Blue Juniata*. Phrases may commence with several small skips or one wide leap upward and end with conjunct movement downward, a feature of **The Bay of Biscay O!*; or begin with conjunct motion, then resort to small skips, seen in **Hours There Were*. The options are many; no one procedure emerges as most favored.

At least half the tunes utilize all seven tones of the major scale (see **How Happy Was My Humble Lot*). The rest are based on gapped scales. To give some instances, **Long Long Ago!* lacks the seventh; **The Blue Juniata,* the fourth. Although all seven scale-degrees are present in **Hazel Dell*'s melody, the seventh is unstressed and treated as a passing tone on the last eighth note of the measure. Several of the most popular tunes, those of **Auld Lang Syne* and Foster's *Nelly Was a Lady* among them, lack the fourth and seventh degree. A few songs, two of them Heath's *The Snow Storm* (Boston, 1843) and Woodbury's *Where is Peace* (New York, 1848), leave out the sixth and seventh degree. Once in a while a piece lacks the sixth, as in Elam Ives' *Come Take Our Boy* (Philadelphia, 1833). No matter what tones are omitted in the melody, all seven are always introduced into the keyboard harmony, where they are needed to define the tonality.

The tunes are mostly in simple duple time and show a unifying rhythmic pattern. For example, four out of the six phases in **The Hazel Dell* have the rhythm:

All four phrases of **The Blue Juniata* begin with

: the first phrase closes with and the rest with .

**How Happy Was My Humble Lot* is unusual in that it has a brief rhythmic pattern that permeates almost every measure:

.

Rarely do melodies neglect to establish a unifying rhythm at the beginning. One song failing to do so is Blockley's **Love Not*!, whose first three phrases have the following rhythms:

Only phrase four and five share a common pattern; they are set to the same line of text:

Immediate repetition of the initial four-measure melodic-rhythmic phrase is common to about two-thirds of the plainer songs. Some compositions have an exact repetition, as in **The Bay of Biscay O!*, whose phrase pattern is A A B C. Other pieces have a somewhat inexact repetition; *Annie Lawrie's* is A A^1 B C. In half the songs that repeat their initial phrase, the first phrase normally ends on the second degree of the scale over a dominant harmony; the second on the first degree over a tonic harmony.

Most tunes that immediately repeat the initial phrase are found to do so again at the song's conclusion, as in Moore's *'Tis the Last Rose of Summer* and *Bayly's *Long, Long Ago*! Both pieces employ the popular A A B A phrase form. When the first two phrases are similar but differ in their endings, it is the music of phrase two that recurs at the close. For example. **Be Kind to the Loved Ones at Home* has four phrases:

Phrase:	A	A^1	B	A^1
Half Phrase:	a b	a c	d e	a c

Each lower-case letter represents two measures of music. The first and third phrases end on the dominant with the melody on the second degree; the second and fourth on the tonic, melody on the first degree.

In some melodies of this type that Americans wrote during Period III, a somewhat different form results. The first two phrases, which are similar to the Woodbury song in construction, are immediately repeated and the second phrase reappears at the song's end, as in **The Hazel Dell:*

Phrase:	A	A^1	A	A^1	B	A^1
Half Phrase:	a b	a c	a b	a c	de	a c

Only a few songs having little melodic repetition ever became popular. One of the exceptions, **Mary's Tears,* is almost entirely through-composed, save for a repetition in measure 19 of four notes heard in measures 16-17.

Tunes which repeat two different phrases are scarce. This kind of repetition occurs in Bishop's *The Mistletoe Bough* (A A B B C) and Wade's **Hours There Were* (A A^1 A A^1 B B^1 A A^1).

Turning next to an examination of the manner of setting texts to music, one finds two-thirds of the melodies composed to fit an eight-line, most of the remainder a twelve-line, stanza. The stanza's predominant rhyme scheme is like that of **The Blue Juniata,* a b c b d e f e, or of **The Hazel Dell,* a b a b c d c d (e f e f). Here, parentheses set off the refrain. Rhyme, of course, functions to link up couplets, quatrains and stanzas.[26] Individual schemes, like the a (b) a (b) c c c (b) of **Long, Long Ago*! are infrequent. Most stanzas are organized into couplets having eight, less seven, even less six, stresses—seen in **Long, Long Ago*!, **Hazel Dell,* and **Blue Juniata,* respectively.

Usually the lyric receives a syllabic setting, one note a syllable with verbal stress and musical accent coinciding. The composer takes care to make every word intelligible. Where the versifier indicates his thought is more or less complete by semicolon or period, normally at the end of the second couplet of each quatrain, the composer makes a full cadential close. The usual rhyme scheme of the stanza also shows this organization into quatrains.

The internal organization of the quatrain is furthered through the use of assonance and alliteration. Assonance refers to similar vowel sounds followed by different consonants; alliteration to identical consonant sounds in neighboring or closely associated words.[27] To give two examples from the Supplement, heard several times in the first quatrain of **Long, Long Ago*! are the *t* sounds in "tell"-"tales"-"to", and the *o* in "long."[28] The first quatrain of **Hazel Dell* exploits the repeated *eue* sounds "Hazel"-"Dell"-"Nelly's," the long *e* in "sleeping"-"keeping," and the *o* sound in "long"-"lost"-"gone."

Now and then the alliteration becomes obtrusive. If sung by a careless performer, the sibilants in the first quatrain of Foster's *Sweetly She Sleeps, My Alice Fair* (Baltimore, 1851) can annoy. The lyric was written by Charles G. Eastman:

> Sweetly she sleeps, my Alice fair,
> Her cheeks on the pillow pressed,
> Sweetly she sleeps, while her Saxon hair,
> Like sunlight, streams o'er her breast.

Refrains of one- to four-line length, normally heard at the end of a stanza, are common in simple British and American songs. The frequent occurrence of choral refrains, about three-quarters of them harmonized in four parts, is a stylistic feature of American compositions from the late forties on.

Choral endings to patriotic American songs had occurred in Period I but only occasionally. Most of these compositions, like *Arise, Arise, Columbia's Sons Arise* (Philadelphia, ca. 1805), end with a "Chorus" which states only one vocal part. Apparently all voices are to join in on the one melody. A few works, one of them *Freedom Triumphant* (Philadelphia, 1796), end each stanza with a harmonized "Chorus" that is not a refrain because the same music is repeated to different words. The non-refrain choral close here is for SATB chorus. The remaining songs like *Rise, Columbia!* (Boston, ca. 1798) do have a harmonized choral refrain.[29]

A scattering of non-patriotic songs also end with a chorus. One of these, Dr. Clarke's *Brignal Banks,* was published in Baltimore, around 1813, with a three-part choral refrain. In 1826 the song was reissued with a four-part refrain. Two other Period-II songs with choral refrains are Bartholomew Brown's *The Pilgrim Song* (Boston, 1821) and *The Archer's Song* (Boston, 1836). Both end on an SSB Chorus.

The practice of ending American songs on a harmonized choral refrain seems to have come into general use only with the minstrel compositions of the early forties—J.W. Turner's arrangement of *Charleston Gals* (Boston, 1844) and Cool White's arrangement of *Lubly Fan* (Boston, 1844) exhibit such refrains. In the thirties a handful of minstrel songs had appeared with an unharmonized "Chorus," as in *Long Time Ago,* "sung by Mr. T. Rice" (Baltimore, 1833). Once in a while a song appeared with a brief harmonized refrain. William Clifton's arrangement of *Long Time Ago* (New York, 1836) is of this type. Its three-part refrain on the words "Long time ago" is heard twice in each stanza.

With the late forties and early fifties, American parlor and minstrel pieces began to resemble each other more and more closely. After 1850 many minstrel songs have the smoother melodies, slower tempos and sentimental texts of parlor songs.[30] At the same time, many parlor songs have the final chorus, normally in four parts, associated with minstrel compositions. This kind of parlor work, called a "Song and Chorus" on the title page of the sheet music, was written by the most popular song composers in America.[31] As minstrel music aped the respectability of parlor works and minstrel men included unabashedly sentimental parlor songs in their shows, the bolder members of the middle class ventured to attend minstrel concerts and thus encouraged a further rapport between the two genres.[32]

We have already observed that keyboard accompaniments are easily executed and always subordinated to the vocal melody. In these accompaniments, a brief figure may be repeated for an entire phrase or strain, and sometimes for an entire song. This figure is written so that the player's hand position remains unchanged for several measures at a time, thus making it convenient for a singer to accompany himself. For example, the hand position in *Blue Juniata* remains the same from measure 9 to 24; in *Hazel Dell,* from measure 9 to the song's conclusion.

What keyboard solos there are occur in the prelude and postlude.

The former provides a short introduction to the vocal melody; the latter an even shorter conclusion to the song. The opening keyboard solo is four to eight measures long, closes on the tonic, and is either a replica of, or a variation on, the first phrase or two in the vocal melody. The concluding keyboard solo usually reproduces only the last half of the prelude's music.[33]

The Period-I compositions appeared during the years when *basso continuo* accompaniments and songs written on two staves were changing to more fully harmonized accompaniments and songs written on three staves. During the last half of the eighteenth century many important European composers, including C.P.E. Bach, Mozart and Haydn, were composing simple, two-stave strophic songs for which the accompanist was encouraged to add a fuller harmony of his own.[34] Haydn's first songs on three staves were the *Six Original Canzonettes,* set to English words and first published in London, in 1794.[35] Arthur Jacobs, English writer on music, claims these Haydn works were among the first such songs to English texts.[36] Nevertheless, in 1794 Benjamin Carr composed and published four songs in Philadelphia that were written on three staves: *When Icicles Hang By the Wall, Take, Oh! Take Those Lips Away, Tell Me Where is Fancy Bred,* and *When Nights Were Cold.* The first three have Shakespeare's words; the last, J.E. Harwood's.

The late eighteenth-century was also a time to be sure when accompaniments from a *basso continuo* became a skill few performers acquired. Daniel Gottlob Turk published one of the last of the century's treatises on the subject, *Kurze Anweisung zum Generalbassspielen,* in 1791. The preface states the realization of a *basso continuo* is an art in general neglect, most of its rules not practised or unknown.[37] Although Turk had the state of German music in mind, his statement was surely applicable to America. Regrettably, no writer in America mentioned a similar neglect among American performers, where almost all Period-I songs were published on two staves. A large majority of American amateurs, no doubt, performed the music as written, having neither the knowledge nor the technical capability of improvising a fuller harmony.

As the years go by one can trace the transition from *continuo* to written-out accompaniment in the sheet-music publications. Throughout the 1780s and 1790s, publishers issued two-stave songs most often as a single line of music on each staff, illustrated by the beginning of *Roslin Castle* (Example 23).[38] At the same time, another form of two-stave accompaniment was seen, one with the left-hand part moving faster than the right, and usually executing arpeggios of the Alberti type, as at the beginning of Benjamin Carr's

Ellen Arise (Example 24).[39] When in 6/8 time arpeggios normally proceed as in von Hagen's *May Morning* (Example 25).[40]

The attempt of composers to provide for the richer harmony that the usual player was unable to supply is evident. The problem also was to avoid the performing difficulties that would discourage players living in an America where competent keyboard instruction was unavailable or scarcely come by in most communities. These left-hand arpeggios do produce a more complete sound, simulate a faster forward movment and make few technical demands.

After 1795 composers occasionally wrote a filled-out treble part, as in Dibdin's *Lovely Nan.*[41] Example 26 reproduces the song's beginning; the small notes are as they appear in the original sheet music. Passages in small notes do not seem intended for keyboard performers. In the example, the middle part awkwardly crosses the bass line (measures 2-3) and is separated from the melody by more than an octave in measure 3. Later, in measure 7, the middle part moves to a *b* natural, a tenth away from the *G* of the bass and from the *d′* of the treble. Although another instrument might have played the small-note line or the line might have been intended to clarify the chords so that the keyboardist could more easily realize the harmonies, in all probability it was an optional part for voice, permitting the song's performance as a vocal duet if desired. Most such middle parts remain completely within one of the ranges of the voice.

The two-stave piece with added notes in each part (Example 27)[42] is extremely rare. In such formats the music might have proved a little confusing for the singer, who continuously had to disentangle the vocal melody from the rest of the music as he performed.

After 1800 more and more songs appeared with an independent treble part for the keyboard. By this date, the number of capable keyboard teachers was augmented daily by new arrivals from Europe. Moreover, the importation and domestic manufacture of pianos was increasing. More Americans had the money to purchase instruments and pay for instruction, and the time to practice an hour or so each day. Amateurs did acquire the modest increase in keyboard facility demanded by the new kind of accompaniment. At first this innovation was treated with caution by composers and arrangers. Thus, Carr's Journal (1800) contains *The Blue Bells of Scotland* in a two-stave version. Immediately following is the same song on three staves, the vocal part different and separate from the keyboard treble part. On the first page of the second version is printed above the music: "N.B.: the superior effect that will be produced by those who can sing one part and play the other as here adapted; [sic] will make an apology unnecessary for the reinserting it in this form."[43]

Amateurs did improve in playing ability. Certainly the piano pieces are more difficult in the later years than in the earlier. Singers, too, began to prefer the added fullness in the accompaniments in the three-stave songs. The dawning of the era of Romanticism, now being experienced in America, induced a craving for the greater richness in sound that the piano could provide. The thin tinkle of the two-stave songs with harpsichord accompaniment was no longer desired. Within the first decade after 1800 most published parlor songs were on three staves. About the time Carr printed the two versions of *The Blue Bell of Scotland,* several other compositions were issued on three staves, among them *Ah! Delia,* by George Jackson and printed for the composer around 1800, *A Poor Little Gypsy,* music by Arnold and published by Trisobio in Philadelphia around 1798, and *The Graceful Move,* Song LX of *The American Musical Miscellany* (1798).[44]

Changes in accompaniment came about slowly, even in the three-stave format. The keyboard treble part of many turn-of-the-century compositions still follows the vocal line, a characteristic of *A Smile and a Tear* (Example 28)[45] and *Aurelia Betray'd* (Example 29).[46]

On occasion the accompaniment's treble is printed above the vocal part—the layout of Braham's *On This Cold Flinty Rock!* (Example 30).[47] If this treble is played on the piano through to the end, the intermittent thickening of chords and the ease with which the player performs the line point to a keyboard rendition. In contrast, when a composer or arranger intends an upper part of this sort for a second instrument, the opening symphony is on three staves and the name of the obbligato instrument is printed above the music. Spofforth's *The Wood Robin* (Example 31)[48] illustrates this procedure.

Though the transition from *continuo* to written-out accompaniment was almost complete in parlor song by the end of Period I, still lacking in a majority of works were accompaniments that show rhythmic and melodic independence from the vocal line. Keyboard parts having this independence were exceptional at first. One exception, Braham's *The Willow,* appeared in America about 1804. Its accompaniment does have an individual rhythmic shape, as can be seen in Example 32.[49]

By the end of Period I, the harpsichord, with its limited capabilities for sustaining sound and realizing different dynamic levels, was supplanted by the piano as the favored instrument. As a first sign of this change, the accompaniments to works issued in the 1790s are described as "for the piano forte or harpsichord."[50]

Gradually the harpsichord submitted to the piano's ascsendency. Amateur singers increasingly sought to purchase pianos. Music stores laid up a stock of them while at the same time banishing harpsichords from their showrooms.[51] Then about 1799-1800 most songs began to appear "for the piano forte," without mention of the harpsichord.[52]

From Period II's beginning on, only the piano, never the harpsichord, is mentioned on title pages as the keyboard instrument for the accompaniment of parlor works. A great majority of musicians held the piano to be the most suitable instrument for enhancing the voice's attempt to project feeling. With this in mind, John W. Moore, noted music teacher and editor, states: "The chief beauty of this instrument [the piano], and which, indeed, constitutes its principal advantage over the harpsichord, is its capacity of obeying the touch, so as to enable the performer to vary and accommodate the expression....It is, of all instruments, preeminently the best for the accompaniment of the voice.[53]

An indication of the piano's growing popularity in the 1820s is given in an article "Piano Fortes," written for the Boston *Euterpeiad* in 1823. The author, who employs the pseudonym "Felix," claims pianos "are now justly considered to be a most important, if not *indispensable* article, to every family that makes any pretensions either to taste or fashion." The writer finds that most young ladies of his acquaintance have taken up its study and use it to accompany their singing.[54]

Beginning with Period II the reed organ also became a favorite instrument for accompanying simple songs. Some music teachers offered lessons on the organ to amateurs of both sexes.[55] It is named as an alternate instrument to the piano here and there in the sheet music.[56] Most important of all, it was within the means of amateurs who desired a keyboard instrument but found the piano unaffordable.[57]

During Period III a small organ called a Melodeon became popular as a parlor instrument.[58] A few professional singers like the Hutchinson Family also employed it. The Melodeon's tone is described as "rather sweet and melodious, but lacking in power and produced from one set of reeds."[59] This instrument was quite adequate for the accompaniment of songs like **The Blue Juniata* and **The Hazel Dell.*

Whether accompanied with a piano or organ, or no instrument at all, the plain parlor song of early America had no problem communicating with a listener. Interest was concentrated on the melody, on the singer not the accompanist. The general feeling among composers was why demand a specific accompanying instrument, a strict adherence to detailed instructions on interpretation, and musicianship encompassing a complex musical vocabulary? Americans were prepared to enjoy only the plainest music, set forth in the simplest terms.

George Root, composer of **Hazel Dell*, observes that in the United States, "many business and professional people, giving very little time or thought to the subject... prefer the simpler music to the end of their days....They must get their fill of the simple—must hear it until they crave something higher—before that which is higher can be of any use to them. It is an axiom that emotional or aesthetic benefit by music can come to a person only though music he likes. By that alone can he grow musically."[60] Root made certain his accompaniments and melodies remained uncomplicated, thus meeting the needs of his fellow citizens.[61]

That his conclusions were correct on what Americans from "business and professional" circles needed and wished, the collections of sheet music from these years amply demonstrate. Most songs in the collections are of the simpler kind. Although some compositions are a little less plain than the ones described in this section, they are pieces easily performed and understood.

By the end of the forties, a broad spectrum of American society had enthusiastically accepted songs by native composers. Furthermore, in an article entitled "Who Writes Our Songs?" appearing in *Dwight's Journal* in 1859, an unidentified reporter claims not only an American but a "world-wide" popularity for native, and particularly Foster, songs. The writer enumerates what he considers the reasons for this popularity: "easy flowing melody, the adherence to plain chords in the accompaniments, and the avoidance of intricacy in the harmony or embarrassing accidentals in the melody."[62] American parlor songs of the fifties almost invariably shared the characteristics described by the *Journal* reporter.

The Complex Parlor Song

Far less often mentioned by contemporary American writers and purchased by amateur musicians were complicated parlor songs. Most of the ones seen today are by British composers. Few complex compositions date from before 1830; most were written after 1840. European-trained singers customarily introduced them to the American public. Normally, the more sophisticated and musically educated American amateurs alone purchased them.

In contrast to the simple pieces, these more involved songs make great use of dynamic marks and other indications of expression, dissonance, chromatically-altered notes, tonal ambiguity, modulation to distant keys, complex chordal structures and deceptive cadences. Apparently the composer expected his public to understand, respect and more-or-less faithfully carry out his instructions. A concomitant feature of these songs is the greater technical facility required to perform both the vocal and instrumental parts

The description just given also fits the art song as it was developed in Austria and Germany in the first half of the nineteenth century.[63] The art songs of Schubert and Schumann, however, explore a greater range of emotions, handle musical material more subtly, make the piano a more equal partner with the voice, and attempt to probe greater psychological depths than do the complex parlor songs.[64]

The most popular song of the complex type was **Kathleen Mauverneen,* words by Mrs. Crawford, music by the British composer Frederick William Nichols Crouch.[65] Published in London in 1840, this work was reprinted in Philadelphia by James Osbourn, among others, around 1841. One crucial difference between **Kathleen Mavourneen* and simple song lies in Crouch's extensive use of a variety of symbols of expression, printed in the piano prelude, interludes and postlude, and in the entire vocal part. Markings such as *p, mf* and symbols for *crescendo* and *diminuendo* occur in 102 of the composition's 112 measures.

Other complex songs sometimes changed their dynamic levels swiftly from one extreme to the other.[66] For example, in measures 45-46 of Crouch's *Would I Were With Thee* (Boston, 1854), at the line "When all seems dark and sad below," the music to the first four words is marked *f,* followed by an abrupt *pp* on "sad" and a *decrescendo* to *ppp* on "below."[67] Just the opposite procedure is followed in Dempster's *Can I Forget to Love Thee, Mary?* (Philadelphia, 1839). Above the music of measures 19-20, at the line "Ere I forget to love thee, Mary," the composer has written "ad lib. Con Express." A *pp* is printed under "Ere," a *crescendo* under the next three words, and an *f* under "love."

In a few compositions, a change in dynamic level occurs simultaneously with a change in tempo. This change frequently takes the form of *crescendo* and *rallentando* before a moment of climax, after which the song resumes its normal tempo, as in measures 15-16 of George Linley's *Why Do I Love Thee Yet?* (Boston, ca. 1850). This method of delineating a climax is seldom indicated on the music of simple songs.

A lesser number of complex songs show a *rallentando* just before a phrase marked *pianissimo* that proceeds in a slower tempo than the rest of the composition. In measures 19-20 of E.J. Loder's

The Church Bell (Boston, ca. 1850), a *rallentando* is written for the music to "Time in life's volume hath reach'd the last page," and the slow passage is marked *pp* for the words that follow: "Still the old church bell with a moral divine/As it tolls from the tow'r shall mark my decline."

A second difference between compositions like **Kathleen Mavourneen* and simple song is the many chromatically altered tones and the modulations in the former in contrast to their absence in the latter. Crouch's prelude employs chromatically raised neighboring-tones and several lowered-sixth degrees of the scale. Next, the raised first and fifth degree occur in the vocal melody. Later, the music of the third phrase enters the submediant key, passes through the dominant key, and returns at last to the original tonality.

Even more than Crouch's composition, other complex songs show a high level of sophistication in the use of chromatic harmony. As a case in point, George Loder's *The Bride,*[68] partly reproduced in Example 33, reveals a subtle use of harmony: the V^0 of V in the first and fifth measure includes three tones (A flat, B natural and D) which become parts of the V^7 of III harmony (G sharp, B natural and D) in measure seven. In the fifth phrase (Example 34), the harmonic changes V - V^7 of V - V - V^7 of V - V are heard over a dominant pedal. This passage is followed by a V^7 of VI. A sudden C-sharp coloring occurs on the word "priceless," another sophisticated touch rare in simple song.

Some British song feature chromatic harmonies in every melody phrase. One composition, Linley's *Why Do I Love These Yet?*[69] in the key of E flat, has the following harmonic design:

Phrase					
	1.	I	$V^{6}_{\substack{4\\3}}$ of V	V^7	I
	2.	I v^6_3	VI $VI^{5\flat}$	V^6_4 V^7 of V	V
	3.	II	V^7 of VI	VI $II^{6\sharp}_5$	V of VI V^7
	4.	I	$V^{6}_{\substack{4\\3}}$ of V	V^7	V^6_5 of VI
	5.	IV V	I $V^{0 9}$ of II $II^{6\flat}_3$	I^6_4 V^7 of V I^6_4 V^7	I

A handful of complex songs employ a chromatically altered chord to harmonize the commencement of the vocal melody, as in Michael Balfe's *The Fair Land of Poland.*[70] (Example 35). Others like Balfe's *'Tis Sad to Leave Our Father-Land*[71] (Example 36) exhibit abrupt modulations to distant keys. Although a few American compositions (one or two of them composed by Elam Ives,

Jr.) attempt complicated procedures like these, the vast majority of parlor songs by American composers eschew such practices.

A third difference between complex and simple song lies in the variety of nonharmonic tones—their conspicuousness in one, their lack of prominence in the other. Aside from weak diatonic passing and neighboring tones and the dominant seventh chord, simple songs are mostly consonant in sound. In contrast, complex works may make use of diatonic and chromatic passing and neighboring tones, appogiaturas, echapees, cambiatas, and anticipations in the melody. They also resort to secondary sevenths and ninths, nondominant sevenths, seventh chords based on the raised subdominant and supertonic and augmented sixth chords in the harmony. In the fifth measure of **Kathleen Mavourneen,* for example, is a 6-5 appogiatura heard above a dominant seventh harmony and a tonic pedal. As the appogiatura sounds, one hears the clash of major-seventh intervals between *a* flat and *g′* and between *E* flat and *d′*, along with an augmented fourth between *a* flat and *d′*.[72] Nothing approximating this dissonance was found in the simple songs. The same 6-5 in the melody is heard above a dominant seventh and tonic pedal in measure 21.[73] Then in the next measure, while the dominant seventh continues to sound above the tonic pedal, the melody skips from *f′* up to a dissonant *c″*.[74]

An instance of how intricate the dissonant harmony can be in a complex parlor song is provided by Balfe's *'Tis Sad to Leave Our Fatherland.* Example 36 gives the portion of the song where it modulates from D minor to A-flat major, then to F major. Out of the eight measures in the example, only the beginning of measure one, the second half of measure two, and measure three have consonant harmonies. Close to 90% of the passage is dissonant.

A fourth difference is found in the construction of the tune of the complex song. **Kathleen Mavourneen's* melody, while attractive, is not easy for an amateur to sing. Its difficulty can be established in the passage (measures 29-30) where the singer must leap up an octave, *e′* flat to *e″* flat, then down an eleventh, *e″* flat to *b* flat. Also, none of the phrase patterns are identical, making it difficult for the singer to recall the tune. Letting a lower-case letter represent two measures of melody, the following rhythmic and melodic phrase pattern results:

Phrase 1 and 2.

3 and 4.

(Next comes a piano interlude of four measures, derived from the prelude.)

Phrase 5 and 6.

7 and 8.

9 and 10.

Unlike the tunes of simple songs, those of works like *Kathleen Mavourneen* require a great deal of effort to grasp and were probably never performed accurately by the majority of amateur vocalists who attempted them.[75]

The singer finds that occasional words in *Kathleen Mavourneen* receive "false" accents for expressive reasons, something rarely done in simple songs. One instance occurs in phrase two, where the second and weak syllable of "Hunter" receives a musical accent; another in phrase nine, where the note for the word "and" is marked with an accent and arrived at through an upward skip of a fourth.[74]

A fifth difference is evident in the piano part. Although assigned a subordinate role and usually designed to provide only a harmonic support for the vocal melody, the accompaniment to a more complicated composition demands greater playing ability than that to a simple song. Unquestionably, *Kathleen Mavourneen*'s piano part contains difficulties not present in, say,

**The Hazel Dell.* In Crouch's prelude, the player must execute chords in both hands at once, or perform passages in thirds for the right hand, or manage quick extensions of the little finger of the right hand to strike a high note while the thumb and index finger play notes a major seventh and fourth below (measures 5-6). Contrast this with Root's prelude, which has an undemanding single-note melody in the right hand, and a facile quarter- and half-note accompaniment in the left.

As the vocalist sings Crouch's melody, the pianist (if the vocalist has the good fortune to have one) plays eighth-note arpeggios; next, reiterated eighth-note chords; the, eighth-note broken chords which require some skill to perform properly, especially in measures 45-51. Root, on the other hand, writes whole- or half-note octaves for the left hand and quarter-note chords in close position for the right—no insuperable difficulties anywhere.[77]

Other songs of the complex type have accompaniment parts where the pianist must perform three eighth notes in the left hand against two in the right (Crouch's *Would I Were With Thee*), broken-chord figures having a span of a tenth or more (Hall's *Ever of Thee*), and arpeggio figures in both hands at once (Dempster's *The Blind Boy*). These hurdles are usually absent from simple song.

In a few complex works, the piano prelude serves as more than a perfunctory introduction to the vocal melody. Though based on melodic motives and harmonies heard in the body of the work, the music of **Kathleen Mavourneen*'s prelude is not a mere variation on the melody but a vital passage for establishing the mood of the composition.[78] Later, a modification of the music from the prelude's first four measures provides the material for the keyboard interlude between phrases four and five of the vocal line. Two other interludes based on the prelude's music are heard between the first and second stanza, and just before the submediant-minor section of the second stanza. For some inexplicable reason, the postlude of the Crouch song sounds indifferent and ends abruptly.

An occasional song even has a recurring motive allotted to the piano accompaniment. One such motive, simulating the sound of a bell, is heard several times in Wallace's *The Bell-Ringer*.[79] It appears in the bass part of measure four and the treble part of measure eight in Example 37. In one song, Glover's *Beautiful Erin* (New York, ca. 1850),[80] the composer has the pianist play not a motive but the first two melodic phrases of *'Tis the Last Rose of Summer* high up in the treble, while the vocalist sings Glover's own tune to the words "I'll sing the songs of my own green land."

Yet, after an examination of the complex songs in the United States before 1860, one must conclude that the pianist never finds himself an equal partner with the singer. It is the rare song that contains anything of importance for him to play. In most songs, the composer regards "the voice-part as the primary consideration."[81]

From one standpoint, **Kathleen Mavourneen* is atypical. Most preludes to complex songs are little more than a presentation of the opening of the vocal melody in right-hand octaves. When the vocalist enters, the pianist normally resorts to arpeggiated figures or repeated eighth-note chords in the right hand, and half- or quarter-note octaves in the left. Occasionally arpeggios are assigned to the left hand, the right playing two- and three-note harmonies. These passages, however, are inconveniently performed by amateurs who have given "little time or thought to the subject."[82]

In constrast to the simplicity of Root's **Hazel Dell,* which is "unpretentious and can be attempted by moderate performers,"[83] a complex work like Crouch's *Would I Were With Thee* "demands an extensive voice, and a qualified singer."[84] It is therefore to be expected that the number of fairly complex compositions constitute less then fifteen percent of the total number of songs now found in American collections.

Some Conventions of Parlor-Song Musical Style

It is safe to say that the composer and his audience observed certain usages in coping with musical style, structure, the setting of the text and the working-out of the accompaniment. In complex compositions, the composer allowed himself some freedoms. In simple songs, he recognized limits upon his choices so as to make his works readily performable and to permit their comprehension in terms familiar to his audience.[85]

Most popular parlor songs from the years before 1860 are neither individual expressions, nor completely formulaic statements. They fall somewhere between. A majority of them, nevertheless, do share characteristics that incline them toward simplicity.[86]

First, with regard to the shared traits of the music itself, songs occupying the broad middle between simple and complex have comparatively few indications of dynamics and expression, chromatically altered tones in the melody, modulations other than passing ones to closely related keys, and intervals awkward to sing. A typical song of the intermediate type is Glover's *Jeannette and Jeannot (The Conscript's Departure).* Its prelude has one p, one *Cres.* and *Dim.;* its postlude, one *Cres.* and *Dim.*; there are no other dynamics. Aside from three *g′* sharps occurring as neighboring tones, no chromatic alterations occur in the vocal part. The harmony, however, does make several passing modulations, three to the dominant, one to the subdominant, and one to the supertonic key. Since in other respects the song is uncomplicated, it cannot be classified as of the complex type. Yet, because of the characteristics just enumerated, neither is it of the simplest type.

Further common traits of intermediate types of songs are their moderate use of dissonance, of harmonies other than I, V and IV, and of nonharmonic tones save for the unobtrusive diatonic passing and neighboring kinds. If Woodbury's intermediate type of song **Be Kind to the Loved Ones at Home* is examined as representative of this large group of works, three V^7 and two V of V chords appear as dissonant harmonies, and in addition the weak clash of a few unaccented passing tones and appoggiaturas. Harmonies are mostly the three principal ones of the home key—the exceptions being a VI, a V of VI, and two V of V chords. Again, one finds insufficient complications for a complex, too many for a simple, song.

Most melodies display the prevalent 4- or 8-measure phrase length, recurring rhythmic and melodic patterns, and major-mode scale structures noticed in simple songs. In the work's middle, the tune may occasionally have the fourth degree raised for a temporary move to the dominant. Normally chromatically-altered tones remain in the accompaniment part. The accompaniment is easily executed, always much less important than the vocal part, and usually provides harmonic support to the melody in the form of one or two brief figures that are constantly repeated.

A few of these figures are found in so many songs composed in the first sixty years of the nineteenth century that they can be considered as formulas. Examples 38 a to l reproduce the twelve figures most often employed by composers of parlor song. Some compositions have one figure accompany almost the entire melody as in Balfe's **I Dreamt that I Dwelt in Marble Halls*. Other works change their figure on the third phrase, at the point where the singer commences singing the second quatrain of a stanza. Spilman's **Flow Gently, Sweet Afton* shows this change. A few songs change their figures more frequently, as in Kiallmark's *Araby's Daughter* (Boston, ca. 1824) and Grannis's *Do They Miss Me at Home?* (Boston, 1852). Rarely, a parlor song appears with a different accompaniment for each stanza. One such exceptional composition is Meineke's *The Bird at Sea* (Baltimore, 1836).

In most cases, keyboard preludes and postludes rather routinely introduce and conclude the singer's melody. The prelude sounds the first phrase or two of the melody, exactly or in a somewhat florid variation, before closing on the tonic; the typical postlude reproduces the last half of the prelude. An example of such an approach is Dempster's *Footsteps of Angels* (Boston, 1848). Several songs start in the fashion just described but end with new music. One of these is Daniel Johnson's *The Carrier Dove* (New York, 1836), whose ending owes nothing to the music of the prelude.

What has just been written should make it clear that most characteristics of intermediate types of song resemble those of simple ones, and differ only in their slightly higher level of complication.

Conclusion

A study of the parlor songs from all three periods shows a change in the secular music of America from the late eighteenth century, when an almost complete dependence on British compositions existed, to the 1850s, when American compositions achieved prominence.

The compositions from Period I include few works by Americans. A study of secular vocal music sung by Americans during these years must concentrate on British works. Though one American, Francis Hopkinson, wrote and published several parlor songs, none won popularity. Not until Period II did the number of American song composers increase. Oliver Shaw, Thomas Wiesenthal, and John Hewitt even succeeded in composing some songs that gained large followings. Yet, the musical styles of these native musicians for the most part remain indistinguishable from those of the British. In addition, the greater number of secular songs published and sung in America continued to be British in origin. Finally, in Period III a considerable body of songs by Americans achieved great popularity among all classes, from the affluent to the citizen of modest means. Possibly because the stylistic features of these pieces differ from those of the British and because American songs are attractive yet easy to execute, they succeeded in winning an equal place beside, and at times supplanting, British compositions in American homes.

In general, most American works are best described as ranging from simple to intermediate types; most British from intermediate to complex. This is not to say that the Americans did not write complex, or the British simple, songs. They did.[87] But these works are less often found. What songs are found and the conclusions concerning their general characteristics, therefore, must reflect both the practices of composers and arrangers and the preferences of the Americans using these songs for their own enjoyment.

Quite a few American musicians specialized in writing simple parlor songs because they felt most of their countrymen wanted and needed them.[88] Some composers, among them Marion Dix Sullivan and Stephen Foster, were probably unable to write more complex songs, because of their limited musical training.[89] And many Americans (Sullivan, Foster, Woodbury, Root, etc.) seem to have had greater success than the British in writing unassuming works that could please American tastes. This success might well have encouraged them to continue in the same style.[90]

The last consideration in this study is a summary of some of the differences between American and British compositions written between 1841 and 1860. The conclusions are based on an examination of about 1200 of the most popular songs as seen in their incidence in the collections. (Appendix A lists the topmost ranking ones.) What follows is essentially an amplification of the several differences already mentioned in this chapter.

Regarding the music—first, most British compositions from Period III do have dynamic indications, chromatically-altered melodic tones, and modulations to one or more keys. Half the American pieces have no, and the remainder have few, symbols of expression or chromatics. Second, British compositions use a variety of harmonies, including chords of the seventh and ninth often altered by chromatics. American works employ mostly I, V, and IV; sometimes II, VI, or V^7 of V, andV^7 of VI. Third, the level of dissonance and the range of melody (an octave or more) in British songs are greater than in American ones, where dissonance is usually that of the dominant seventh in the home key, and the melodic range is an octave or less

Concerning the text, British songs have mostly three, less often two, sometimes as many as eight, stanzas. American works normally have two stanzas, but may employ as many as five, rarely six or more, stanzas. The stanzas in British pieces are in eight, some in four to twelve, lines. Few end on refrains. On the other hand, one to four lines in each stanza may be repeated to new music at the conclusion of the verse. American pieces have stanzas mainly in eight or twelve lines, although some are in four, others up to fourteen, lines. Lines are hardly ever repeated. Rather, they usually close with a refrain of one to four lines in length. In the 1850s this refrain is entitled "Chorus" and harmonized for four, less often three or two, voices. In a few instances, though the word "Chorus" heads the refrain, no harmony parts for voice are seen.

Turning to the keyboard accompaniments, while none are really difficult to play, more technique is required for British songs. Native composers tend to vary their accompaniment figures less than British composers do. One figure is repeated eight to sixteen measures at a time before changing. There are, of course, exceptions. Indeed, some American songs like Woodbury's *He Doeth All Things Well* change figures frequently. Some British songs like Balfe's **I Dreamt that I Dwelt in Marble Halls* repeat one figure for most of the work.

These differences between the two nationalities become even more apparent when the most popular compositions by non-native musicians held in the highest esteem (Crouch, Wallace, Dempster and Balfe) are contrasted with the very popular American compositions (Foster, Woodbury and Root). By the mid-nineteenth century these three Americans had each written several songs whose wide acceptance was phenomenal. These three men are among the principal composers represented in the extant parlor song literature. The American composer had at last established himself in the field of popular music and in the affections of his countrymen.

Whether the parlor songs are qualitatively excellent compositions is not a question as easily answered as some latter-day critics of the genre might think. In the first place, several virtues can be singled out that show this music to have merit. Not the least of these virtues is the absence of superfluous notes inserted to expand artificially a song's length. Moreover, a parlor composition rarely attempts to be more than it should; that is, it hardly ever goes beyond the bounds imposed by its basic matter, verbal and musical. In its own day this popular form of recreation was considered a sensitive reflector of natural human emotions and an embodiment of civilized taste. It was tested again and again in the crucible of contemporary concerns and experiences, and what it had to say was found worthy of widespread support. When today's listener hears these works constantly and accepts them on their own terms, he finds they do come alive for him and can illumine aesthetic and emotional corners of the psyche which nowadays remain neglected.

Any attempt to dismiss parlor song lightly, as inconsequential or as an aberration from standards based on what is musically estimable raises the issue of the premises upon which such a judgment rests. Every age, including our own, has redefined excellence in the arts to suit its own precepts of fitness, function and universality. One wonders how Americans one hundred years from now will regard our own popular and artistic creations.

To condemn parlor song because it fails to correspond to a later generation's divergent opinions on taste and fashion, or to the grand creations of a Bach or Beethoven, or to the products of the jazz and rural-folk world is manifestly unfair. This modest music was written to meet the necessities of a younger society living in a different period in America's history. Furthermore, it no more resembles the symphonies of Beethoven than a Salem ship-carpenter's exquisite carvings in a sea captain's mansion resemble the majestic *David* of Michelangelo. Yet, both are beautiful in their own way. And why should the popular music of the nineteenth-century middle class be less vital an expression because it did not come from the throats of blacks or the inhabitants of Appalachia?

Music by American composers once gave intense pleasure to thousands of our early citizens, among them America's outstanding political, business, intellectual, literary, scientific and artistic leaders. Walt Whitman, Mark Twain, Oliver Wendell Holmes, Henry Wadsworth Longfellow, Emily Dickinson and William Sidney Mount were delighted, moved and comforted by this music. Surely their high estimation is not to be dismissed as owing to inexperience on their part, or to a lack of discernment about music.

Recent concerts featuring parlor songs, carefully prepared and seriously presented, have begun to elicit renewed praise for the melodies. Less enthusiasm has been generated for some of the lyrics, which contain a coefficient of sentimentality too sizeable for some today to accept. Fortunately the sentimentality of Schubert's Lieder can take refuge in the German language; of Bellini's arias, in the Italian. Half-understanding these languages permits Americans to enjoy the music more, worry about the emotional overtones of the texts less. Parlor song is in perfectly understandable English and today suffers for it. The connotational implications of sentimentality, so pregnant with meaning for nineteenth-century men and women, is lost on the more cynical, hard-boiled members of twentieth-century society. Whether the twenty-first century will usher in a climate more receptive to the kind of personal emotionalism valued by yesterday's Americans remains to be seen.

Meanwhile, at least a few people have come to love the genre for itself, and not merely for its historical importance or for its nostalgic evocations. One hopes more and more men and women will become ready to take an initial step toward the sympathetic understanding of the idiom.

It is not, however, only that present-day Americans should appreciate and love the old songs; at least on one level—and in one way—that is immaterial. But it is imperative that Americans of today, if they are to be musically or culturally educated, at least know about and understand the parlor song. To fail to do that is to turn a deaf ear to our musical past. And to do that is to embrace an intolerable ignorance and indifference.

Notes

1. George Root, *The Story of a Musical Life* (Cincinnnati, 1891), pp. 96-97. George Root is the only American composer active in the first half of the nineteenth century who wrote at length on why and how popular songs were composed.

2. Ibid., p. 97.

3. New York *Musical Review,* 10 January 1857, p. 6.

4. Boston *Euterpeiad,* 10 March 1821, p. 193. The songs of Henry Bishop, an English composer, were extremely popular in America at this time.

5. Some other songs with the skip up to 8 and the descent 7-6 are Fostor's *Gentle Annie* (New York, 1856), Septimus Winner's *What Is Home Without a Mother?* (New York, ca. 1838), and John Davy's *The Red, Red Rose* (Boston, ca. 1827). Three that skip up to 8, then descend 6-5, are W. Irving Hartshorne's *Cora Lee* (Boston,1855), Stephen Foster's *Lily Ray* (New York, 1850) and Thomas Wiesenthal's **The Ingle Side* (New York, ca. 1850).

6. Further examples of this melody type are Thomas Comer's *Alone, Alone* (Boston, 1847), Thomas Haynes Bayly's *I'd Be a Butterfly* (New York, ca. 1830) and George Barker's *Where Are the Friends of My Youth?* (New York, ca. 1850).

7. Similar to it are Coote's *A Barque Upon the Waters* (New York, ca. 1830), Richard Storrs Willis' *It Came Upon a Midnight Clear* (New York, 1850), Hodson's *Annat Lyle* (New York, 1830), Root's **Rosalie* (Boston, 1855). Only one earlier song, Braham's *Fair Ellen* (New York, ca. 1802), was found to resemble Shaw's tune. The melodic outline of *Mary's Tears,* 3 down to 5, then up for a close on 2 or 1, can also be found in the Moore-Stevenson *Oft in the Stilly Night* (New York, n.d.), Lowell Mason's *Nearer My God to Thee* (New York, 1859), Wallace's *Why Do I Weep for Thee?* (Boston, 1850), Baker's *My Trundle Bed* (Chicago, 1860) and Howe's *Cara Lee* (Boston, 1854).

8. See, for example, Barnett's *The Spot Where I was Born* (Boston, ca. 1833), Russell's *We Have Been Friends Together* (New York, 1840), Barker's *The Graves of a Household* (Boston, 1848) and Hewitt's *The Betrothed* (Philadelphia, 1840).

9. James J. Fuld, *The Book of World-Famous Music,* rev. ed. (New York, 1971), pp. 115-16; Henry George Farmer in *Grove's* s.v. "Auld Lang Syne."

10. For the remainder of the chapter, the place of publication and date of a song will be given only the first time the title occurs.

11. See Bach's *Sinfonia Concertante in C,* ed.C.R.F. Maunder (London, n.d.), the facsimile reprint of the opera *Amadis des Gaules* (London, 1772), and the *Quartet in G,* ed. Walter Bergmann (Mainz, 1951). For a history of expression marks, see Rosamond Harding, "On the Origins and History of the Forte and Piano," *Musical Time and Expression* (London, 1938), pp. 85-107; and David Boyden, "Dynamics in Seventeenth- and Eighteenth-Century Music," *Essays on Music in Honor of Archibald Thompson Davison* (Cambridge, Mass., 1957), pp. 185-93. Both Harding (p. 105) and Boyden (p. 193) state that the entire system of dynamics was well understood by composers writing at the end of the eighteenth century.

12. James Hewitt's *Pot Pourri* for piano, published in Benjamin Carr's *Musical Journal for the Piano Forte,* II (Philadelphia, ca. 1801), 25-32, and Hewitt's song *Ellen Weep Not So My Love* (New York, ca. 1804) contain a variety of dynamic marks, both of the terraced and graded type. On the other hand, most of Hewitt's vocal pieces have either no dynamic indications at all, as in *The Primrose Girl* (New York, ca. 1794) and *When First Maria Won My Heart* (New York, 1807), or only a few in the keyboard prelude and postlude, as in *Advice to the Ladies* (New York, ca. 1803) and *Thou Art False to the Zephyr that Flies* (New York, ca. 1807.

Benjamin Carr's *Rondo* for piano, in the *Journal,* II (ca. 1801), 13-14, and his long and elaborate non-strophic song, *Ah, How Hapless is the Maiden,* in the *Journal,* I (ca. 1801), 41-48, contain many expression marks. Yet none occur in Carr's shorter strophic songs, like *Shakespeare's Willow* (I, 20-21) and *The Poor Flower Girl* (II, 42).

13. See Chapter 4, on the performance of parlor songs.

14. See, for instance, the Boston *Musical Magazine,* 21 November 1840, p. 400; New York *Musical Times* 27 December, 1851, p. 118.

15. Joseph and Horace Bird, *The Singing School Companion* (Boston, 1852), p. 2.

16. Usually these songs have no keyboard prelude and a very brief postlude; see, for instance, Ware's *Until Fifteen Dull Years,* Vol. 2, 8 December 1821; Moore's *Come Rest in This Bosom,* Vol. 2 [?], ca. 1821; and Braham's *Is There a Heart That Never Loved?* Vol. 2 [?], ca. 1821. Concerning the dates these songs were published, see Wolfe, #2721.

17. For example, see the two piano pieces sent to subscribers in 1821, *The Zephyr Waltz,* which has the following expression marks: *f, fz, diminuendo;* and *The Prussian March,* which contains three *pianos* and three *fortes* in its 32 measures.

18. See Baker, p. 5.

19. The failure to teach American students to read music, and the prevalent rote learning of songs is referred to in the prefaces of Artemus N. Johnson's *The Normal Song Book* (Boston, 1855), and of Joseph and Horace Bird's *The Singer's First Book* (Boston, 1845).

20. James Hewitt's *Sweet Are the Flowers* (New York, ca. 1807) provides another instance of a very simple parlor song, otherwise containing no complications, whose keyboard prelude, in measures 5-7, has an unusual passage: $V^7$of IV-IV-IV^{3b} I-V^7 of V, V^7 of IV-IV-V^7, I. The song is in G major.

21. See Francis Collinson, *The Traditional and National Music of Scotland* (London, 1966), p. 3, and David Johnson, *Music and Society in Lowland Scotland in the Eighteenth Century* (London, 1972), p. 130.

22. Collinson, pp. 2-5.

23. Johnson, p. 152.

24. Ibid., pp. 150-57.

25. In his article on "Melody," in *Music and Letters,* V (1924), 272-85, H.J.Watt, after analyzing many melodies, particularly those of the Schubert songs, concludes that the most used melodic interval is the second, and that the larger the interval, the less often it occurs in a tune.

26. Harold Whitehall in the *Princeton Encyclopedia of Poetry* s.v. "Rhyme."

27. The employment of assonance and alliteration in poetry in general, is discussed by Ulrich K. Goldsmith in the *Princeton Encyclopedia* s.v. "Assonance" and "Alliteration." Goldsmith writes that alliteration became a commonly employed device in English poetry only with the beginning of the Romantic movement, about 1800, and that it "often occurs in combination with alliteration."

28. The pronunciation symbols and the diacritics are those in *Webster's Third New International Dictionary.*

29. *Rise, Columbia!,* the words by Thomas Paine, and adapted to the air of *Rule, Brittania,* appears as a song with an SSB choral refrain in several of the early songbooks, such as *The American Musical Miscellany* (Northampton, 1798), pp. 103-05, *The Baltimore Musical Miscellany* (Baltimore, 1804), pp. 127-29, and *The Nightingale* (Portsmouth, 1804), pp. 103-06.

30. Examples are *Chloe's to be My Wife,* "as sung by the Ethiopian Serenaders" (New York, 1849), *Mary Blane,* "as sung by the Ethiopian Serenaders" (New York, 1847), and *Nancy Till,* "written for, and sung by, White's Serenaders" (New York, 1851). Several of Stephen Foster's songs are of this type: *Nelly Bly, *Nelly Was a Lady* and *Old Folks at Home.*

31. See the several examples in the Musical Supplement. In the fifties, some of

the important parlor song composers in America, besides Foster, were T. Brigham Bishop, John Fletcher, Fred Buckley, L.V.H. Crosby, Luther O. Emerson, Patrick Gilmore, S.M. Grannis, Benjamin Hanby, "Alice Hawthorne" (Septimus Winner), E.A. Hosmer, George C. Howard, John P. Ordway, "Wurzel" (George Root), H.S. Thompson and Joseph Webster.

32. New York *Musical World*, 31 October 1852, p. 137. Hans Nathan, in "Dixie," *Musical Quarterly,* XXXV (1949), p. 62, states that in the fifties a typical minstrel show started out with sentimental "white" ballads, and later in the show featured comic minstrel songs.

33. Typical examples are the keyboard symphonies of **Long, Long Ago!* and **The Blue Juniata.* In **The Hazel Dell,* Root omits the postlude and ends the song with a *pianissimo* repetition of the choral refrain.

34. Philip Radcliffe, in *A History of Song,* ed. Denis Stevens (New York, 1960), pp. 231-33; Karl Geiringer, *Haydn,* rev. ed. (Berkeley, 1968), pp. 327-28.

35. Geiringer, pp. 362-63.

36. Arthur Jacobs, in *A History of Song,* p. 148.

37. See F.T. Arnold, *The Art of Accompaniment from a Thorough-Bass,* I (London, 1931), pp. 318-19.

38. *Roslin Castle* (Philadelphia, ca. 1796).

39. *Ellen Arise,* words by J.E. Harwood, music by Benjamin Carr (Philadelphia, ca. 1798).

40. *May Morning,* music by Peter A. Von Hagen (Boston, ca. 1802).

41. *Lovely Nan,* words and music by Charles Dibdin (n.p., n.d.).

42. *Anna,* music by Peter A. Von Hagen (Boston, ca. 1802).

43. Both versions may be found in the 1 December 1800 issue of the *Musical Journal for the Piano Forte,* II (Philadelphia, 1800),2-4.

44. *The American Musical Miscellany,* pp. 158-9.

45. *A Smile and a Tear,* words by M.P. Andrews, music by Miss Abrams (London, n.d.).

46. *Aurelia Betray'd* words by J. Hutton, music by John Bray (Philadelphia, ca. 1809).

47. *On This Cold Flinty Rock!,* music by John Braham (Philadelphia, ca. 1809).

48. *Musical Journal,* I, no. 11.

49. *The Willow,* words by Thomas Dibdin, music by John Braham (Baltimore, ca. 1808).

50. In 1798 American publishers were still advertising "favorite songs for the piano forte or harpsichord"; see Sonneck under "Ah! Seek to Know It."

51. During the 1790s, Carr of Philadelphia, Gilfert of New York and Von Hagen of Boston were offering "imported piano fortes" for sale. See, for example, James Hook's *As Forth I rang'd the Bank of Tweed,* published in Boston by Von Hagen, around 1799. The first page of the composition prints the information that at the Von Hagen store "may be had...a great variety of warranted piano fortes." Also see Storace's *As Wrapt in Sleep I Lay,* published in Philadelphia by Carr, around 1794, at whose store "may be had all the newest music, reprinted from European publications; likewise and elegant assortment of piano fortes."

Daniel Spillane, in *The History of the American Pianoforte* (New York, 1890), p. 69, writes that the "first legitimate pianoforte and music store...was Gilfert's [in New York], and this was in existence as early as 1786." During Period I, a small number of pianos of American manufacture was produced; see Spillane, pp. 34-83. By 1829, about 2500 American-made pianos a year were being produced, according to Spillane, p. 84. The number of imported pianos is not known.

In the New York *Musical Pioneer,* 1 April 1857, p. 103, Isaac B. Woodbury, the editor, writes: "It is estimated that there are 760,000 pianos in use in our country at the present time." The source for the figure given is not revealed.

52. For example, Von Hagen of Boston published *Adams and Liberty* in 1799, "for the piano forte"; in 1800 Benjamin Carr of Philadelphia began publication of his *Musical Journal for the Piano Forte.*

53. John W. Moore, *Encyclopedia of Music* s.v. "Piano-Forte." George Hogarth, *Musical History, Biography, and Criticism* (New York, 1848), p. 169, writes that "its [the piano's] powers of *sostenuto* and expression, of which the harpsichord was destitute, led to the abandonment of that instrument."

54. Boston *Euterpleiad,* February 1823, p. 180. The same writer criticizes the performances of the young ladies as ones "managing both *playing* and *singing* into one confused heap."

55. See,for example, Mr. S.P. Taylor's advertisement in the Boston *Euterpeiad,* 7 October 1820, p. 112.

56. To give two instances, *Oh! Thou Who Dry'st the Mourner's Tears,* words by Thomas Moore, "the music composed and arranged for the organ or piano forte by Thomas Wiesenthal" (Philadelphia, ca. 1818), and *O My Love's Like the Red Rose,* "arranged for the organ and piano forte," published in the Boston *Euterpeiad,* 3 March 1821, p. 196.

57. For example, in the Boston *Euterpeiad,* 24 November 1821, p. 143, pianos are advertised ranging in price from $225 to $474; a table organ for $120. In the New York *Musical Review,* 19 January 1854, p. 17, pianos are advertised ranging in price from $200 to $600; on p. 18, melodeons (a type of small organ) meant for use in either "church or parlor" are advertised as ranging in price from $75 to $200.

58. Christine Merrick Ayers, *Contributions... by the Music Industries of Boston, 1640 to 1936* (New York, 1933),. 135; Jones, *Handbook* s.v. "Organ, Reed," "Melodeon," and "Mason & Hamlin Organ and Piano Company." See also, the New York *Musical Review,* 26 January 1856, p. 18.

59. Jones, s.v. "Melodeon."

60. Root, *The Story,* pp. 19-20. Much the same thing is stated in the article "Artistic Music and People's Music," in the New York *Musical Review*, 14 July 1855, p. 228.

61. Root, *The Story,* p. 96. See also the New York *Musical Review,* 16 February 1854, pp. 57-8.

62. *Dwight's Journal of Music,* 14 May 1859, pp. 51-52.

63. See Radcliffe, in *A History of Song,* pp.241-42, 247.

64. Maurice Brown, *Schubert* (New York, 1966), pp. 28-29, 47-48, 144-45; Eric Sams, *The Songs of Robert Schumann* (New Haven, 1967); Radcliffe, pp. 242-47.

65. Most of the complex parlor songs do not seem to have been popular with amateur singers. Usually each of these works is found in no more than one or two collections from these years, and number very few copies among the sheet-music that is not bound. However, one complex song reproduced in the Musical Supplement, *Kathleen Mavourneen,* was extremely popular and is found in a great many collections.

66. What is referred to here is not the commonly seen *p* to *f* and *f* to *p* terraced dynamic change, but a change between two greater extremes in dynamic level.

67. To discourage the singer from taking a *decrescendo* in measure 45, Crouch writes an *f* under "When" and another under "dark."

68. *The Bride,* words by H.P. Grattan, music by George Loder (New York, 1849).

69. *Why Do I Love Thee Yet?*, words and music by George Linley (New York, ca. 1850).

70. *The Music of the Bohemian Girl* (Philadelphia, 1845), no. 3.

71. Ibid., no. 6.

72. Crouch continues the tonic pedal and delays the resolution of the dominant

seventh until measure 9.

73. Appoggiaturas are also heard in measures 15, 28, and 29. Chromatic neighboring-tones occur in measures 2 and 4, and changing-notes in measure 27. Measure 30 begins with an unresolved appoggiatura (*e″*-flat) that skips down to *b*-flat, followed by changing-notes (*e′*-flat to *g′*).

74. The *c″* could also be interpreted as the ninth of a dominant ninth chord.

75. That this statement is true was confirmed several times when the author rehearsed these songs with half-trained "ballad singers." After one rehearsal, singers were able to reproduce the tunes of the two simple songs with ease from memory. The tune of **Kathleen Mavourneen* required many rehearsals. When these songs were then sung before an audience, the singers of **Kathleen Mavourneen* still made several errors. These "ballad singers" had the same difficulties learning to sing Loder's *The Bride.* Moreover, the singers were able to accompany themselves on the simple songs; unable to do so on the two complex ones.

76. Other examples of "false" accent are found in measures 38 and 42 on "forgotten," measure 48 on "ever," measure 50 on "silent," and measure 51 on "of."

77. See the last sentence of note 75 above.

78. The skip in the treble part, from *b*-flat to *g′*, in measures 1, 3, 5 and 6, the passages in thirds with the accent on the second eighth-note of each measure, in measures 2 and 4, the unresolved dissonances in measures 5-8, and the tone of the lowered-sixth degree in measures 5-7 contribute to a feeling of restlessness in the prelude, which is not dispelled until measures 15-16, when the *g′* descends to *e′*-flat, written as a dotted half-note over a tonic harmony.

79. *The Bell-Ringer,* words by J. Oxenford, music by William Vincent Wallace (New York, 1859).

80. The words are by Mrs. Weelington Boate.

81. Mrs. Edmond Wodehouse, in the first edition of *Grove's,* III (London, 1883) s.v. "Song: English." She is referring to the songs of composers like Knight, Wallace and Balfe. One of the songs mentioned is *The Bell-Ringer.* As a contrast to the predominance of the melody in British parlor songs, one notes an observation Joan Chissell makes concerning Schumann's art songs, in *Schumann* (New York, 1962), p. 148: "It was the general atmospheric effect which mattered to him more than the creation of beautiful melody *per se,* and following the example of Schubert, it was invariably on the piano that he relied most to achieve this."

82. Root, *The Story,* p. 19.

83. From a review of *The Hazel Dell,* in the New York *Musical Review,* 7 December 1854, p. 425. The reviewer is unidentified.

84. From a review of *Would I Were with Thee,* in the New York *Musical Review,* 3 August 1854, p. 278.

85. See "The Acquiring of a Taste for Refined Music," Boston *Euterpeiad,* 10 June 1820, p. 43; Thomas Hastings, *Dissertation,* p. 169; Ronald Pearsall, *Victorian Popular Music* (London, 1973), pp. 95-96.

86. See the unsigned article "Music," in the *Atlantic Monthly,* XXIX (1872), p. 764; Montague, "Horn," pp. 75-89; Barrett, *Balfe,* pp. 300-302.

87. An example of a complex song by a Bostonian is J.C.D. Parker's *Come into the Garden, Maud* (Boston, 1855). For a simple British song that sounds like a precursor of Foster's *Oh! Susannah,* see William Dempster's *If You're Waking Call Me Early,* Part Second of the secular cantata *The May Queen* (Boston, 1845).

88. See the New York *Musical Review,* 16 February 1854, pp. 57-58; Root, *The Story,* pp. 19-20, 96.

89. See, for example, Howard, *Stephen Foster,* pp. 81, 107, 131.

90. See *Dwight's Journal of Music,* 14 May 1859, pp. 51-52.

Appendix A

The Most Popular Songs In The Extant Collections Of Music

Listed alphabetically by title; including, if known, the poet, composer and year of first publication in the United States

1. *Absence,*m. Jean Jacques Rousseau, arr. Johann Baptist Cramer (ca. 1820).
2. *Ah! Don't Mingle One Human Feeling,* m. adapted from *La Sonnambula* of Vincenzo Bellini (1835).
3. *Alice Gray,* m. Mrs. P. Millard (ca. 1830).
4. *Allan Percy or It Was a Beauteous Lady* (1851).
5. *All's Well,* w. Thomas Dibdin, m. John Braham (ca. 1804).
6. *The Angel's Whisper,* w. and arr. Samuel Lover (ca. 1836).
7. *Annie Lawrie,* m. Lady John Scott (ca. 1845).
8. *The Arab Maid,* w. W. McGhie, m. George Alexander Hodson (ca. 1830).
9. *Araby's Daughter,* w. Thomas Moore, m. George Kiallmark (ca. 1824).
10. *As I View These Scenes So Charming,* m. adapted from *La Sonnambula* of Vincenzo Bellini (ca. 1835).
11. *Auld Lang Syne,* w. in part by Robert Burns (ca. 1805).
12. *Auld Robin Gray,* w. Lady Anne Barnard, m. Alexander Lee (ca. 1833).
13. *Away, Away to the Mountain's Brow,* m. Alexander Lee (ca. 1833).
14. *The Banks of the Blue Moselles,* w. Edward Fitzball, m. George Herbert Rodwell (ca. 1830).
15. *The Bay of Biscay O!* w. Andrew Cherry, m. John Davy (ca. 1805).
16. The Beautiful Maid, w. Thomas Dibdin, m. John Braham (ca. 1803).
17. *Be Kind to the Loved Ones at Home,* w. and m. Isaac Baker Woodbury (1847).
18. *Behold! How Brightly Breaks the Morning,* m. Daniel Francois Esprit Auber (ca. 1830).
19. *Believe Me, If All Those Endearing Young Charms,* w. Thomas Moore, m. arr. Sir John Andrew Stevenson (ca. 1809).
20. *The Bird at Sea,* w. Mrs.Felicia Hemans, m. Christopher Meineke (1836).
21 *The Blind Boy,* w. Hannah F. Gould, m.William R. Dempster (1842).
22. *Blue Eyed Mary* (ca. 1817).
23. *The Blue Juniata,* w. and m. Marion Dix Sullivan (1844).
24. *Bonnie Doon* (ca. 1803).
25. *The Bride's Farewell,* w. Miss M.L. Beevor, m. Thomas Williams (ca. 1830).
26. *Brignal Banks,* w. Walter Scott, m. Dr. Clarke (ca. 1827).
27. *Bring Flowers,* w. Mrs. Felicia Hemans, m. arr. J. Worsley (1827).
28. *The Campbells are Coming,* arr. G.T.C. (ca. 1830).
29. *A Canadian Boat Song,* w. and m. arr. Thomas Moore (ca. 1807).
30. *The Captive Knight,* w. Mrs. Felicia Hemans, m. Miss Browne (ca. 1832).
31. *The Carrier Dove,* m. Daniel Johnson (1836).
32. *The Carrier Pigeon,* w. James Gates Percival, m. Peter K. Moran (ca. 1823).
33. *Come Rest in This Bosom,* w. and m. arr. Thomas Moore (ca. 1820).

34. *Comin' Thro' the Rye* (ca. 1825).
35. *Dark-Eyed One,* w. Thomas Haynes Bayly, m. adapted from Daniel Francois Esprit Auber (1833).
36. *Darling Nelly Gray,* w. and m. Benjamin Russell Hanby (1856).
37. *The Dashing White Sergeant,* w. General Burgoyne, m. Henry Rowley Bishop (ca. 1825).
38. *The Deep, Deep Sea,* m. Charles E. Horn (ca. 1830).
39. *Do They Miss Me at Home?* w. and m. S.M. Grannis (1832).
40. *The Evening Gun,* w. Thomas Moore, m. arr. Charles Zeuner (1831).
41. *Ever of Thee,* w. George Linley, m. Foley Hall (ca. 1852).
42. *Eve's Lamentation,* m. Mathew Peter King (ca. 1818).
43. *Farewell to My Harp,* m. Charles E. Horn (ca. 1827).
44. *The Field of Monterey,* m. Marion Dix Sullivan (1846).
45. *Flow Gently, Sweet Afton,* w. Robert Burns, m. James E. Spilman (1838).
46. *Fly to the Desert,* w. Thomas Moore, m. George Kiallmark (ca. 1818).
47. *Friend of the Brave,* w. Thomas Campbell, m. John Wall Callcott (ca. 1834).
48. *Gaily the Troubadour,* w. and m. Thomas Haynes Bayly (ca. 1830).
49. *Gentle Annie,* w. and m. Stephen C. Foster (1856).
50. *Go Forget Me Why Should Sorrow,* w. Rev. Charles Wolfe, m. from *Don Giovanni* by Wolfgang Amadeus Mozart (ca. 1832).
51. *The Grave of Bonaparte,* w. Henry S. Washburn, m. Lyman Heath (1843).
52. *The Green Hills of Tyrol,* w. George Linley, m. Gioacchino Rossini (ca. 1832).
53. *The Hazel Dell,* w. and M. George Frederick Root (1853).
54. *He Doeth All Things Well,* w. F.M.E., m. Isaac Baker Woodbury (1844).
55. *Henry's Cottage Maid,* m. Ignaz Pleyel (ca. 1807).
56. *Here's a Health to Thee, Mary,* w. Barry Cornwall, m. George Herbert Rodwell (ca. 1836).
57. *A Highland Minstrel Boy,* w. Harry Stoe Van Dyk, m. John Barnett (ca. 1835).
58. *Hinda's Appeal to Her Lover,* w. Thomas Moore, m. George Kiallmark (ca. 1827).
59. *Home Again,* w. and m. Marshall S. Pike, arr. John P. Ordway (1850).
60. *Home! Sweet Home!,* w. John Howard Payne, m. Henry R. Bishop (ca. 1823).
61. *Hours There Were,* w. and m. Joseph Wade (ca. 1825).
62. *Hurrah! for the Bonnets of Blue,* m. Alexander Lee (ca. 1827).
63. *I Dreamt that I Dwelt in Marble Halls,* w. Alfred Bunn, m. Michael W. Balfe (1844).
64. *I Left Thee Where I Found Thee, Love,* m. Charles Gilfert (ca. 1823).
65. *I See Them on Their Winding Way,* w. Bishop Reginald Heber, m. B. Hime (ca. 1825).
66. *I'd Be a Butterfly,* w. and m. Thomas Haynes Bayly (ca. 1827).
67. *I'd Offer Thee This Hand of Mine,* m. L.T. Chadwick (1848).
68. *I'll Hang My Harp on a Willow Tree,* arr. W. Guernsey (ca. 1845).
69. *The Indian's Prayer,* m. Isaac Baker Woodbury (1846).
70. *The Ingle Side,* w. H. Ainslie, m. Thomas Van Dyke Wiesenthal (1826).
71. *Isabel,* w. Thomas Haynes Bayly, m. Henry R. Bishop (ca. 1824).
72. *'Tis Midnight Hour,* m. by an Amateur (1843).
73. *'Tis the Last Rose of Summer,* w. Thomas Moore, m. arr. Sir John Andrew Stevenson (ca. 1814).
74. *I've Left the Snow-Clad Hills,* w. and m. George Linley (ca. 1850).
75. *The Ivy Green,* w. Charles Dickens, m. Henry Russell (1838).
76. *Jamie's on the Stormy Sea,* m. Bernard Covert (1847).
77. *The Conscript's Departure,* w. Charles Jeffreys, m. Charles W. Glover (ca.

1850).

78. *Joys that We've Tasted* (1843).

79. *Jessie, The Flow'r O' Dumblane,* w. Robert Tannihill, m. Robert A. Smith (ca. 1817).

80. *John Anderson, My Jo,* m. arr. Jan Antonin Kozeluch (ca. 1803).

81. *Kate Kearney,* w. Miss Owenson, m. arr. John Davy (ca. 1807).

82. *Kathleen Mavourneen,* w. Mrs. Annie Crawford, m. F. Nicholls Crouch (ca. 1840).

83. *Kathleen O'Moore* (ca. 1833).

84. *Katy Darling,* w. J.C.Greenham (1851).

85. *The Knight Errant,* w. and m. Hortense de Beauharnais, trans. Walter Scott (ca. 1820).

86. *The Lament of the Irish Emigrant,* w. Mrs. Price Blackwood, m. William R. Dempster (1840).

87. *The Last Man,* w. Thomas Campbell, m. William H. Callcott (ca. 1840).

88. *Let Us Haste to Kelvin Grove,* w. John Sim, m. arr. Robert A. Smith (ca. 1840).

89. *Life Let Us Cherish,* m. Hans Georg Naegeli (1801).

90. *A Life on the Ocean Wave,* w. Epes Sargent, m. Henry Russell (1838).

91. *The Light Bark,* w. Miss A. Mahony, m. John Thomas Craven (ca. 1837).

92. The Light of Other Days, w. Alfred Bunn, m. Michael W. Balfe (ca. 1837).

93. *Like the Gloom of Night Retiring,* m. Henry R. Bishop (ca. 1819).

94. *Lilly Dale,* w. and m. H.S. Thompson (1852).

95. *Listen to the Mocking Bird,* w. Septimus Winner, m. Richard Milburn, arr. Septimus Winner (1855).

96. *Long, Long Ago!,* w. and m. Thomas Haynes Bayly (ca. 1833).

97. *The Lone Starry Hours,* w. Marshall S. Pike, m. James Power (1849).

98. *Love Not!* w. Mrs. Caroline Norton, m. John Blockley (ca. 1836).

99. *Love's Young Dream,* w. Thomas Moore, m. arr. Sir John Andrew Stevenson (ca. 1811).

100. *The Maid of Llangollen,* m. James Clarke (ca. 1830).

101. *The Maltese Boatman's Song,* m. L.Devereaux (ca. 1830).

102. *The Marseilles Hymn,* w. and m. Claude Rouget de Lisle (ca. 1803).

103. *Mary of Argyle,* w. Charles Jeffreys, m. Sidney Nelson (ca. 1839).

104. *Mary's Tears,* w. Thomas Moore, m. Oliver Shaw (1817).

105. *The May Queen,* w. Alfred Tennyson, m. William R. Dempster (1845).

106. *The Meeting of the Waters,* w. Thomas Moore, m. arr. Sir John A. Stevenson (ca. 1820).

107. *The Mellow Horn,* w. C.W. Hyatt, m. Mr. Jones (1831).

108. *The Minstrel's Return from the War,* w. and m. John H. Hewitt (1827).

109. *The Mistletoe Bough,* w. Thomas Haynes Bayly, m. Henry B. Bishop (ca. 1834).

110. *Molly Bawn,* w. and m. Samuel Lover (ca. 1843).

111. *My Boyhood's Home,* w. J.T. Haines, m. William M. Rooke (ca. 1842).

112. *My Heart and Lute,* w. and m. arr. Thomas Moore (ca. 1824).

113. *My Home, My Happy Home,* m. George A. Hodson (ca. 1847).

114. *My Soul is Dark,* w. Lord Byron, m.Cyrus E. Phillips (1828).

115. *My Sister Dear,* w. J. Kenny, m. from *Masaniello* by Daniel Francois Esprit Auber (ca. 1835).

116. *Near the Lake Where Drooped the Willow,* w. George P. Morris, m. arr. Charles E. Horn (1839).

117. *Nelly Bly,* w. and m. Stephen C. Foster (1849).

118. *Nelly Was a Lady,* w. and m. Stephen C. Foster (1949).

119. *No More by Sorrow,* m. John Braham (ca. 1803).

120. *Oft in the Stilly Night,* w. Thomas Moore, m. arr. Sir John A. Stevenson (ca. 1818).

121. *Oh! No, We Never Mention Her,* w. Thomas Haynes Bayly, m. arr. Henry R. Bishop (ca. 1828).

122. *Oh, Were I a Bird,* w. and m. J.T.D. Sullivan (1846).

123. *Oh Cast that Shadow from Thy Brow* (ca. 1948).

124. *O Cold Was the Climate,* m. John Monro (ca. 1823).

125. *Oh! Say Not Woman's Heart is Bought,* m. John Whitaker (ca. 1920).

126. *The Old Arm Chair,*W. Eliza Cook, m. Henry Russell (1849).

127. *Old Dog Tray,* w. and m. Stephen C. Foster (1853).

128. *Old Folks at Home,* w. and m. Stephen C. Foster (1851).

129. *The Old Granite State,* w. and m. The Hutchinson Family (1843).

130. *The Old Sexton,* w. Park Benjamin, m. Henry Russell (1841).

131. *The Origin of the Harp,* w. Thomas Moore, m. arr. Sir John A. Stevenson (ca. 1810).

132. *Pensez a Moi,* m. James G. Drake (ca. 1837).

133. *The Pilgrim Fathers,* w. Mrs. Felicia Hemans, m. Miss Browne (ca. 1825).

134. *A Place in Thy Memory, Dearest,* m. Miss Smith (ca. 1837).

135. *The Recall,* w. Mrs. Felicia Hemans, m. Miss Browne (ca. 1827).

136. *Robin Adair,* w. Lady Caroline Keppell (ca. 1812).

137. *Rocked in the Cradle of the Deep,* w. Mrs. Willard, m. Joseph Philip Knight (1840).

138. *Rory O'Moore,* w. and m. arr. Samuel Lover (ca. 1831).

139. *Rosalie, the Prairie Flower,* w. and m. George Root (1855).

140. *The Rose of Allandale,* w. Charles Jeffreys, m. Sidney Nelson (ca. 1830).

141. *Said a Smile to a Tear,* m. John Braham (ca. 1807).

142. *She Wore a Wreath of Roses,* w. Thomas Haynes Bayly, m. Joseph Philip Knight (ca. 1837).

143. *The Soldier's Bride* (ca. 1817).

144. *The Soldier's Grave,* w. Thomas Haynes Bayly, m. Thomas Williams (ca. 1829).

145. *The Soldier's Tear,* w. Thomas Haynes Bayly, m. Alexander Lee (ca. 1830).

146. *Some Love to Roam O'er the Dark Sea Foam,* w. Charles Mackay, m. Henry Russell (1836).

147. *The Song of Fitz-Eustace,* m. Dr. John Clarke (ca. 1812).

148. *The Spring Time of the Year is Coming,* w. and m. C. Thompson (ca. 1834).

149. *Sweet Gratitude,* w. Dibdin, m. James Sanderson (ca. 1817).

150. *Take This Rose,* m. Thomas Van Dyke Wiesenthal (ca. 1818).

151. *There Is No Home Like My Own,* m. Madame Malibran (ca. 1834).

152. *There's Nothing True but Heaven,* w. Thomas Moore, m. Oliver Shaw (1829).

153. *Tho' Love is Warm Awhile,* m. John Braham (ca. 1817).

154. *Thy Blue Waves O'Carron,* w. Mr. Rannie, m. John Ross (ca. 1808).

155. *The Twilight Dews,* w. Thomas Moore, m. Sir John A. Stevenson (ca. 1830).

156. *Tyrolese Evening Hymn,* w. Mrs. Felicia Hemans, m. Miss Browne (1828).

157. *The Watchman,* w. Thomas Moore (ca. 1830).

158. *Watchman Tell Us of the Night,* w. Bowring, m. Lowell Mason (1830).

159. *We Have Been Friends Together,* w. Mrs. Caroline Norton, m. Henry Russell (ca. 1836).

160. *When Stars are in the Quiet Skies,* W. Edward Lytton Bulwer, m. Alexander Ball (1838).

161. *We Have Lived and Loved Together,* w. Charles Jeffreys (ca. 1835).

162. *We Met!* w. and m. Thomas Haynes Bayly (ca. 1830).

163. *The Wedding Day,* m. James Hook (ca. 1804).

164. *When the Swallows Homeward Fly,* m. Franz Abt (ca. 1850).
165. *Why Does Azure Deck the Sky?* w. Thomas Moore, m. R. Humfrey (ca. 1808).
166. *William Tell,* m. John Braham (ca. 1818).
167. *The Willow Song,* w. J. Wesley Hanson, m. I.N. Metcalf (1841).
168. *Wind of the Winter Night, Whence Comest Thou?* w. Charles Mackay, m. Henry Russell (1836).
169. *Within a Mile of Edinburgh,* w. Tom D'Urfey, m. James Hook (ca. 1802).
170. *Woodman! Spare that Tree,* w. George P. Morris, m. Henry Russell (1837).

Appendix B.

A Selective Bibliography Of Works Consulted

Abrahams, Roger D. "Patterns of Structure and Role Relationships in the Child Ballad in the United States," *Journal of American Folklore* LXXIX (1966), 448-62.

Abrahams, Roger D. and George Foss. *Anglo-American Folksong Style.* Englewood Cliffs, 1968.

Adolphus, John. *Memoirs of John Bannister, Comedian,* 2 vols. London, 1839.

The American National Song Book, music arr. Uncle Sam. Boston, 1842.

American Society of Composers, Authors and Publishers. *How the Public Gets Its New Music.* New York, 1933.

Anna, Countesse de Bremont. *The World of Music.* New York, 1892.

Avison, Charles, *An Essay on Musical Expression.* London, 1775.

Ayars, Christine Merrick. *Contributions to the Art of Music in America by the Music Industries of Boston, 1640 to 1936.* New York, 1937.

Barrett, William Alexander. *Balfe: His Life and Work.* London, 1882.

Bayly, Thomas Haynes. *Songs, Ballads, and Other Poems,* ed. by his Widow with a memoir of the Author. London, 1844.

Bayly, Thomas Haynes. *Songs of the Affections,* ed. W.L. Hanchant. London, 1932.

Beale, Willert. *The Light of Other Days,* 2 vols. London, 1890.

Belden, H.M. ed. *Ballads and Songs Collected by the Missouri Folk-Lore Society,* 2nd. ed. University of Missouri Studies, XV, 1. Columbia, Mo. 1955.

Bernard, Kenneth A. *Lincoln and the Music of the Civil War.* Caldwell, Idaho, 1966.

Bingley, William. *Musical Biography,* 2 vols. London 1834.

Bio-Bibliographical Index of Musicians in the United States of America Since Colonial Times, 2nd. ed., prepared by the District of Columbia Historical Survey, Division of Community Services Programs, Works Projects Administration. Washington, D.C., 1956.

Boas, George, ed. *Romanticism in America.* New York, 1940.

Bode, Carl. *The Anatomy of American Popular Culture, 1840-1861.* Berkeley, 1959.

The Boston Musical Miscellany. Boston, 1811.

The Boston Musical Miscellany, 2 vols. Boston, 1815.

Bradbury, William B. *The New York Glee and Chorus Book.* Boston, 1855.

Breathnach, Breandon. *Folkmusic and Dances of Ireland.* Dublin, 1971.

Brink, Carol. *Harps in the Wind, the Story of the Singing Hutchinsons.* New York, 1947.

Bronson, Bertrand Harris. *The Ballad as Song.* Berkeley, 1969.

Bronson, Bertrand Harris. *The Traditional Tunes of the Child Ballads,* 4 vols. Princeton, 1959-71.

Brooks, Henry M. *Olden-Time Music.* Boston, 1888.

Brooks, Van Wyck. *The Times of Melville and Whitman.* New York, 1947.

Brown, James D. *Biographical Dictionary of Musicians.* London, 1886.

Brown, James D., and Stephen S. Stratton. *British Musical Biography.* Birmingham, 1897.

Bunting, Edward. *A General Collection of the Ancient Irish Music.* Dublin, 1796.

_______. *A General Collection of the Ancient Music of Ireland.* London, 1809.

Burns, Robert. *The Complete Poetical Works,* ed. Willliam Ernest Henley and Thomas F. Henderson. Boston, 1897.

Burton, Robert J. "Copyright and the Creative Arts," in *One Hundred Years of Music in America.* ed. Paul Henry Lang. New York, 1961.

Busby, Thomas. *Concert Room and Orchestra Anecdotes,* 3 vols. London, 1825.

Cantrick,Robert P. "The Blind Men and the Elephant: Scholars on Popular Music," *Ethnomusicology,* IX (1965), 100-14.

Champlin, John Denison, Jr., and William Foster Apthorp, eds. *Cyclopedia of Music and Musicians,* 3 vols. New York, 1880-90.

Chappell, William. *Popular Music of the Olden Time.* 2 vols. London, 1859.

Chase, Gilbert. *America's Music,* rev. ed. New York, 1966.

The Christy's Minstrels' Song Book, 2 vols. London, n.d.

The Christy Minstrel Album, ed. Edward F. Rimbault. London, 1861.

Clapp, William W., Jr. *A Record of the Boston Stage.* Boston, 1853.

[Clemens, Samuel]. *The Autobiography of Mark Twain,* ed. Charles Neider. New York, 1959.

Clifton, Arthur. *New Vocal Instructor.* Philadelphia, 1820.

Coffin, Tristram P. *The British Traditional Ballad in North America,* rev. ed. Publications of the American Folklore Society. Bibliographical Series, II. Philadelphia, 1963.

Cowell, Joseph. *Thirty Years Passed among the Players in England and America.* New York, 1845.

[Cowell, Mrs. Sam]. *The Cowells in America,* ed. Y. Willson Disher. London, 1934.

Crawford, Mary Caroline. *Romantic Days in Old Boston.* Boston, 1910.

Curtis, John Gould. *History of the Town of Brookline, Massachusetts.* Boston, 1933.

[Cushman, Charlotte]. *Charlotte Cushman: Her Letters and Memoirs of Her Life,* ed. Emma Stebbins. Boston, 1879.

Custis, George Washington Parke. *Recollections and Private Memoirs of Washington.* New York, 1860.

Davey, Henry. *History of English Music.* London, 1895.

Davis, Arthur Kyle, Jr., ed. *Traditional Ballads of Virginia.* Charlottesville, 1957.

Denisoff, R. Serge. "The Religious Roots of the American Song of Persuasion," *Western Folklore,* XXIX (1970), 175-84.

Dibdin, Charles. *The Professional Life of Mr. Dibdin, written by Himself, Together with the Words of Six Hundred Songs Selected from His Works,* 4 vols. London, 1803.

Dibdin, Charles, the Younger. *Professional and Literary Memoirs,* ed. George Speaight. London, 1956.

Dibdin, Thomas. *Reminiscences,* 2 vols. London, 1827.

Dichter, Harry, and Elliott Shapiro. *Early American Sheet Music . . . 1768-1889.* New York, 1941.

Dickinson, Emily. Letters, ed. Mabel Loomis Todd. New York. 1931.

Doley, James Edward. "Thomas Hastings: American Church Musician." Ph. D. diss., Florida State University, 1963.

Drew, Elizabeth. *Poetry.* New York, 1959.

[Dunlap, William]. *Diary of Willilam Dunlap, 1766-1839,* 3 vols. Collections of the New York Historical Society for the Year 1929, LXII. New York, 1969.

Dunlap, William. *A History of the American Theatre.* New York, 1832.

Durang, Charles. "The Philadelphia Stage, from 1749 to 1821," Philadelphia *Sunday Dispatch*(1854-60).

Ellis, S.M. *The Life of Michael Kelly...1762-1826.* London, 1930.

Ellsworth, Ray. "Jenny Lind and Ole Bull in America," *Hi-Fi Stereo Review* (Sept., 1965), 58-62.

Elson, Louis C., ed. *Vocal Music and Musicians.* University Musical Encyclopedia, VI. New York, 1912.

Epstein, Dena J. *Music Publishing in Chicago before 1871: the Firm of Root and Cady, 1858-1871.* Detroit Studies in Music Bibliography, XIV. Detroit, 1969.

Ewen, David. *History of Popular Music.* New York, 1961.

Farmer, Henry George. *A History of Music in Scotland.* London, 1947.

Father Kemp's Old Folks Concert Music. Boston, n.d.

Fatout, Paul. "Threnodies of the Ladies' Books," *Musical Quarterly,* XXXI (1945), 464-78.

Finkelstein, Herman. *Public Performance Rights in Music and Performance Right Societies,* rev. ed. New York, 1961.

Finley, Ruth E. *The Lady of Godey's, Sarah Josepha Hale.* Philadelphia, 1931.

Fisher, William Arms. *The Music that Washington Knew.* Boston, 1931.

———. *Notes on Music in Old Boston.* Boston, 1918.

———. *One Hundred and Fifty Years of Music Publishing in the United States.* Boston, 1933.

Fithian, Philip Vickers. *Journal and Letters, 1767-1774,* ed. John Rogers Williams. Princeton, 1900.

Fitzball, Edward. *Thirty-Five Years of a Dramatic Author's Life,* 2 vols. London, 1859.

Fitzgerald, Percy. *Music Hall Land.* London, n.d.

Fitz-gerald, S.J. Adair. *Stories of Famous Songs,* 2 vols. Philadelphia, 1901.

The Forget Me Not Songster. New York, n.d.

Fuld, James J. *The Book of World-Famous Music,* rev. ed. New York, 1971.

Gagey, Edward McAdoo. *Ballad Opera.* New York, 1937.

Gamble, William. *Music Engraving and Printing.* London, 1923.

Gardner, William. *Music and Friends,* 3 vols. London: I and II, 1838; III, 1853.

The Gem of Song, ed. by an Amateur. Boston, 1846.

Gentle Annie Melodist. New York, 1858.

Gerson, Robert A. *Music in Philadelphia.* Philadelphia, 1940.

Gilbert, Henry F. "Folk Music and Art-Music, A Discussion and a Theory," *Musical Quarterly,* III (1917), 577-601.

Gombosi, Otto. "Stephen Foster and 'Gregory Walker'," *Musical Quarterly,* XXX (1944), 133-46.

Goodwin, Thomas. *Sketches and Impressions.* New York, 1887.

Greenway, John. *American Songs of Protest.* New York, 1960.

Hale, Edward Everett. *James Russell Lowell and His Friends.* Cambridge, Mass., 1899.

Haskins, John C. "John Rowe Parker and the *Euterpeiad,*" *Notes of the Music Library Association* (1951), 447-56.

Hastings,Thomas. *Dissertation on Musical Taste.* New York, 1853.

Hehr, Milton Gerald. "Musical Activities in Salem, Massachusetts: 1783-1823." Ph.D. diss., Boston Univ., 1963.

Hewitt, John H. *Shadows on the Wall.* Baltimore, 1877.

Hipsher, Edward Ellsworth. *American Opera.* Philadelphia, 1927.

Hitchcock, H. Wiley. "An Early American Melodrama: The Indian Princess of J.N. Barker and John Bray," *Notes of the Music Library Association* (1955), 375-88.

Hogan, Ita Margaret. *Anglo-Irish Music, 1780-1830.* Cork, 1966.

Hogarth, George. *Musical History, Biography and Criticism.* New York, 1845.

Hopkins, Kenneth. *English Poetry: A Short History.* Philadelphia, 1962.

Houghton, Walter E., and G. Robert Stange. *Victorian Poetry and Poetics.* Boston, 1959.

Howard, John Tasker. "The Hewitt Family in American Music," *Musical Quarterly,* XVII (1931), 25-39.

_______ "The Literature of Stephen Foster," *Notes of the Musical Library Association,* Second series, I (1944), 10-15.

.... "Discovered Fosteriana," *Musical Quarterly,* XXI (1935), 17-24.

_______ *Stephen Foster, America's Troubadour.* New York, 1953.

_______ *Our American Music,* 4th ed. New York, 1965.

Ireland, Joseph N. *Records of the New York Stage from 1750 to 1860,* 2 vols. New York, 1866-67.

Jackson, George Pullen. "Stephen Foster's Debt to American Folk-Song," *Musical Quarterly,* XXII (1936), 154-69.

Jackson, George Stuyvesant. *Early Songs of Uncle Sam.* Boston, 1933.

Jarvis, Charles, ed. *Lady's Musical Library,* 2 vols. Philadelphia, 1842-43.

Johnson, H. Earle. "The Adams Family and Good Listening," *Journal of the American Musicological Society,* XI (1958), 165-76.

_______ *Musical Interludes in Boston, 1795-1830.* New York, 1943.

Johnson, Helen Kendrick. *Familiar Songs.* New York, 1881.

Jones, F.O., ed. *A Handbook of American Music and Musicians.* Canaseraga, N.Y., 1886.

Jones, Howard Mumford. *The Harp That Once.* New York, 1937.

Lacy, Dan. "The Quagmire," *TheSaturday Review* (27 November 1971), pp. 24-28.

Lahee, Henry C. *Annals of Music in America.* Boston, 1922.

Laws, G. Malcolm, Jr. *American Balladry from British Broadsides.* Publications of the American Folklore Society, VIII. Philadelphia, 1957.

_______ *Native American Balladry,* rev. ed. Publications of the American Folklore Society, I. Philadelphia, 1964.

Leach, MacEdward, ed. *The Ballad Book.* New York, 1955.

Lenhart, Charmenz S. *Musical Influence on American Poetry.* Athens, Ga., 1956.

Levy, Lester S. *Grace Notes in American History.* Norman, OK., 1967.

Loesser, Arthur. *Men, Women, and Pianos.* New York, 1954.

Lowens, Irving. *Music and Musicians in Early America.* New York, 1964.

Ludlow, Noah M. *Dramatic Life as I Found It.* New York 1966.

Mackerness, E.D. *A Social History of English Music.* London, 1964.

Montague, Richard A. "Charles E. Horn, His Life and Works." D. Ed. diss., Florida State Univ., 1959.

Moore, John W. *Complete Encyclopedia of Music.*Boston, 1854.

[Moore, Thomas]. *A Selection of Irish Melodies with Symphonies and Accompaniments by Sir John Stevenson, Mus. Doc, and Characteristic Words by Thomas Moore, esqr.* Numbers 1-7. London, 1808-18.

_______ *A Selection of Irish Melodies with Symphonies and Accompaniments by Henry R. Bishop, and Characteristic Words by Thomas Moore.* Numbers 8-10, and Supplement. London, 1821-34.

_______ *National Airs, and Other Songs.* London, 1858.

_______ *A Selection of Popular National Airs,* music arr. Sir John Stevenson. London, [1818].

Mornweck, Evelyn Foster. *Chronicles of Stephen Foster's Family,* 2 vols.

Pittsburgh, 1944.

[Moscheles, Ignatz]. *Recent Music and Musicians,* ed. Mrs. Moscheles, adapted from the original German by A.D. Coleridge. New York, 1873.

The MusicalCarcanet. New York, 1832.

Nathan,Hans. *Dan Emmett and the Rise of Early Negro Minstrelsy.* Norman, Ok., 1962.

——— *"Dixie," Musical Quarterly,* XXXV (1949), 60-84.

——— "The Tyrolese Family Rainer and the Vogue of Singing Mountain-Troupes in Europe and America," *Musical Quarterly,* XXXII (1946), 63-79.

Nevin, Robert P. "Stephen C. Foster and Negro Minstrelsy," *The Atlantic Monthly,* XX (1867), 608-16.

Nicholson, Margaret. *A Manual of Copyright Practice.* *Rosalie, the Prairie Flower Melodist.* Boston, 1859.

Russell, Henry. *Cheer! Boys, Cheer!.* London, 1895.

Ryan, Thomas. *Recollections of an Old Musician.* New York, 1899.

The Scots Musical Museum, 6 vols.Edinburgh, 1787-1803.

Shemel, Sidney, and M. William Krasilovsky. *This Business of Music,* rev. ed. edited by Paul Ackerman. New York, 1971.

Simpson, Harold. A Century of Ballads, 1810-1910. London, 1910.

The Singer's Companion. New York, 1854.

Sonneck, Oscar. *A Bibliography of Early Secular American Music,* rev. William Treat Upton. New York, 1964.

——— *Early Concert-Life in America, 1731-1800.* Leipzig, 1907.

——— *Francis Hopkinson...and James Lyon.* Washington, D.C., 1905.

——— *Suum Cuique.* New York, 1916.

Spaeth, Sigmund. *A History of Popular Music in America.* New York, 1948.

——— *Read 'Em and Weep,* rev. ed. New York, 1945.

——— *Weep Some More, My Lady.* Garden City, 1927.

St. Leger's Reminiscences of Balfe. London, 1870.

Stevens, Denis, ed. *A History of Song.* New York, 1961.

Stevenson, Robert. "Opera Beginnings in the New World," *Musical Quarterly,* XLV (1959), 8-25.

Stone, Henry Dickinson. *Personal Recollections of the Drama, or Theatrical Reminiscences.* Albany, 1873.

Stone, James. "Mid-Nineteenth-Century American Beliefs in the Social Values of Music," *Musical Quarterly,* XLII (1957), 38-99.

Stoutamire, Albert. *Music of the Old South.* Rutherford, N.J. 1972.

Thompson, Harold W., ed. *A Pioneer Songster.* Ithaca, 1958.

Turner, Michael R. *The Parlour Song Book.* New York, 1972.

Upton, George. *Musical Memories.* Chicago, 1908.

Upton, William Treat. *Art Song in America.* Boston, 1930.

Warren,Alba H., Jr. *English Poetic Theory, 1825-1865.* New York, 1966.

Waters, Edward N. "John Sullivan Dwight," *Musical Quarterly,* XXI (1935), 69-88.

Weichlein, William J. *A Checklist of American Music Periodicals, 1850-1900.* Detroit Studies in Music Bibliography, XVI. Detroit, 1970.

Wellek, Rene. *The Romantic Age. A History of Modern Criticism,* II. New Haven, 1955.

Wells, Evelyn Kendrick. *The Ballad Tree.* New York, 1950.

Wemyss, Francis Courtney. *Theatrical Biography.* Glasgow, 1848.

——— *Twenty-Six Years of the Life of an Actor and Manager,* 2 vols. New York, 1847.

White, Eric Walter. *The Rise of English Opera.* New York, 1951.

Wilson, Arthur Herman. *A History of the Philadelphia Theatre, 1835-1855.* Philadelphia, 1935.

Winsor, Justin, ed. *The Memorial History of Boston... 1630-1880,* 4 vols. Boston, 1881.

Wolfe, Richard J. *Secular Music in America, 1801-1825,* 3 vols. New York, 1964.

Wood, William B. *Personal Recollections of the Stage.* Philadelphia, 1855.

Wordsworth, William. *Poetical Works,* ed. Thomas Hutchinson. Rev. ed. Ernest De Selincourt. London, 1936.

Wunderlich, Charles Edward. "A History and Bibliography of Early American Musical Periodicals, 1782-1852." Ph. D. diss., Univ. of Michigan, 1962.

Appendix C.

Musical Examples

Ex. 1: Grannis, Do They Miss Me at Home?

Do they miss me at home, Do they miss me? 'Twould be an assurance
most dear,

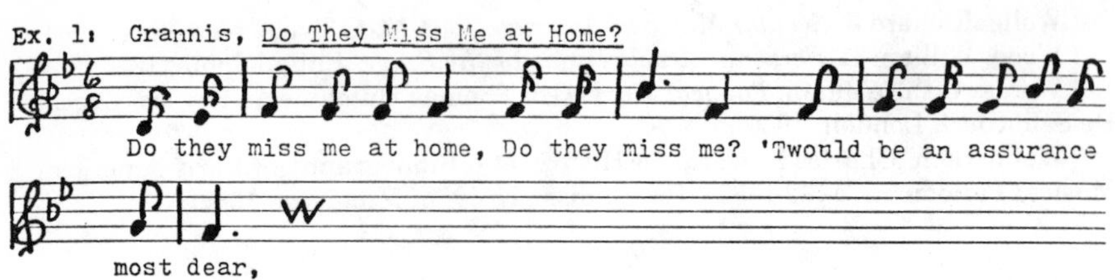

Ex. 2: Foster, Massa's in de Cold Ground.

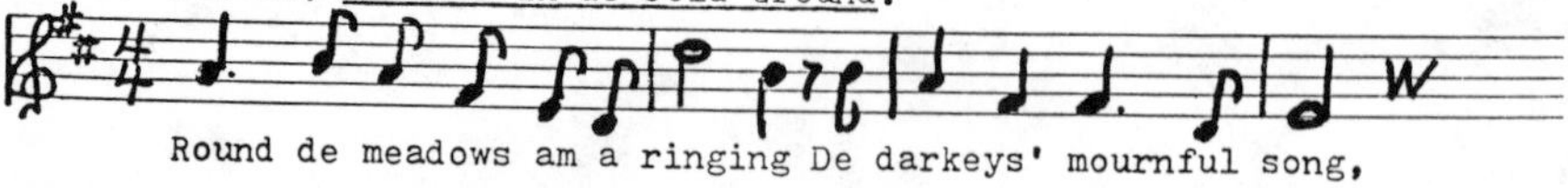

Round de meadows am a ringing De darkeys' mournful song,

Ex. 3: Cole, O'er the Far Blue Mountain.

O'er the far blue mountain, O'er the white sea foam,

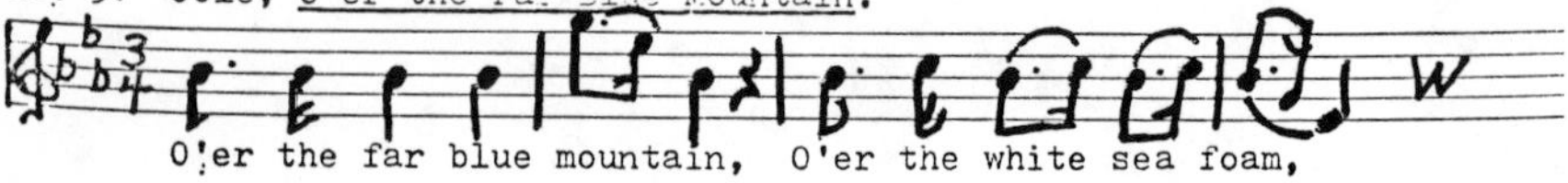

Ex. 4: Foster, The Voice of By Gone Days.

Ah! the voice of by gone days Will come back a-gain,

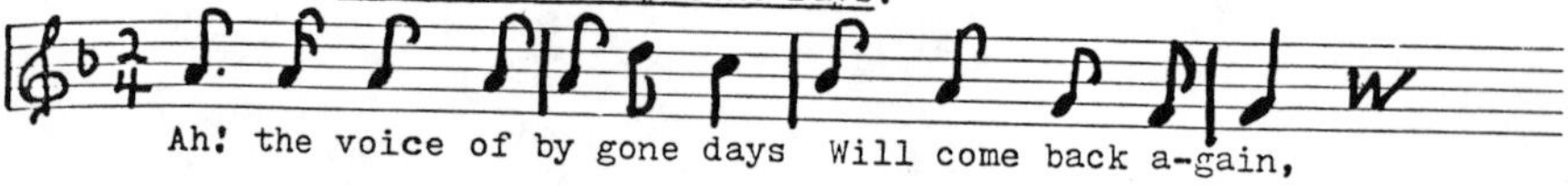

Ex. 5: Russell, The Old Arm Chair.

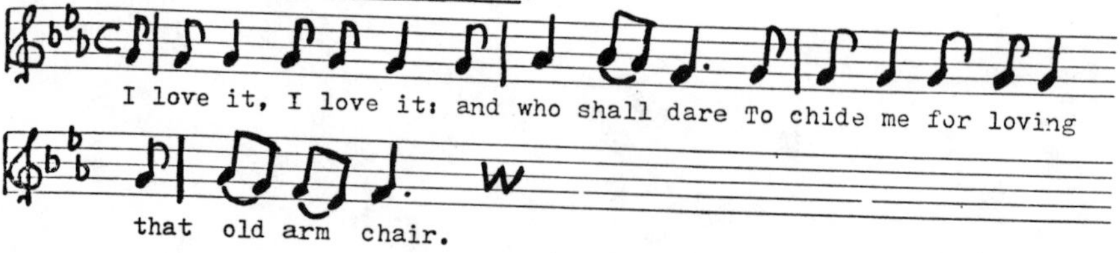

I love it, I love it: and who shall dare To chide me for loving
that old arm chair.

Ex. 6: Dempster, The Blind Boy.

Oh! tell me the form of the soft summer air, That tosses so
gently the curls of my hair!

Ex. 7: Wallace, The Bell-Ringer.

Ex. 8: Foster, Old Folks at Home.

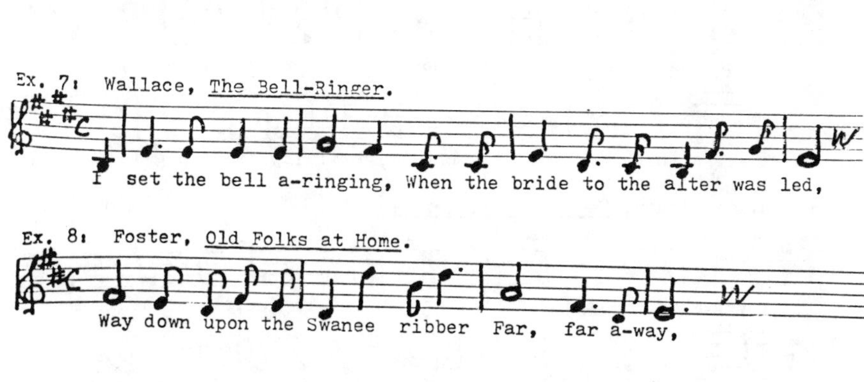
I set the bell a-ringing, When the bride to the alter was led,
Way down upon the Swanee ribber Far, far a-way,

Ex. 9: Foster, Farewell, My Lilly Dear.

Oh! Lilly dear, it grieves me The tale I have to tell;

Ex. 10: Foster, The Village Maiden.

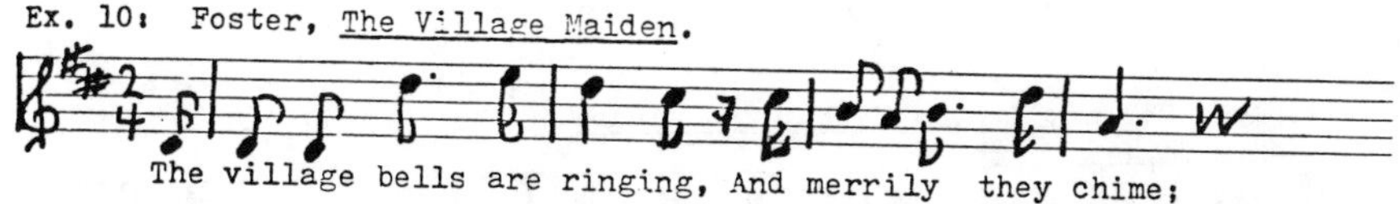
The village bells are ringing, And merrily they chime;

Ex. 11: Scott, Annie Lawrie.

Max---welton's banks are bonny, where early falls the dew.

Ex. 12: A Young Lady of Georgia, No More.
Oh tell me not of future peace Nor let my wand'ring fancy soar
Ex. 13: Lover, My Mother Dear.
There was a place in child hood, That I remember well, And
there a voice of sweetest tone bright fairy tales did tell,
Ex. 14: Woodbury, He Doeth All Things Well.
I remember how I lov'd her, when a little guiltless child, I
saw her in the cradle As she look'd on me and smil'd,
Ex. 15: Horn, The American Indian Girl.
O give me back my forest shade, Where once I roam'd so blithe and gay
Ex, 16: Carter, I Seen Her at the Window.
Last Sunday night as I walk'd out, I know I was quite lazy,
Ex. 17: Hagen, Anna.
The morning was fair and the Ham--let look'd gay,

Ex. 18a: Blewitt, Come to the Highlands (Boston, ca. 1830).
b: Brown, The Song My Mother Sings (Boston, 1845).
c: Balfe, The Light of Other Days (New York, ca. 1835).
d: Bowker, Jenny Dale (Boston, 1854).
e: Buckley, Kiss Me Quick and Go (New York, 1856).
f: Poulton, Willie Bell (Buffalo, 1854).
Ex. 19a: Hyme, Wilt Thou Meet Me? (Boston, ca. 1830).
b: Hargreaves, Song of the Bedouin Maid (Philadelphia, ca. 1835).
c: Allen, The Ocean Burial (Boston, 1850).
Ex. 20: James Hewitt, Advice to the Ladies (New York, ca. 1805).
No more along the daisy Mead, I meet my fickle Swain, Whose
Auld Lang Syne (New York, ?).

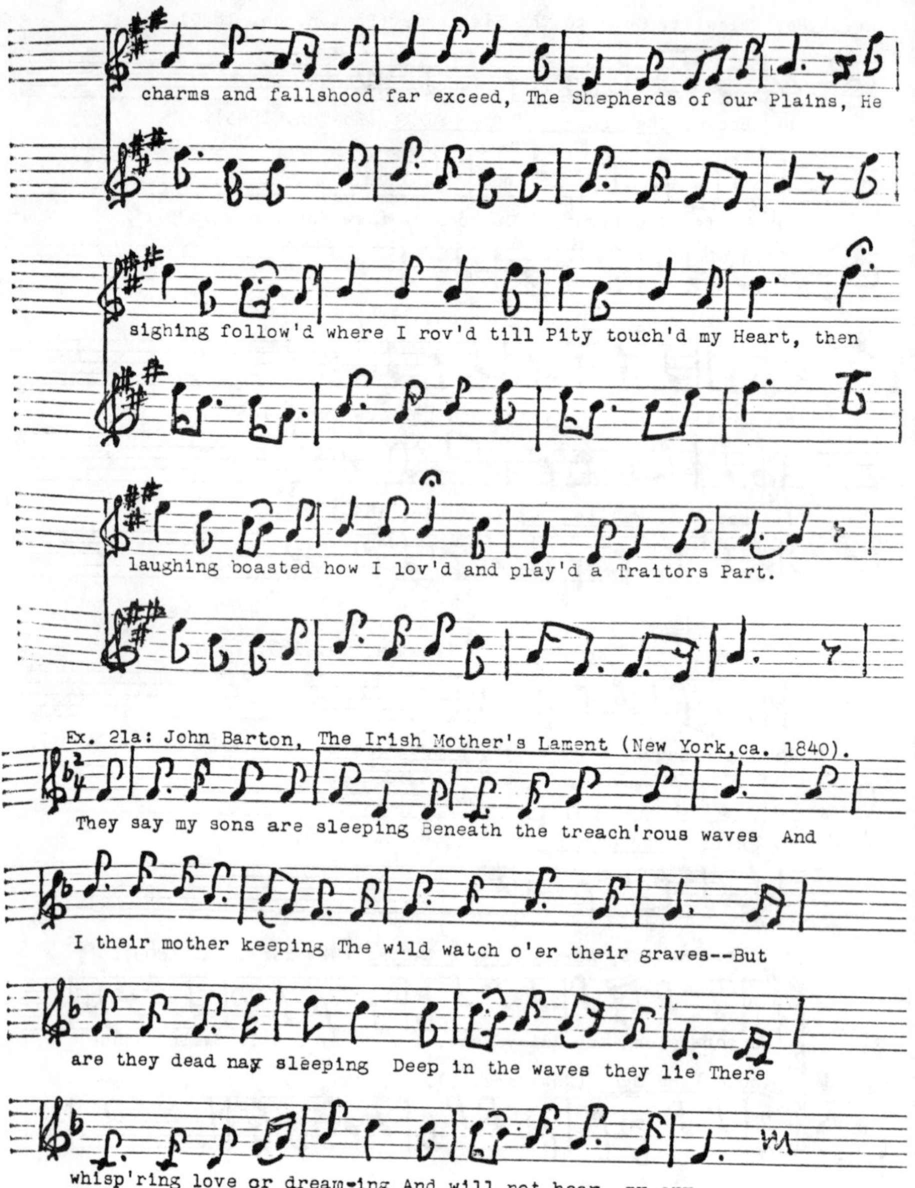
charms and fallshood far exceed, The Shepherds of our Plains, He
sighing follow'd where I rov'd till Pity touch'd my Heart, then
laughing boasted how I lov'd and play'd a Traitors Part.

Ex. 21a: John Barton, The Irish Mother's Lament (New York, ca. 1840).

They say my sons are sleeping Beneath the treach'rous waves And
I their mother keeping The wild watch o'er their graves--But
are they dead nay sleeping Deep in the waves they lie There
whisp'ring love or dream-ing And will not hear my cry.

b: J.K., The Yellow Rose of Texas (New York, 1858).

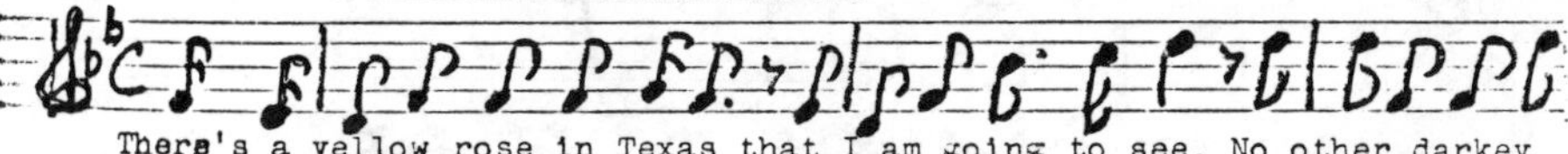

There's a yellow rose in Texas that I am going to see, No other darkey

knows her, no darkey only me; She cried so when I left her, it like to

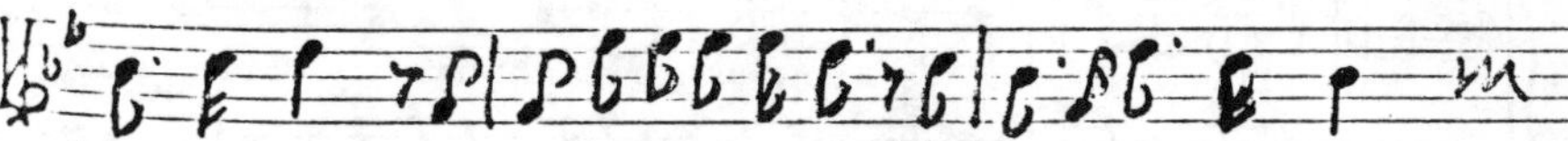

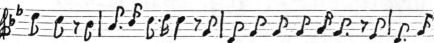

broke my heart, And if I ever find her we never more will part.

Ex. 22: Yellow Rose, first half of tune.

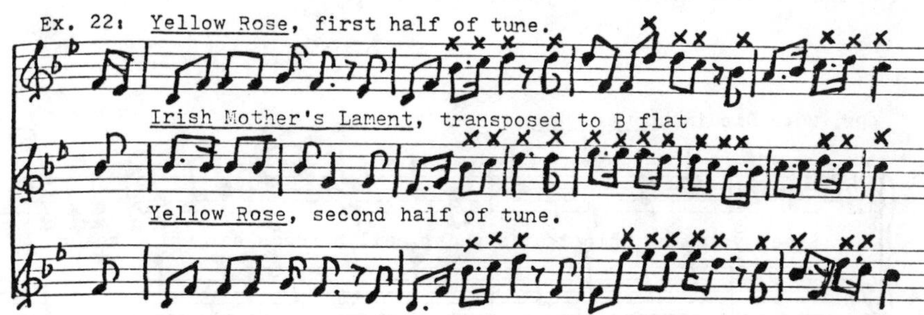
Irish Mother's Lament, transposed to B flat
Yellow Rose, second half of tune.

Ex. 23: Roslin Castle.

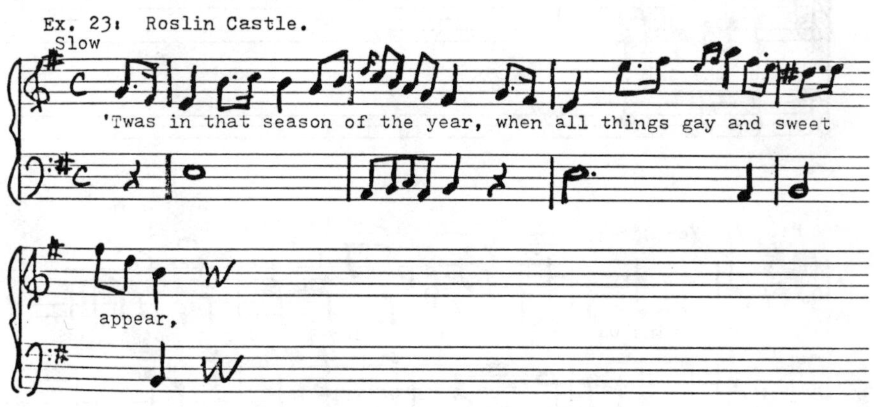
Slow
'Twas in that season of the year, when all things gay and sweet
appear,

Ex. 24: Carr, Ellen Arise.
See from yon cot---tage win---dow plays
Ex. 25: Von Hagen, May Morning.
The mellow lustre of the Morn,was mingling with the Golden beam,
Ex. 26: Dibdin, Lovely Nan.
Sweet is the Ship that's under sail,Spreads her white bosom
to the Gale,
Ex. 27: Von Hagen, Anna.
The morning was fair and the Ham-let look'd gay not a cloud

Ex. 28: Abrams, A Smile and a Tear.
You own I'm complacent, but tell me I'm cold,
Ex, 29: Davy, Aurelia Betray'd.
Aurelia was the sweetest maid that cheer'd the hallow vale
Ex. 30: Braham, On This Cold Flinty Rock!
(Braham cntd.)
On this cold flinty rock I will lay down my head,

Ex. 31: Spofforth, The Wood Robin.
Flute
Pastorale
Ex. 32: Braham, The Willow.
Oh take me to your arms my love, For keen the wind doth blow,
Ex. 33: Loder, The Bride.
She's thine for ever now thine own, My beautiful! my best, I
pp
give her freely, yet I feel Deep sorrow at my breast,

Ex. 34: Loder, The Bride.
From infancy her life hath seemed The very life of mine, The
pp
ad libitum
priceless treasure of my soul; The altar maketh thine! yes
colla Voce
Ex. 35: Balfe, The Fair Land of Poland.
When the fair land of Po-land was plough'd by the hoof
Ex. 36: Balfe, 'Tis Sad to Leave Our Fatherland.
Yet hard as are such ills to bear, And deeply though they smart, Their
Accello. il tempo
cresc.

(Balfe cntd.)

pangs are light to those who are the orphans of the heart 'Tis
pp
Ex. 37: Wallace, The Bell-Ringer.
I set the bell aringing, When the bride to the altar was led, And I
PP
p
p
fz
lov'd to hear it swinging So merrily over my head; The children flung
f>
gay garlands round

Ex. 38: Accompaniment Patterns.
a.
b.
c.
d.
e.
f.
g.
h.
i.
j.
k.
l.

Appendix D

Musical Supplement

A collection of sixteen representative parlor songs from Periods I (1790-1810), II (1811-1840) and III (1841-1860). They are listed below alphabetically by title, followed by the date of first publication in the United States and the page number. The compositions were selected as those best calculated to illustrate the text. They also number amongst the most popular song of early America.

(Note: None of the compositions of Stephen Foster are included since the music is widely available and published in its original format by Da Capo and others.)

AULD LANG SYNE.

a favorite Scotch Song

New York Engraved Printed & Sold by E. Riley, No. 29 Chatham Str.
Andante
Should Auld acquaintance be for-got, And ne-ver brought to mind Should
Auld acquaintance be for-got, And days O Lang Syne. For Auld Lang
Syne my dear for Auld Lang Syne, We'll take a Cup O' kind-ness yet for
Auld Lang Syne.

2

We twa ha'e run about the braes,
And pued the gowans fine;
But we've wandered mony a weary foot,
Sin Auld Lang Syne.
For Auld Lang Syne, &c.

3

We twa ha'e paidlet i' the burn,
Frae morning Sun till dine;
But Saes between us braid ha'e roar'd
Sin Auld Lang Syne.
For Auld Lang Syne, &c.

4

And there's a hand my trusty feire,
And gie's a hand o' thine;
And we'll tak' a right gude willie waught,
For Auld Lang Syne.
For Auld Lang Syne, &c.

5

And surely you'll be your pint stoup,
And surely I'll be mine;
And we'll take a Cup O' kindness yet,
For Auld Lang Syne.
For Auld Lang Syne, &c.

Auld Robin Gray
Affettuoso
Young JAMIE loo'd me weel, and sought me for his Bride, but
saving a Crown he had nae thing else be-side, To mak' his crown a poun' my
JAMIE went to Sea, and the crown and the poun' were baith for me. He
had nae been gane but a Year and a day, when my Father brak' his Arm & our
Cow was stoun a-wa' my Mither she fell sick and JAMIE at the Sea, and
Auld ROBIN GRAY came a courting to me.

(2)

My Father coudna' work, and my Mither coudna' spin,
I toiled day and night, but their bread I coudna' win,
Auld Robin fed them baith, and wi' tears in his ee
Said, JENNY, for their sakes, Oh! marry me.
My heart it said na, and I look'd for JAMIE back,
But the wind it blew high, and the Ship it was a wreck,
The Ship it was a wreck, why didna' JAMIE die?
And why do I live to say, Ah! wae's me.

(3)

My Father urg'd me sair; my Mither didna' speak,
But she look'd in my face, till my heart was like to break,
So they gi'ed him my hand, tho' my heart was on the Sea,
And Auld ROBIN GRAY is gude man to me.
I hadna' been wife a week but only four
When sitting sae mournfully at mine ain door,
I saw my JAMIE'S Ghaist; for I coudna' think it he,
Till he said, I'm come back, love, to marry thee.

(4)

Sair sair did we greet, and little could we say,
We took but ae kiss, and we tore ourselves away,
I wish I were dead; but I'm nae like to die
And why do I live to say, Ah! wae's me?
I gang like a Gaist, and I care na' to spin,
I darena' think on JAMIE, for that wou'd be a sin,
But I'll do my best a gude wife to be,
For Auld ROBIN GRAY, is sae kind to me.

The Bay of Biscay O!

As Sung by Mr INCLEDON

In Spanish Dollars or the Priest of the Parish;

Composed by JOHN DAVY.

Price 25 Cts.

NEW YORK: Publish'd by Wm DUBOIS No 126 Broadway.

MODERATO
EXPRESSIVO
p
f
Loud roar'd the dreadful thun-der, The
rain a de-luge showers; The clouds were rent a-sun-der, By
light'ning's vi-vid pow'rs; The night both drear and dark, Our

poor de lu-ded bark Till next day There she lay In the BAY of BISCAY
O.

2

Now dash'd upon the billow,
Our op'ning timbers creak;
Each fears a wa'try pillow,
None ftop the dreadful leak.
To cling to flipp'ry fhrouds,
Each breathlefs feaman crowds,
As fhe lay
Till the day
In the BAY of BISCAY O!

3

At length the wish'd-for morrow,
Broke thro' the hazy fky,
Absorb'd in silent sorrow
Each heav'd the bitter figh,
The dismal wreck to view,
Struck horror to the crew;
As fhe lay
On that day
In the BAY of BISCAY O!

4

Her yielding timbers sever
Her pitchy seams are rent,
When heav'n all bounteous ever
Its boundlefs mercy sent.
A fail in sight appears
We hail her with three cheers
Now we sail
With the gale
From the BAY of BISCAY O!

BE KIND TO THE LOVED ONES AT HOME

Song

Composed and Arranged for the

PIANO FORTE

AND

AFFECTIONATELY INSCRIBED TO

HIS MOTHER

By

J. B. Woodbury.

25 cts. nett.

BOSTON

Published by MARTIN & BEALS 131 Washington St.

BE KIND TO THE LOVED ONES AT HOME.

Music composed by
I. B. WOODBURY.
ANDANTE
ESPRESSIVO.
Be kind to thy father—for when thou wert young, Who loved thee so fondly as
he? He caught the first accents that fell from thy tongue, And joined in thy innocent
glee. Be kind to thy father, for now he is old, His locks in-termingled with

gray; His footsteps are feeble, once fearless and bold, Thy father is passing a -
way Be kind to thy mother—for lo! on her brow May
traces of sor-row be seen; Oh well may'st thou cherish and
comfort her now, For lov - ing and kind hath she been. Re -

member thy mother—for thee will she pray, As long as God giveth her breath; With
accents of kindness then cheer her lone way, E'en to the dark valley of death.
Be kind to thy brother—his heart will have dearth, If the
smile of thy joy be withdrawn; The flowers of feeling will fade at their birth, If the

dew of affection be gone. Be kind to thy brother- wherever you are, The
love of a brother shall be An or - nament purer and
richer by far Than pearls from the depth of the sea.

4

Be kind to thy sister—not many may know
The depth of true sisterly love;
The wealth of the ocean lies fathoms below
The surface that sparkles above.
Be kind to thy father, once fearless and bold,
Be kind to thy mother so near;
Be kind to thy brother, nor show thy heart cold,
Be kind to thy sister so dear.

THE BLUE JUNIATA
MARION DIX SULLIVAN.
E. L. WHITE.
Wild rov'd an Indian girl, Bright Alfa - rata, Where sweep the waters Of the
blue Juni - ata. Swift as an Antelope, Thro' the forest going

Loose were her jetty locks In wavy tresses flowing.

2

Gay was the mountain song
  Of bright Alfarata,
Where sweep the waters
  Of the blue Juniata.
Strong and true my arrows are
In my painted quiver,
Swift goes my light canoe
Adown the rapid river.

3

Bold is my warrior good
  The love of Alfarata,
Proud waves his snowy plume
  Along the Juniata.
Soft and low he speaks to me,
And then his war-cry sounding,
Rings his voice in thunder loud
From height to height resounding.

4

So sang the Indian girl,
  Bright Alfarata,
Where sweep the waters
  Of the blue Juniata.
Fleeting years have borne away
The voice of Alfarata,
Still sweeps the river on
  Blue Juniata.

FLOW GENTLY SWEET AFTON,
(A Ballad)

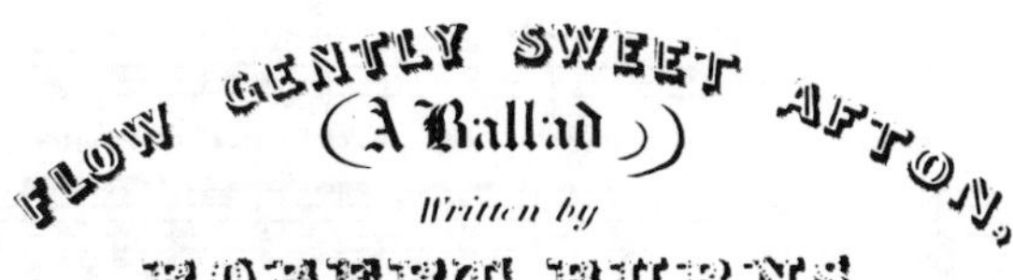

Written by

ROBERT BURNS

MUSIC

Composed and Arranged

by

J. E. SPILLMAN.

Philadelphia. George Willig 171 Chesnut Street.

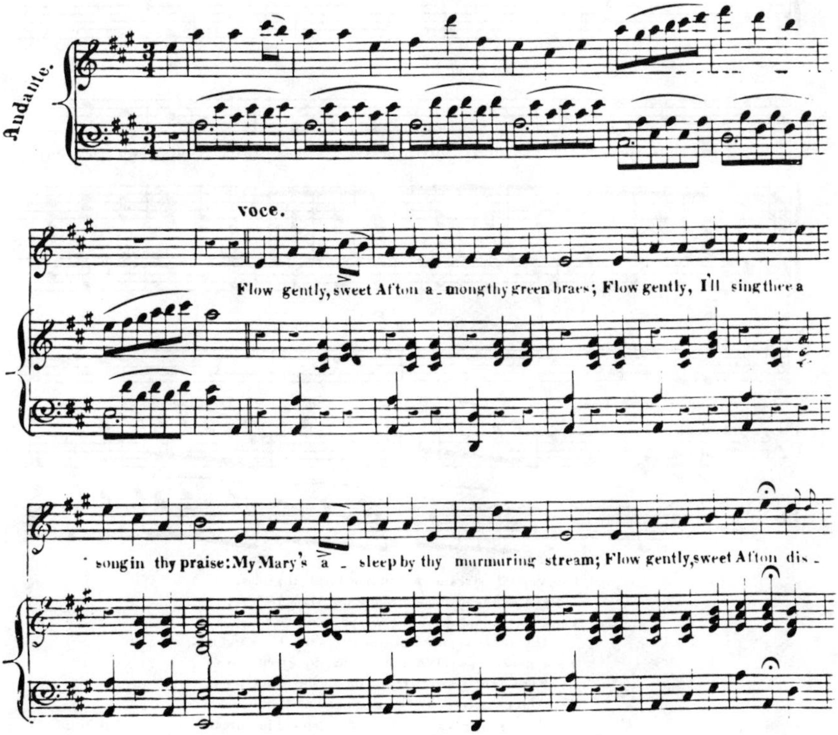

Andante.
voce.
Flow gently, sweet Afton a _ mong thy green braes; Flow gently, I'll sing thee a
song in thy praise: My Mary's a _ sleep by thy murmuring stream; Flow gently, sweet Afton dis _

turb not her dream. Thou dove, whose soft e_cho re_sounds from the hill, Thou
green crested lap_wing, with noise loud and shrill, Ye wild whistling
war_blers your mu_sic for_bear I charge you dis_turb not my
slumber_ing fair.

Thy crystal stream, Afton how lovely it glides;
And winds by the cot where my Mary resides;
There, oft as mild ev'ning weeps over the lea,
Thy sweet scented groves shade my Mary and me.
Flow gently, sweet Afton among thy green braes
Flow gently sweet river, the theme of my lays,
My Mary's asleep by thy murmuring stream.
Flow gently sweet Afton, disturb not her dream.

THE

Hazel Dell

SONG and CHORUS

BY

WURZEL.

Pearson, Sc. 25 Cts. nett.

Published by WILLIAM HALL & SON, 239 Broadway. New York

DRESSLER & CLAYTON, 288 Broadway.

Boston, HENRY TOLMAN. Phil^a LEE & WALKER.

"THE HAZEL DELL."

WURZEL.
Moderato.
In the Ha - zel Dell my Nelly's sleep-ing, Nelly lov'd so long! And my
lone-ly, lone-ly watch I'm keep-ing, Nel-ly lost and gone; Here in

moon-light oft-en we have wan-der'd Thro' the si-lent shade, Now where
lea-fy branches drooping down-ward, Lit-tle Nel-ly's laid.
CHORUS 2nd time PP.
AIR.
All a-lone my watch I'm keep-ing In the Ha-zel Dell, For my
ALTO.
TENOR.
All a-lone my watch I'm keep-ing In the Ha-zel Dell, For my
BASS.
PIANO.

2710

dar - ling Nelly's near me sleep - ing, — Nelly dear, fare - well.
dar - ling Nelly's near me sleep - ing, — Nelly dear, fare - well.
2nd Verse. In the ha - zel dell my Nelly's sleep - ing, Where the flow - ers
3rd " Now I'm wea - ry, friendless and for - sa - ken, Watch - ing here a -
wave, And the si - lent stars are nightly weep - ing O'er poor Nel - ly's
lone, Nel - ly thou no more will fondly cheer me, With thy lov - ing
grave; Hope that once my bo - som fondly cher - ish'd Smile no more for
tone; Yet for - ev - er shall thy gen - tle im - age In my mem - 'ry
2718
me, Ev - ry dream of joy a - las has per - ish'd, Nelly dear with thee.
dwell, And my tears thy lone - ly grave shall moist - en, Nelly dear, fare - well.

Hours there were
A Favourite
Song
written & arranged for the
PIANO FORTE
by
Joseph Wade Esq.
Philadelphia Published & sold by G.Willig 171 Chestnut Street.
TENDERLY.
Hours there were to mem_ry dear_er, Than the sunbright scenes of day;
Friends were fond_er, joys were near_er, But a_las they've fled a_way.

Oh! 'twas when the moonlight play_ing, O'er the val_leys si_lent grove,
Told the bliss_ful hour for straying, With my fond, my faith_ful love.
mf
pp
ppp

2.

Oft when ev'ning faded mildly,
O'er the wave our bark would rove;
Then we've heard the night-bird wildly
Breathe his vesper tale of love.—
Songs like his, my love would sing me,
Songs that warble round me yet.—
Ah! but where does mem'ry bring me,
Scenes like those I must forget.

3.

But in dreams let love be near me,
With the joys that bloom'd before;
Slumb'ring then 'twill sweetly cheer me,
Calm to live my pleasures o'er.
Then perhaps some hope may waken,
In this heart deprest with care,
And like flow'rs in vale forsaken,
Live a lonely beauty there.

How happy was my humble lot

A FAVORITE BALLAD

Sung by Mrs Old-mixon & Miss Broadhurst

Composed by J.Hewitt

Andante
mf
f
_How happy was my humble lot when Carlos first came wooing
I knew not of those wily arts men practice for our ruin He vow'd he lov'd and I be
liev'd he vow'd it o'er & o'er for him I left my father's Cot where I was bless'd tho' poor where I was
bless'd tho' poor.

2

Alas. the day when I with him, did leave my parent dear,
Behind me oft I caſt my eyes, he kiſs'd the guſhing tear,
I view'd the Seat of rural bliſs, I view'd it o'er and o'er,
For him I left my Father's Cot, where I was bleſs'd tho poor

3

Oft has he ta'en me in his arms, and vow'd eternal love,
He ſwore the Sun ſhould ceaſe to ſhine, ere he'd inconſtant prove;
Yet he alas! is from me flown; Lifes Sunſhine is no more,
Ah. why did I leave my father's Cot, where I was bleſs'd tho poor

For the Flute

For the Guittar

NEW YORK Printed & Sold by J. HEWITT No. 23 Maiden Lane. —— Price 25 Cents.

Anne Seguin
Edward Seguin
M. W. Balfe

I DREAMT THAT I DWELT IN MARBLE HALLS

THE POPULAR SONG,

as Sung with great applause by

Mrs. Seguin.

IN

BALFE'S Celebrated OPERA,

THE

BOHEMIAN GIRL,

as Performed at the

Park Theatre.

Pr. 25 Cents.

NEW YORK.
Published by ATWILL, *201 Broadway.*
ATWILL *has Published all the Music of the* BOHEMIAN GIRL

I DREAMT THAT I DWELT IN MARBLE HALLS.

Composed ———————————————— by Balfe.

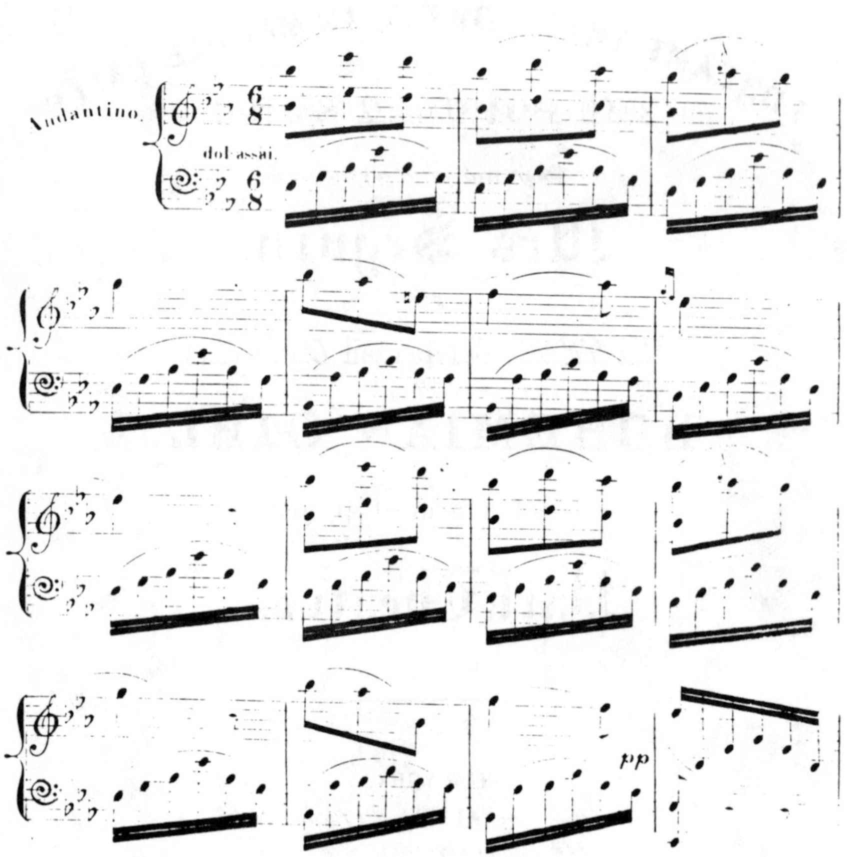

ARLINE. 2. V. I dreamt that kind sui _ tors sought my
1. V. I dreamt that I dwelt in mar _ ble
8.
8.
hand, That knights up _ on ben _ ded knee;
halls, With vas _ sals and serfs at my side;
And with vows no maid _ en heart could with _
And of all who as _ sem _ bled with _ in those
stand, They pledg'd their faith to me,
walls, That I was the hope and the pride;

And I dreamt that one of that no ble
I had riches too great to count, could
host, Came forth my hand to claim,
boast, Of a high an ces tral name.
But I &c.
But I al so dreamt, which pleas'd me
8va
pp
most, That you lov'd me still the same, that you

lov'd me, you lov'd me still the same, that you
lov'd me, you lov'd me still the same.
cres
f
1st time
2d time
f
8.
8.

Price 50 Ct.

Philad.ª OSBOURN'S MUSIC SALOON, 30 S. 4th St.

mf
mf
mf
Kath _ leen Mavour _ _ neen! the grey dawn is breaking, The
horn of the Hunter is heard on the hill The lark from her
light wing the bright dew is sha _ _ _ king Kathleen Mavourneen! what
slum _ bring still. Oh
mf

mf
hast thou for_gotten how soon we must sever? Oh hast thou for_
Espressivo e legato.
mf
__gotten this day we must part, It may be for Years, and it
Colla voce.
may be for ever Oh why..... art thou si_ lent, thou voice of my
cres
-heart, It may be for Years and it may be for ever, Then

mf
why art thou si _ lent Kathleen Ma _ vour _ _ neen.
mf
mf
Kath _ _ leen Ma _ vour _ _ neen! A _
mf
_ wake from thy slumbers, The blue mountains glow in . . . . . . the Suns golden
mf
mf
light, Ah! where is the spell that once hung on my numbers, A _

rise in thy beauty, thou star of my night A_rise......... in thy
cres
Slentando.
beauty thou star........ of my night.
Tempo.
Rallent:
Con mf amore affetto.
Ma_vour_ _neen, Mavourneen, my sad tears are
pp
falling, To think that from E_ _rin and thee I must part, It
mf
fz
mf
f

may be for Years, and it may be for ever, Then why art thou
pp
Sempre legato.
Semplice
mf
si_lent thou voice of my heart, It may....... be for Years and it
mf
may be for ever, Then why..... art thou si_lent Kath_leen Ma_
Rallent: diminuendo
_vour_neen.
Pia

LONG' LONG AGO!

BALLAD

Composed by

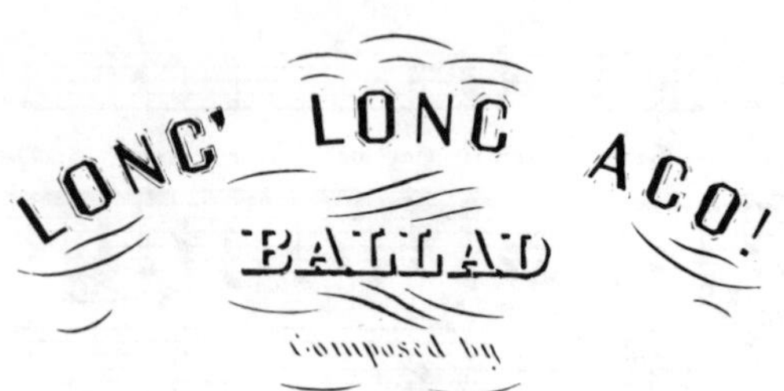

THOS H. BAYLY, ESQ.

BOSTON; Published By C. H. KEITH. 67 & 69 Court St

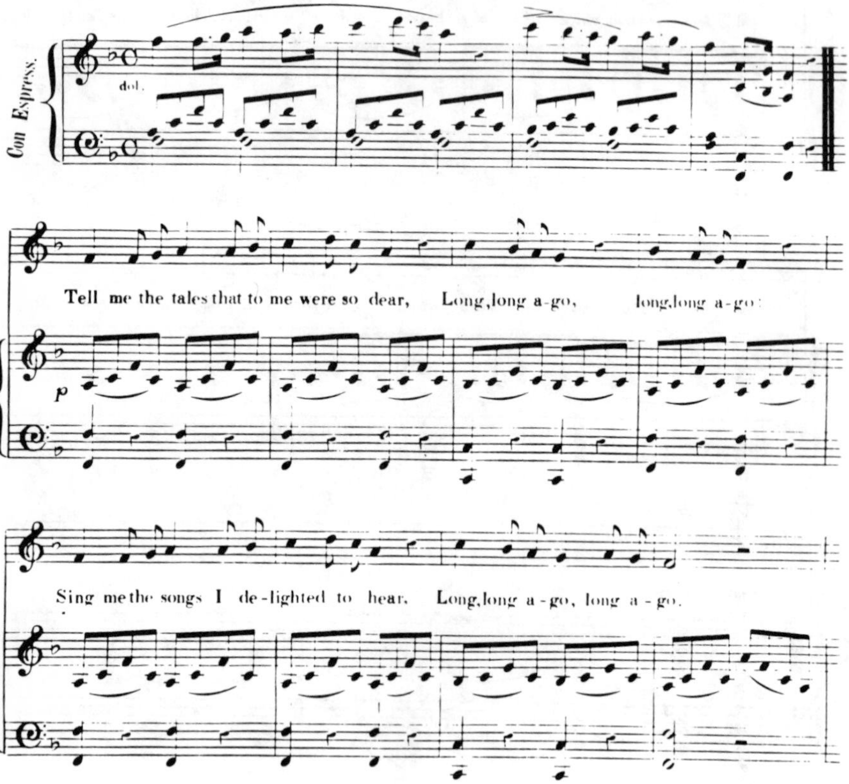

Con Espress.
dol.
Tell me the tales that to me were so dear, Long, long a-go, long, long a-go:
p
Sing me the songs I de-lighted to hear, Long, long a-go, long a-go.

Now you are come all my grief is remov'd, Let me forget that so
long you have rov'd; Let me believe that you love as you lov'd;
Long, long a-go, long a - go.
mf

2

Do you remember the path where we met,
Long, long ago, long, long ago!
Ah! yes, you told me you ne'er would forget,
Long, long ago long ago
Then to all others my smile you prefer'd,
Love when you spoke gave a charm to each word
Still my heart treasures the praises I heard,
Long, long ago, long ago

3

Though by your kindness my fond hopes were raised,
Long, long ago, long, long ago,
You, by more eloquent lips, have been prais'd,
Long, long ago, long ago.
But by long absence your truth has been tried,
Still to your accents I listen with pride,
Blest as I was when I sat by your side,
Long, long ago, long ago.

LOVE NOT!
Written by Mrs. Norton
Composed for the
Piano Forte
BY
BLOCKLEY.

New York Published by E. RILEY. *29 Chatham St.*

ANDANTINO CON EXPRESSION
Love not! Love not! Ye hapless sons of clay,
Hope's gayest wreaths are made of earth_ly flow'rs;
f
(2)

Things that are made to fade and fade a_ _ way, Ere they have
blossom'd for a few short hours, Ere they have
ad lib.
blossom'd for a few short hours. Love not! Love not!

2

Love not! love not! the thing, you love, may die,
May perish from the gay and gladsome earth,
The silent stars, the blue and smiling sky,
Beams on its grave, as once upon its birth. _ _ Love not!..

3

Love not! love not! the thing you love may change,
The rosy lip may cease to smile on you,
The kindly beaming eye grow cold and strange,
The heart still warmly beat yet not be true. _ _ Love not!..

4

Love not! love not! oh warning vainly said
In present hours, as in years gone by:
Love flings a halo round the dear one's head,
Faultless, immortal, till they change or die. _ _ Love not!..

(Love not. 2.)

MARY'S TEARS

Composed by

O. Shaw

Sung at the Oratorio performed by the Handel & Haydn Society in Boston July 5th 1817

in presence of the

PRESIDENT OF THE UNITED STATES,

PROVIDENCE, Published and sold by the AUTHOR No. 70 Westminster Street.

LARGHETTO.
Were not the sin_ful Ma_ry's tears, An
off'_ring wor_thy heav'n An off'_ring wor__thy heav'n,

2

When o'er the faults of for_mer years She wept and was for_
giv'n! She.......... wept and was for_giv'n!

2.

When bringing every balmy sweet
Her day of luxury stored,
She o'er her Saviour's hallowed feet
The precious perfume poured,-

3.

And wip'd them with that golden hair,
Where once the diamond shone,
Though now those gems of grief were there
Which shine for God alone!

4.

Thou that hast slept in error's sleep,
Oh! would'st thou wake in heaven,
Like Mary kneel, like Mary weep,
"Love much," and be forgiven!

NB this Air forms No. of a Series of National Melodies Pr. 50 Cts

NEW YORK Published by HEWITT & JAQUES 239 Broadway

NEAR THE LAKE WHERE DROOP'D THE WILLOW.

Sung by Mrs C. E. Horn.

Arranged by Charles E. Horn.

Dwelt a maid, be-lov'd and cherish'd, By high and low;

ad lib:

But, with au-tumn's leaf, she perish'd, Long time a-go!

f *f*

Rock, and tree, and flow-ing water, Long time a-go!

Bird, and bee, and blos--som--taught her, Love's spell to know!
While to my fond words she listend,-- Mur---mur---ing low,--
ad lib:
Ten--der--ly her dove eyes glisten'd, Long time a----go!
mf
f

Mingled were our hearts forever! Long time a---go! Can I now for--

ad lib:

get her? never! No, lost one, no! To her grave these tears are given,

ad lib:

E------ver to flow! She's the star I miss'd from heaven, Long time a---

go!

mf

G.W. Quidor Engr.

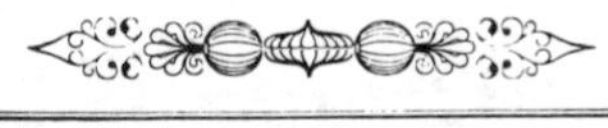

SEVEN POPULAR SONGS,

BY

WURZEL.

(GEO. F. ROOT.)

1. Glad to get home.
2. The Honeysuckle Glen.
3. Rosalie the Prairie Flower.
4. The Church within the Wood.
5. All together again.
6. Proud world, Good bye! I'm going home.
7. Father John.

Price 25 Cents each.

PUBLISHED BY
RUSSELL & RICHARDSON, at the MUSICAL EXCHANGE,
No. 291 Washington Street, Boston.

Rosalie the Prairie Flower.
3
Moderato.
Wurzel. (G. F. R.)
1. On the dis - tant prai - rie, Where the heath - er wild In its qui - et beau - ty
2. On that dis - tant prai - rie, When the days were long, Trip - ping like a fai - ry,
3. But the sum - mer fa - ded, And a chil - ly blast, O'er that hap - py cot - tage
lived and smiled, Stands a lit - tle cot - tage, And a creep - ing vine
sweet her song, With the sun - ny blos - soms And the birds at play,
swept at last, When the au - tumn song - birds Woke the dew - y morn,

4
Loves a-round its porch to twine ; In that peaceful dwelling was a love - ly child,
Beau - ti - ful and bright as they ; When the twi-light shadows gathered in the west,
Lit - tle prai-rie flower was gone ! For the an - gels whispered soft-ly in her ear,
With her blue eyes beam - ing soft and mild, And the wav - y ring - lets
And the voice of na - ture sunk to rest, Like a che - rub kneel - ing
" Child, thy Fa - ther calls thee ; stay not here." And they gent - ly bore her,
of her flax - en hair, Float - ing in the sum - mer air.
seemed the love - ly child, With her gen - tle eyes so mild.
robed in spot - less white, To their bliss - ful home of light.

Chorus. (repeat pp)
Air.
1. Fair as a li - ly, joy - ous and free, Light of that prai - rie home was she.
Alto.
2. Fair as a li - ly, joy - ous and free, Light of that prai - rie home was she.
Tenor.
3. Though we shall nev - er look on her more, Gone with the love and joy she bore.
Bass.
Piano.
Eve - ry one who knew her, felt the gen - tle power of Ros - a - lie the prai - rie flower.
Eve - ry one who knew her, felt the gen - tle power of Ros - a - lie the prai - rie flower.
Far a - way she's blooming, in a fade - less bower, sweet Ros-a - lie the prai - rie flower.

Index